Music Fundamentals

Third Edition

Music Fundamentals: A Balanced Approach, Third Edition combines a textbook and integrated workbook with an interactive website for those who want to learn the basics of reading music. Intended for students with little or no prior knowledge of music theory, it offers a patient approach to understanding and mastering the building blocks of musical practice and structure. Musical examples range from Elvis Presley songs to Filipino ballads to Beethoven symphonies, offering a balanced mixture of global, classical, and popular music.

The new edition includes:

- Additional vocabulary features and review exercises
- Additional musical selections and 1-, 2-, or 3-hand rhythmic exercises
- The addition of guitar tablature
- A revised text design that more clearly designates the different types of exercises and makes the Workbook pages easier to write on
- An improved companion website with added mobile functionality

The author's balanced approach to beginning music theory engages student interest while demonstrating how music theory concepts apply not only to the Western classical canon but also to popular and world music. With the beginner student in mind, *Music Fundamentals: A Balanced Approach*, Third Edition is a comprehensive text for understanding the foundations of music theory.

Sumy Takesue is an Instructor at Santa Monica College, teaching theory and class piano. She has taught at the University of Hawai'i (Hilo) and the University of Southern California.

Music Fundamentals

A Balanced Approach

Third Edition

Sumy Takesue

Routledge
Taylor & Francis Group

NEW YORK AND LONDON

Third edition published 2018
by Routledge
711 Third Avenue, New York, NY 10017

and by Routledge
2 Park Square, Milton Park, Abingdon, Oxon OX14 4RN

Routledge is an imprint of the Taylor & Francis Group, an informa business

First edition published by Routledge 2010
Second edition published by Routledge 2014

Library of Congress Cataloging in Publication Data
Names: Takesue, Sumy, author.
Title: Music fundamentals : a balanced approach / Sumy Takesue.
Description: Third edition. | New York ; London : Routledge, 2018. |
Includes bibliographical references and index.
Identifiers: LCCN 2017000182 (print) | LCCN 2017001460 (ebook) |
ISBN 9781138654402 (hardback) | ISBN 9781138654419 (pbk.) |
ISBN 9781315623269 (ebook)
Subjects: LCSH: Music—Instruction and study. | Music theory.
Classification: LCC MT6 .T133 2018 (print) | LCC MT6 (ebook) |
DDC 781.2—dc23
LC record available at https://lccn.loc.gov/2017000182

ISBN: 978-1-138-65440-2 (hbk)
ISBN: 978-1-138-65441-9 (pbk)
ISBN: 978-1-315-62326-9 (ebk)

Typeset in Melior
by Keystroke, Neville Lodge, Tettenhall, Wolverhampton

Visit the companion website: www.routledge.com/cw/takesue

CONTENTS

APPENDICES

The following appendices can be found on the companion website:

A VISUAL TOUR OF *MUSIC FUNDAMENTALS: A BALANCED APPROACH*

Pedagogical Features

Music Fundamentals: A Balanced Approach, Third Edition offers a number of features to help students in this introductory course in music theory.

CULTURAL AND HISTORICAL NOTES

> **Historical note: English "rownde"**
>
> The title of this piece is written in old English. Here, the "rownde" is not a musical "round" as known today (for example, songs like "Sumer Is Icumen In" or "Are You Sleeping?"). Instead, the rownde is a multi-sectional piece where the first section repeats after the second section is played; that is, the piece "goeth rownde."
>
> This keyboard piece is part of the earliest known collection of English Renaissance music (1450–1600), and like a few other pieces in the group, is attributed to Hugh Aston, a composer known for his progressive keyboard writing.

Throughout the text you will find shaded boxes indicating a note of cultural or historical information. These are intended to provide cultural and historical context to the theory, giving a more rounded and engaging approach for those encountering music learning for the first time.

VOCABULARY NOTES AND IN-TEXT EMBOLDENED TERMS

> **Vocabulary note**
>
> **PENTATONIC**
>
> A pentatonic melody only uses five different pitches. Many melodies from around the world are pentatonic, including folk melodies from Japan, China, Korea, Hungary, Indonesia, Greece, and African countries. Many American folk songs, blues melodies, and spirituals are also pentatonic.

Boxed vocabulary notes explain common music terms and directions. Terms emboldened in the text indicate where further explanatory notes can be found at the back of the book.

IN-TEXT EXERCISES

> **Exercise 10**
>
> Name the notes below.
>
> 1. Write the letter names below the staff.
> 2. Then cover your answers and say the note names out loud. Work for speed and accuracy.
> 3. Starting with the given note, name the two additional ascending notes, skipping every other letter. For example, beginning on C, the names of the two notes skipping up will be C E G.

Exercises illustrate and reinforce topics as students progress through the book.

WORKBOOK SECTION

WORKBOOK – MODULE 1

Name _____

Exercise 1.1

On the staff below, draw a **treble clef** and all the **ascending** notes on the staff from the **ledger line middle C**, up to the **fifth line F**. Then **descend**, returning to middle C. Use whole notes (𝅝). Label the letter names below each note.

At the end of each module is a Workbook of exercises reviewing the material presented in the module. These sections are available to tear out and hand in for assessment if required. There are several exercises per worksheet and between 7 and 19 exercises per module.

FOLD-OUT KEYBOARD

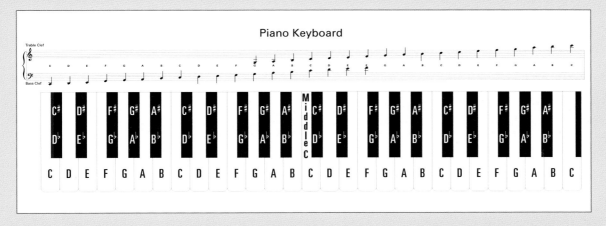

Useful for identifying notes on the keyboard, and understanding scales, the keyboard can be used to simulate actual playing.

Companion Website

www.routledge.com/cw/takesue

Throughout the text this logo indicates where pertinent exercises can be found on the website to consolidate what has been learned in the book.

Audio excerpts to accompany the exercises are also available where this logo is found in the margin.

Visit the companion website at **www.routledge.com/cw/takesue** for a whole host of additional resources for students and instructors.

PREFACE

A "Balanced Approach"

Welcome to the study of music fundamentals! This book is designed for the semester or quarter-long course in the college curriculum that concentrates on learning how to read and write music. All introductory music theory books begin with the study of two basic rudiments: rhythm and pitch. They proceed through the study of the major and minor scales, intervals, triads and seventh chords, and conclude with the study of musical form and harmonizing melodies. However, there are many differences in emphasis in the available books, with one veering toward drill work with very little explanatory text, another toward a reliance on outside sources with few exercises in the textbook, and another emphasizing keyboard, singing, and ear training drills to help explain concepts.

How does *Music Fundamentals* provide a *balanced approach*? This book *balances* textbook with drills, and provides media tools that are integral to the process. It is *balanced* as a combination textbook, workbook and interactive instructional website in order to address the needs of different kinds of learners. Written for the non-music major wanting to "learn about music," and the fledging music major, *Music Fundamentals* serves the student with little or no prior knowledge of music, as well as the music student needing review. By reinforcing musical concepts with numerous written examples, offering a more balanced mixture of global, classical, and popular music, and providing a comprehensive, interactive website, *Music Fundamentals: A Balanced Approach, Third Edition* is a great fit for today's more diverse, technology-savvy students.

I am a teacher "in the trenches." As a piano and music theory instructor for over 20 years, I have taught preparatory students, serious music majors at the university level, and retired senior citizens stretching their intellectual horizons. My current college classes include a diverse ethnic and cultural mix of students. Finding an engaging textbook for all these students—with the appropriate presentation and manner of delivering content—has been challenging. My background puts me in a unique position to draw from a global perspective. I am a Japanese-American, born and raised in Hawaii, schooled in Boston, and teach in a Los Angeles community college. As in many American colleges, my students come from a variety of backgrounds: they are young and old, immigrants, working parents, and those intending to transfer to a four-year university. It is not only possible, but also critical, to connect with students by presenting music in a new and different way, drawing from as many types of music as possible, and providing ample music examples. I chose to create this textbook to address the changing needs of my students. Not infrequently I hear beginning theory students exclaim: "Oh, *that's* how it's supposed to be played (or sung)!" It is for these students that I wrote this book.

Features of *Music Fundamentals*

Music Fundamentals features a combination of modular text with drills, supplemented by a pull-out keyboard, an interactive website, and access to audio examples that relate directly to the text. It includes:

- *Explanations of musical concepts and definitions*, followed by a *variety of exercises* which help students transform knowledge into practice.
- An understanding of pitch, scales, intervals, and chords, whereby students also *listen and sing* to train their ears.
- *Keyboard drills*, constructed to be played on an electronic keyboard, or a piano, or if neither is available, on a "true" sized 50-key paper keyboard, provided in the inside cover. References to the keyboard give students a better visual understanding of what can be the "dry" theoretical basis of music.
- *Numerous clapping and counting exercises* so that students not only have a cerebral understanding, but also a visceral feeling for pulse and rhythm.
- *Workbook exercises* are given at the end of each module to facilitate progress to the next module. The review also includes exercises from previous modules, reinforcing the idea that repeated review reinforces learning.
- *Vocabulary words* are interspersed throughout the text to assist students in the study of music examples. For example, in Module 1 (Pitch), "pentatonic" is introduced to identify songs that students hear. In Module 2 (Rhythm), students learn about "motives." Later, various repeat signs and articulation signs are discussed. New words are integrated into the text to give students a richer understanding of musical concepts.
- *A good mix of music examples*: approximately 45% classical music, 20% American pop, rock and jazz, and 35% global music. They range from Stevie Wonder songs to Beethoven symphonies, from rhythmically challenging African and syncopated Brazilian *choro* songs, to humorous Filipino ballads and Schubert lieder.

Organization

This book is constructed in modules, each with discrete units that allow the instructor flexibility to organize the course. The modules alternate between pitch and rhythm studies. The book may be taught in a variety of ways. For example, in a 16-week course, the book could be divided into four sections:

1. Modules 1–4
2. Modules 5–8
3. Modules 9–12
4. Modules 13–16

In a ten-week course, the book could be divided into units of three to four modules. Module 16 is included to round out a student's understanding of how music is "put together" and also may be introduced earlier at the instructor's discretion.

An instructor may wish to complete one module in its entirety before going on to the next. I integrate the modules so that pitch or scale material is studied in tandem with rhythmic material, or concepts from earlier modules are postponed and discussed later, and vice versa. For example, I postpone the introduction of the double sharp and double flat (Module 4) until those accidentals are used in minor scales (Module 9) or augmented and diminished triads (Module 11). Likewise, I introduce perfect and major intervals (Module 10) and major triads (Module 11) earlier during the second quarter of the course. The modular nature of the book allows for this flexibility.

Pedagogy

All sets of exercises begin from the relatively easy to those requiring more thought. For example, beginning exercises for note reading in Module 1 include alphabet drills; those for counting in Module 2 include drawing stems. By the end of Module 2, students are composing their own rhythms, as well as singing and clapping Western music, such as that of J.S. Bach, and global music, such as music from the Philippines. Drills are included throughout the modules and on the website to ensure that students are given sufficient repetitive practice.

The book provides three other kinds of notes, as shown in the "Visual Tour" section:

1. *Cultural notes* discuss musical genres or place musical examples in a cultural context;
2. *Historical notes* place material in a historical context (for example, the development of the natural);
3. *Vocabulary notes* discuss musical signs or terms. These notes provide contextual background and give students a richer appreciation and understanding of what may otherwise be "dry" information.

Appendices

These can be found in two places. At the end of the textbook, you will find an appendix of Musical Terms that includes additional musical concepts and exercises, as well as appendices on Acoustics, C Clefs, Modes, Other Seventh Chords, and Basic Guitar Chords. Other appendices—which include Keyboard Exercises and several musical analyses of short, *complete* examples of music from the eighteenth to twentieth centuries, and an African piece that uses 8/8 meter—are placed on the companion website. Questions on scales, intervals, triads, form, and rhythm are provided. Instructors may choose to use these as discussion topics, or ask students to submit their answers as homework assignments or quizzes.

Ancillaries

 The companion website to *Music Fundamentals* is a wonderful tool for students. We worked hard to create a dynamic, interactive site. The web address is:

www.routledge.com/cw/takesue

The Routledge Music Theory Trainer has been redeveloped to be compatible with modern web browsers and accessible on mobile devices. It includes:

1. *Exercises of progressive difficulty*
2. *Customized drills* where students work on one or more parameters; for example, students may select to be quizzed on diminished triads, or on up to all four triad qualities. New exercises include notating compound intervals, and exercises utilizing the grand staff
3. *Rhythm exercises for one or two hands* allowing students to listen to a correct playback and have their tapping graded. Students may select their own tempo
4. *Listening drills* test scales, rhythms, and triads. Interval exercises begin by quizzing ascending and descending "steps" and "skips" (corresponding to Module 1); later exercises examine all qualities of intervals (Modules 10)
5. *Keyboard quizzes* to reinforce students' knowledge of the grand staff, accidentals, whole and half steps, scales, and triads
6. *Email submission of scores* directly from student to instructor, with the option to print them out

7. *Audio excerpts of music examples*—classical, pop, and global music is streamed to the companion website. Other audio files reinforce singing and tapping exercises presented in the book

8. *Additional appendices*, as noted in the above section describing the appendices. An instructor's access code to audio files and information on the website is available through the sales office.

9. The site content is *available in the major Virtual Learning Environments* (VLEs), such as Blackboard or Moodle, upon request to the sales office.

• An *Instructor's Manual* is available on the website. Sample tests and accompanying answers are now provided for every module.

New to this Edition

• New vocabulary exercises and review exercises have been added to every module.

• To expand the student's musical experience, additional selections have been added and changed from the earlier editions' mix of standard Classical repertoire, pop, and global music examples.

• A new appendix on Basic Guitar Chords has been added, including chord diagrams (fretboard charts) and exercises with examples of popular songs.

• On the companion website, the Music Theory Trainer has been redeveloped to run on HTML5 instead of Flash, ensuring that it is compatible with modern web browsers and accessible on mobile devices.

• An expanded interactive web site provides additional exercises for tapping, listening, and writing, including exercises quizzing alto and tenor clefs, modes, and seventh chords other than the dominant seventh. A progress bar now shows the student's place in the drill.

• Sample tests with answers are provided for every module in the Instructor's Manual found online.

• Now available on Blackboard or Moodle and other VLEs.

To the Instructor

Music Fundamentals is written as a fresh approach to America's changing student demographics. Many students are recent immigrants or the children of immigrant parents, and some are older students returning to school. Younger students have been raised with laptops, smart phones and MP3 players. Because of the varied population, students have a wide range of math, reading and writing backgrounds. Fewer have had music instruction in the lower grades or heard American folk songs or classical music.

With this diverse student body in mind, this book presents concepts using simple, clear and concise language. Using a wide range of music examples, students are challenged to count, clap, sing, and compose. Review exercises are given at the end of every module. These may be used to measure students' knowledge, prepare them to move onto the next module, or assigned as additional exercises to augment those given earlier in the module. The accompanying audio files offer audio samples of classical, pop and global music that students may listen to or sing along with, and this can be done at home or in class. The Routledge Music Theory Trainer on the companion website is interactive so that students are drilled and immediately corrected. If you wish to track their progress, they may print out their scores or email them to you. The *Instructor's Manual* offers suggestions for classroom exercises.

Not all concepts in the book need be covered. For example, one reviewer felt that dominant seventh chords should be taught at the next theory level, while another wanted more discussion of all seventh chords. One reviewer felt that singing should not be included at this level; several were pleased that it was. But should one teach solfège? Numbers? Or sing "La"? I have tried to balance the numerous musical concepts with the demands placed on the student, and to provide a variety of material to give the instructor more options and greater flexibility.

A word on rhythm: this may be the most difficult component of music for students to grasp, especially for those who haven't worked sufficiently with simple math functions. I help students with rhythm in three ways.

1. When first discussing rhythm, students are asked to write the note value *above* each note, dot, or rest (for example: "1" for quarter note in 3/4 time). They are instructed to write the consecutive counts *below* the notes (such as "1 2 3"). Some students may not need to "show their work" above the music, while others find it helpful to write the note values. I have found that this process is especially helpful to students when the pulse note changes or when students begin to work with syncopated rhythms.
2. When dealing with compound meter, I give two methods of counting (neither of which is "1 la le 2 la le").
3. In the instructor's manual, suggested classroom exercises may incorporate rhythm instruments. One reviewer stated it was a grade school exercise to use percussion instruments. If you find this to be the case, you may want to use any "found" instrument: tapping with pens or on different parts of the body, clapping, and foot stamping. In my own classroom, I have noticed that students are intrigued by the sounds created by percussion instruments, particularly finger cymbals, guiros, drums and maracas, and are especially attentive when a fellow student conducts the ensemble. (Be prepared for disaster as well, which is also part of the fun of creating music.)

A note about the choice of music examples: I had hoped to include more music from around the world, but the rhythms did not always work to illustrate basic "Western" concepts. Additionally, I wished to include more contemporary jazz, pop/rock and classical selections, but permissions were sometimes denied, or the fees were outside our budget; the publisher and I had vowed to price the book as low as possible, lower than other major books on the market.

To the Student

As Edgard Varèse said, "Music is organized sound." Music is everywhere: it comes to you blaring out of open car windows, or piped from loudspeakers in supermarkets and elevators. As you walk around campus you're plugged into your devices that are smaller than a deck of cards; as you do your homework you listen to music streaming from your laptop. You listen (and perhaps sing along with) your favorite pop singers: you ask yourself, how did they get started? You may also want to compose your own music but ask yourself: how do I get started?

Music Fundamentals: A Balanced Approach, Third Edition is written for you. It is a "hands on" book that includes music examples from all genres: pop, spirituals, classical, songs from around the world, many of which may be familiar to you. You will learn to read and perform music and begin to compose your own music. Every musical concept, whether it's reading, writing, counting or singing, is followed by exercises that begin with easy drills and progress to more challenging ones. Additionally, you can go online to the website at **www.routledge.com/cw/takesue** and listen to or sing with the tracks that are provided, or complete the interactive exercises. The book is designed for you to play exercises such as scales or triads on your own keyboard or on the 50-key pullout paper keyboard. As in learning any new language, the more you involve yourself in these activities, the better you will master the language of music.

By the end of the book, you will have the tools to read, write, and perform music. With a better understanding of music theory, I hope you will have a better appreciation and understanding of music when you hear it, perform it, or compose it yourselves.

Acknowledgments

This book would not have been possible without the help of Cody Fisher and Louise Savage who painstakingly pored over my manuscript, red pen in hand; Sally Perry who helped me "connect the dots;" the support and encouragement of my colleagues at Santa Monica College, particularly David Goodman and James Martin; and the many anonymous reviewers who read and refined my work through this process.

Many, many thanks to Constance Ditzel, my senior editor at Routledge, for her guiding hand in the previous two editions; to editor Genevieve Aoki for her leadership in bringing this present edition to fruition; to Peter Sheehy for his invaluable assistance in technical matters; to Alexandra McGregor for her assistance in editing; and to Harris Lapiroff and the Little Weaver Web Collective for their work on the website. I am also grateful to my production editor Katie Hemmings and to Chester See and Ryan Dorin for their assistance with the audio files. Ryan also performs on new piano tracks.

Very special thanks to Ric Alviso, Jim Bergman, Miyuki Brazina, Terry Carter, Caroline Chang, Lin-San Chou, Brian Driscoll, Keith Fiddmont, Lori Geller, David H. Gilbert, Gudrun Gotschke, Mark and Terisa Green, Huatao Guo, Jim Harmon, Leah Komaiko, Barbara and Takeo Kudo, Barbara Lamperti, Joanna Li, Ying Ma, Peter Morse, Harmony and Sunshine Richman, Eric Risner, Jon Saul, Jory Schulman, Michael Sherman, Edith Tanaka, Susan Wang, and Gary Washburn for their help in obtaining music from around the world (and sometimes translating their lyrics or helping with obtaining music copyright permission), for their assistance in taming the computer or editing material outside of my musical expertise.

Thanks also to the various instructors who gave their time to review draft material including the following: Lynda Reid, Professor of Music, South Plains College; Jason Roland Smith, Professor of Music, Ohio University; Jeremy Ribando, DMA, Professor and Chair of Performing Arts, Northwest Florida State College; Jeannie Barrick, Texas Tech University, Texas; Brenda J. Lang, Professor of Music & Worship, Cincinnati Christian University; Professor Philip Ewell, Hunter College and the CUNY Graduate Center; Professor Jessica Portillo, Ithaca College School of Music; Melinda O'Neal, Professor of Music, Dartmouth College; G. Bradley Bodine, Lecturer, Purdue University; Professor Richard Lavenda, Shepherd School of Music, Rice University; Denise Grupp-Verbon, Owens State Community College, Ohio.

Also, particular thanks to my parents who encouraged my music study, to my sisters, Lucy and Amy, and my son, Kitaro, who gave me invaluable support, and to my college students who were the inspiration for this book.

Sumy Takesue
March 2017

MODULE 1

BASICS OF PITCH

The Musical Alphabet

Music is a language consisting of sounds and silences. When learning a new language, one must learn grammar, pronunciation, vocabulary, and sometimes a different alphabet. Music is written with an alphabet consisting of the letters A through G. Each letter represents a different sound or **pitch**. Just as words consist of letters, musical melodies consist of **pitches**.

- When melodies *ascend* to higher pitches, the alphabet moves forward from A to G.

  A B C D E F G

Listen to the track or your instructor playing these pitches for you. Then sing the pitches, using the first seven letters of the alphabet. Notice that the pitches are ascending consecutively; we call this singing "ascending by **steps**."

🔊 **TRACK 1**

    1. Ascending pitches by steps: A B C D E F G

Melodies may ascend, sometimes by steps or larger leaps. Listen, then sing the beginning of the melody "Oh When the Saints" and notice how the first four words (and the pitches) ascend; only the last three pitches move by step. Also sing the opening of the Hawaiian melody "Aloha Oe;" the pitches of the first four syllables also ascend but only the first two pitches move by step.

1

🔊 **TRACKS 2–3**

    2. "When the Saints Go Marching In"
    3. "Aloha Oe" (Queen Liliuokalani)

- When melodies *descend* to lower pitches, the musical alphabet moves backward through the first seven letters of the alphabet.

G F E D C B A

Listen to the track or your instructor playing these pitches for you. Then sing the pitches, using the first seven letters of the alphabet backward from G to A. Notice that the pitches are descending consecutively; we call this singing "descending by **steps**." We are comfortable saying our alphabet forward from beginning to end, but we rarely say it in the opposite direction.

🔊 **TRACK 4**

    4. Descending pitches by steps: G F E D C B A

Listen, then sing the beginning of the melody "Joy to the World." Notice how the pitch of the first eight words descends, all by steps. In the Mexican folk song "La Bamba," after the repeated "La's," the pitch descends, but only the first two pitches descend by step.

🔊 **TRACKS 5–6**

    5. "Joy to the World"
    6. "La Bamba"

Listen, then sing the first line of "Deck the Halls with Boughs of Holly." After first descending by steps, the music ascends. Because music ascends and descends, it is important to know and say the alphabet in both directions with ease.

🔊 **TRACK 7**

    7. "Deck the Halls with Boughs of Holly"

Exercise 1 Class Exercise

Say the musical alphabet *backwards* as quickly as you can, by memory.

It is useful to be able to skip every other letter. (See the section on the names of lines and spaces on the staff later in this module, and triads in Module 11.)

To skip every other letter beginning from F, you will skip over the G when going from F to A, skip B when going from A to C, and skip D when going from C to E.

2

These letters together, which spell "FACE," will be useful later in this module.
    We can also skip down every other letter.

Exercise 2 Class Exercise

Going up from the given letter, skip every other letter of the alphabet two times. Repeat this exercise several times so that your answers flow easily and quickly, and are memorized. For example, to skip every other letter from D, you will say "D F A."

1. D F A   2. C _____   3. B _____   4. G _____   5. F _____   6. E _____   7. B _____   8. A _____

9. D _____   10. C _____   11. G _____   12. A _____   13. E _____   14. B _____   15. F _____

The Keyboard

Knowledge of the keyboard is very helpful for the study of music theory. It is not necessary to be able to perform on the keyboard, but access to a keyboard can assist in the study of note names because it has a wide range and is capable of sounding notes simultaneously. Using a keyboard also helps one to hear and visualize many musical concepts since all notes and their relationship to each other are exposed. Exercises utilizing the keyboard will be given throughout this book to assist in your study. (The guitar is also a helpful instrument because it is capable of producing several notes at the same time.)

- The keyboard consists of white and black keys.
- The black keys are grouped alternately by twos and threes.
- This arrangement of black keys can assist in identifying the white keys.

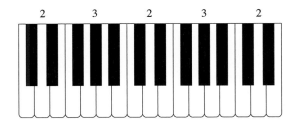

White Keys

The **groups of two black keys** make it easy to find the note C. The white keys immediately to the left of the group of two black keys are named C. The white keys to the right of the two blacks are named E; the white keys in the middle are D. (The names of the black keys will be discussed in Module 4.)

Exercise 3

1.   On the keyboard below, locate and label the keys C D E in relationship to any group of two black keys.
2.   On a keyboard or the paper keyboard provided with this book, play these white keys. When ascending, play C D E. When descending, play the notes in the opposite direction: E D C.

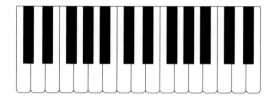

The **groups of three black keys** make it easy to find F. The white keys immediately to the left of each group of three black keys are named F. The white keys to the right of each group are named B. The white keys G and A are in the middle.

Exercise 4

1.   On the keyboard below, locate and label the keys F, G, A, and B in relationship to any group of three black keys.
2.   On a keyboard, play these notes. When ascending, play F G A B. When descending, play the notes in the opposite direction: B A G F.

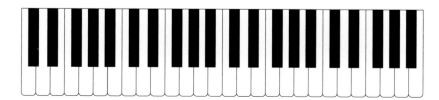

Exercise 5

On the keyboards below, label the keys marked with an **X**.

1.
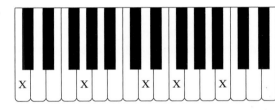

E __ __ __ __

2.
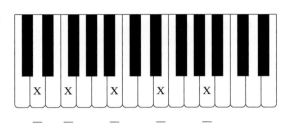

__ __ __ __ __

3.
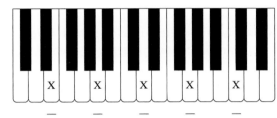

__ __ __ __ __

4.

__ __ __ __ __

Exercise 6

On a keyboard, pitches to the right are higher; pitches to the left are lower. The manufacturer's name of the piano or keyboard is written near the middle of the keyboard just above a group of two black keys. The C to the left of this group is **middle C**. On a full-sized keyboard, this is the fourth C from the bottom.

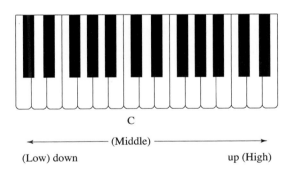

C

←———— (Middle) ————→

(Low) down   up (High)

• Do the following keyboard exercises. (If you do not have a keyboard, use your paper keyboard.)

1. Beginning with the lowest note on the left, play **up** the keyboard (to the **right**).

   • Point to or play each white note and name it, saying the alphabet **forward**.
   • If you are playing a full-sized piano, begin at the left end of the keyboard with the letter A.
   • Find and play **middle C**.
   • Repeat the exercise. **Work for speed and accuracy.**

2. Beginning with the highest note on the right, play **down** the keyboard (to the **left**).

- Point to or play each white note and name it, saying the alphabet **backward**.
- If you are playing a full-sized piano, begin at the top with the letter **C**.
- Find and play **middle C**.
- Repeat the exercise. **Work for speed and accuracy**.

3. Point to or play up the keyboard skipping every other white key. Name the keys. Repeat the exercise, always working for speed and accuracy.

The Staff

A system for notating **pitch** developed in the West during the Middle Ages (sixth century CE–1450). The development of a precise system of notation enables a person to read and perform music without hearing it first.

Historical note on notation

The use of notation in Western Classical music contrasts with the absence of precise musical notation in genres like jazz, blues, and global music, which frequently are not notated. If the music is written down, the notation may specify only the contour of the melody, previously known by the performer.

In modern notation, **pitch** is written as notes on a **staff**. Initially (around the ninth century), only one line was used and higher pitches were placed above this line, and lower pitches were placed below the line. By the eleventh century, four lines were utilized with one line designated F or C. The staff today (plural: staves) consists of five lines and four spaces numbered from the bottom to the top.

The seven letters of the musical alphabet represent pitches in ascending order from lowest to highest. The staff lines and spaces may represent any letter as determined by the **clef**, but the letters must always be in their consecutive order.

Clefs

A **clef** sign drawn at the beginning of each staff indicates the letter name of each line and space. These clef signs represent the pitches F and G. An additional clef sign, less frequently used, will be discussed in Appendix 3.

The G Clef (Treble Clef) (𝄞)

When the **G clef** (usually called the **treble clef**) is placed at the beginning of the staff, the second line from the bottom of the staff represents the pitch G. All other pitches follow in alphabetical order, ascending (forward) or descending (backward) from G. The G clef is usually used to indicate higher sounding pitches.

The following is an example of pitches written on the staff as whole notes (𝅝). Whole notes are discussed in Module 2.

G Line →

C D E F G A B C D E F   F E D C B A G F E D C

<h2 style="background:#555;color:#fff;display:inline-block">Exercise 7</h2>

Draw **G clefs** on the staff below. Notice how the G clef circles around the second line, therefore indicating that the second line represents the pitch G.

G Line →

The Octave

The octave (**octa** = eight) spans eight notes, beginning and ending with the same letter name. (See Appendix 2 for a detailed discussion of frequency and pitch, including octaves.)

A B C D **E** F G A B C D **E** F G A B C D **E** F G A

E   E

Ledger Lines

The five lines and four spaces of one staff can represent only nine letter names. In order to extend the range of the staff, notes above and below the staff are written using ledger lines.

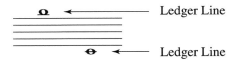

Ledger Line

Ledger Line

- Ledger lines are short. The ledger line for one note does not connect to the ledger line of another note.

Incorrect   Correct

Ledger lines too long

- The distance between the lines and spaces of ledger lines is the same as those of the staff.

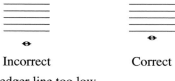

Incorrect   Correct

Ledger line too low

- Ledger lines are used only when needed. For example, notes written above the staff only use the ledger lines that pass through or **below** the note; conversely, notes written below the staff only use ledger lines that pass through or **above** the note.

Incorrect   Correct

Unnecessary ledger line

- The note C written on a ledger line below the treble clef is "middle C."

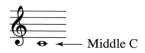 — Middle C

Exercise 8 Class Exercise

On the staff below, draw a **treble clef** and all the **ascending** notes on the staff from **the ledger line middle C**, up to **the fifth line F**. Use whole notes (**𝅝**). Write the letter names below each note.

Notice that:

* The letters of the alphabet are written below, beginning with middle C. All letters must be consecutive.
  C D E F G A B C D E F
* The G clef gives the second line its name: G.
* All letter names are capitalized.

Using your own staff paper, repeat this exercise.

Exercise 9

On the staff below, draw a **treble clef** and all the **descending** notes on the staff from the **fifth line F to middle C.**
Use whole notes (**o**). Write the letter names below each note.

When using the treble clef, notice:

* The letters of the alphabet are written backward beginning with F. All letters must be consecutive.
  F E D C B A G F E D C
* The G clef gives the second line its name: G.
* All letter names are capitalized.

Using your own staff paper, repeat this exercise.

Note Reading in the G Clef

Study the names of the lines and spaces in the G clef (treble clef).
  *Letter names of the **lines:***

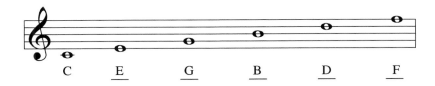

The ledger line below the staff is **middle C.** The names of the five lines of the treble clef can be remembered by
the mnemonic "**E**very **G**ood **B**oy **D**oes **F**ine."
  *Letter names of the **spaces:***

Exercise 10

Name the notes below.

1. Write the letter names below the staff.
2. Then cover your answers and say the note names out loud. Work for speed and accuracy.
3. Starting with the given note, name the two additional ascending notes, skipping every other letter. For example, beginning on C, the names of the two notes skipping up will be C E G.

Notes on lines:

Notes on spaces:

Notes on lines and spaces:

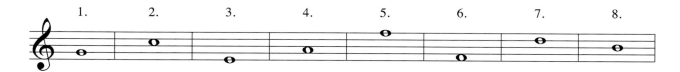

Exercise 11 Class Exercise

The following examples are songs from different countries. Write the letter name of the pitch below each note and then sing the exercise. These exercises contain musical notation that has not been covered, but will be discussed in later modules. Students whose voices are outside the range notated in the exercises may sing pitches an octave higher or lower than the written notes.

Historical note: English "rownde"

The title of this piece is written in old English. Here, the "rownde" is not a musical "round" as known today (for example, songs like "Sumer Is Icumen In" or "Are You Sleeping?"). Instead, the rownde is a multi-sectional piece where the first section repeats after the second section is played; that is, the piece "goeth rownde."

This keyboard piece is part of the earliest known collection of English Renaissance music (1450–1600), and like a few other pieces in the group, is attributed to Hugh Aston, a composer known for his progressive keyboard writing.

1. "The Short Mesure off My Lady Wynkfyld's Rownde" (attributed to Hugh Aston, *c.* 1550)

Brackets are placed around notes in the first two measures. Locate and bracket two other measures that are similar to the opening ones. Compare and contrast the bracketed measures.

Vocabulary note

PENTATONIC

A pentatonic melody only uses five different pitches. Many melodies from around the world are pentatonic, including folk melodies from Japan, China, Korea, Hungary, Indonesia, Greece, and African countries. Many American folk songs, blues melodies, and spirituals are also pentatonic.

---

2. "Hamachidori" ("Beach Plover") (R. Hirota), Japanese **pentatonic** melody
   Identify the five different pitches used in this melody.

3. "Nel Cor Più Non Mi Sento" Variations (L.v. Beethoven)

4. "Fountain of Sorrow" (J. Browne)

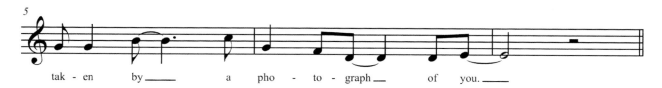

🔊 **TRACKS 8–11**

Listen, and then sing the letter names of these excerpts from Exercise 11.

8. *"The Short Mesure off My Lady Wynkfyld's Rownde" (attributed H. Aston)*
9. *"Hamachidori" (R. Hirota)*
10. *"Nel Cor Più Non Mi Sento" Variations (L.v. Beethoven)*
11. *"Fountain of Sorrow" (J. Browne)*

Exercise 12

Draw the following notes (use 𝅝) being careful to place the notes precisely through the lines or in the spaces. There will be two notes for C, D, E, F, and G in different octaves.

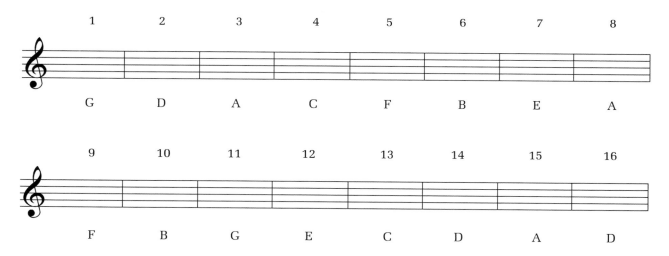

Relating the Treble Clef to the Keyboard

Each note on the staff corresponds to one key on the keyboard. The G clef at the beginning of the staff determines which specific keys of the keyboard represent the notes of that staff. In the G clef, the ledger line **middle C** corresponds to the fourth highest C on a standard keyboard of 88 keys.

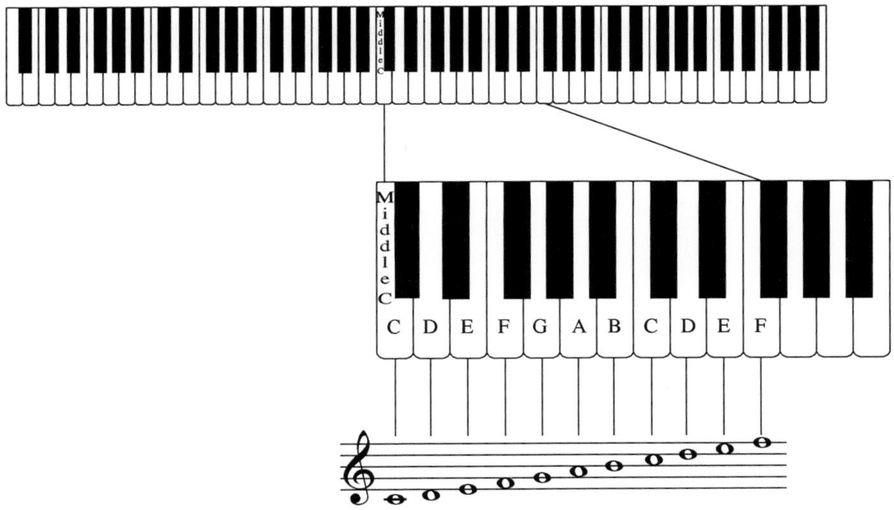

Study the relationship between each note of the treble clef with the note on the keyboard.

Exercise 13

Draw each pitch on the staff (𝅝). Then write the letter name below each note.

Example

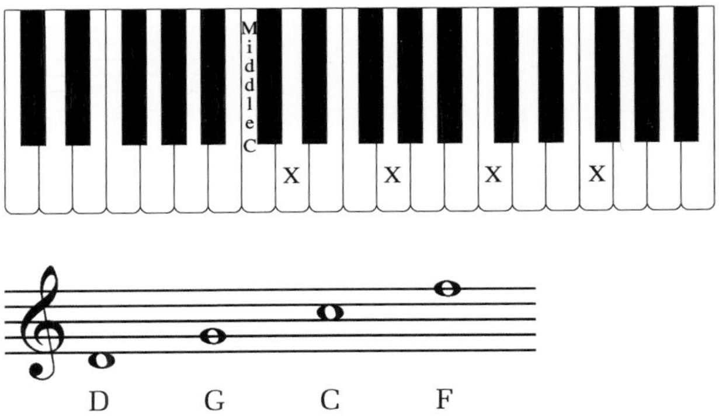

1.

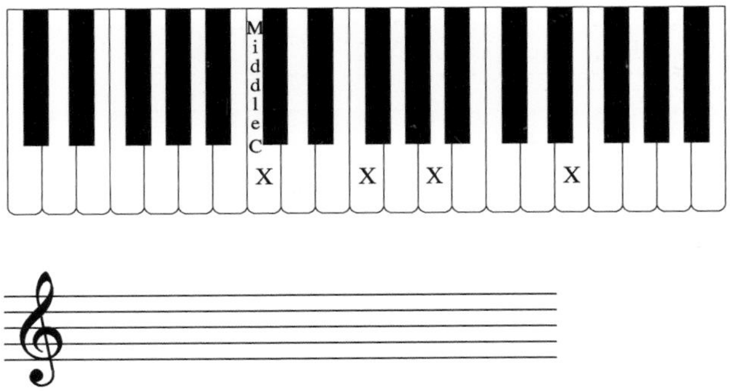

2.   3.

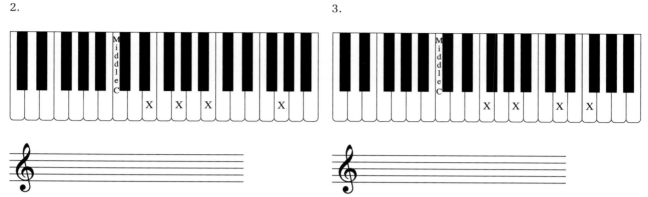

Exercise 14

Write the letter name of the note below the staff. Above, place an **X** on the corresponding key and draw an arrow connecting the three as shown in the example.

Example   1.

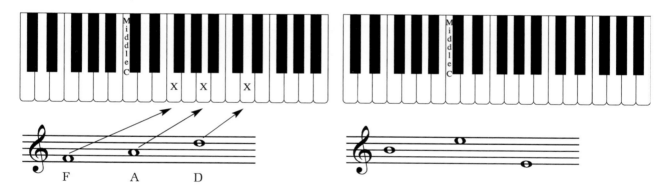

F   A   D

2.   3.

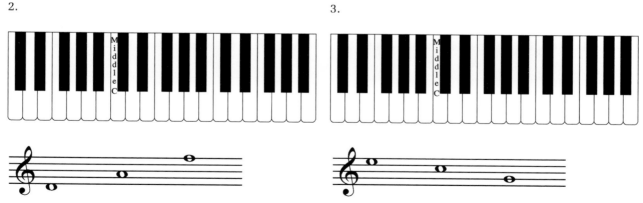

Workbook Exercises 1.1–1.5

 Theory Trainer

Exercise 1a Find white keys on the staff (treble clef).
Exercise 1b Find white keys on the keyboard (treble clef).

Introduction to Singing—Why Sing?

Singing, next to speaking, is the second most important means of verbal communication.

- Singing is important in all cultures around the world; melodies run the gamut from religious songs to popular songs, including songs about love, work, nature, and family life. Songs are used to inspire (national anthems or college school songs) and to teach (how to count). Songs mark celebrations like weddings, rites of passage like bar and bat mitzvahs, as well as funerals and processions.
- Singing is an important expressive form of art along with painting, dancing, drama, poetry, and literature. Singing, with its use of language, gives music a distinctive artistic dimension. Singing, however, may be expressive, even without the use of words (for example, jazz scat singing).
- Singing is an important aid in the study of music theory and does not require additional resources for practice.

Singing exercises will be included throughout this book. It is not important that one's singing be "beautiful"—"beauty" is culturally determined. Instead, it is important to listen carefully to match one's pitch with the pitch on the track or played by the instructor. Your instructor may use one of several methods for singing: solfège (the use of syllables), numbers, letter names, or perhaps a repeated syllable like "La."

Singing in the Treble Clef

Musicians in many countries do not use the alphabet to name pitches; instead, they use syllables, called solfège, or solfeggio. Guido d'Arezzo, a medieval monk, devised a syllabic system (or possibly codified it) around the eleventh century. He used the first syllable of each line of a Latin hymn to name consecutive ascending pitches. Originally only six syllables were used and the seventh (Ti or Si, pronounced "See") was added later.

- For these first singing exercises we are using the pitch C as the central note, also called the "tonic." If C is the tonic then it is called "Do" (originally "Ut" in the Middle Ages), D is named "Re" and so forth.
- The word "solfège" is a combination of the two syllables, Sol and Fa.

	C	D	E	F	G	A	B	C
	Do	Re	Mi	Fa	Sol	La	Ti (Si)	Do
Pronounced:	Doh	Ray	Mee	Fah	Sol	Lah	Tee	Doh

- Numbers may be substituted for either solfège syllables or alphabet letters.

C	D	E	F	G	A	B	C
1	2	3	4	5	6	7	8

- Your instructor will tell you the method to use for singing.

Exercise 15 Class Exercise

Sing the following exercises using solfège, letter names, or numbers.

To the student: If you have a keyboard outside of the classroom, first play the pitches yourself as you slowly sing each exercise; i.e. play and sing along, always matching your pitch to the keyboard accompaniment. Then sing each exercise without the accompaniment. Repeat all exercises several times.

1. Track 12

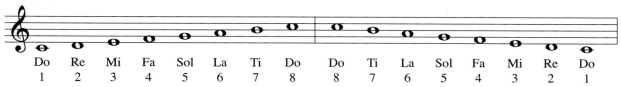

2. Track 13

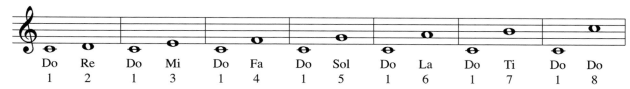

3. Track 14   4. Track 15

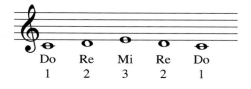
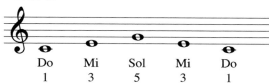

5. Track 16

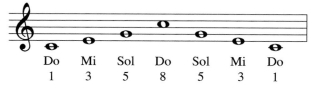

6. Track 17

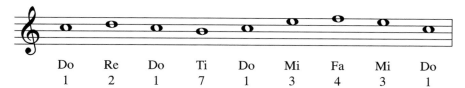

🔊 **TRACKS 12–17**

Listen, then sing: each of the above exercises will be played twice at a slow tempo. Listen the first time, then sing the second time, matching each pitch.

Exercise 16 Class Exercise: Ear Training

Your instructor will play or sing three notes. Place a check in the appropriate blank below, indicating whether the notes are ascending (going up) or descending (going down). You will hear each example twice.

- Try to match the pitches by singing to yourself.
- If you are unsure of the answer, write down the first answer that comes to mind. (First impressions are frequently correct.)

Ascending	Descending
1. _____	_____
2. _____	_____
3. _____	_____
4. _____	_____
5. _____	_____
6. _____	_____

 Theory Trainer

(Your instructor will assign the number of exercises to complete.)

Exercise 1c Listen to three notes and identify ascending or descending steps or skips.

The F Clef (Bass Clef) (𝄢)

The **F clef**, usually called the **bass clef**, is used to indicate voices or instruments that sing or play low pitches including male voices, the cello, and the tuba. When the F clef is placed at the beginning of the staff, the fourth line from the bottom is named F. All other pitches follow in alphabetical order above or below the F.

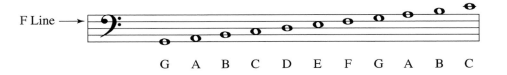

F Line →

G   A   B   C   D   E   F   G   A   B   C

Exercise 17

Draw F clefs on the staff below. Notice how the F clef begins on the fourth line. In modern notation, the two dots are always placed above and below the F line in the third and fourth spaces.

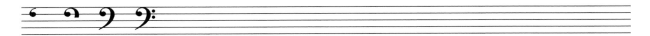

Exercise 18 Class Exercise

Draw an **F, or bass clef** and the **ascending** notes on the staff from the **first line (G)** to the **middle C ledger line**. Use whole notes (𝅝). Write the letter names below each note. Repeat the exercise on your own staff paper.

Remember that:

- The F clef begins on the fourth line and curves around like a backwards C.
- Two dots are placed in the third and fourth spaces.
- The F clef gives the fourth line its name: F.
- The letters of the alphabet will be written ascending beginning with the bottom line: **G A B C D E F G** etc.

Exercise 19

Draw a **bass clef** and the **descending** notes on the staff from the **middle C ledger line** down to the **first line (G)**. Use whole notes (**o**). Write the letter names below each note.

Note Reading in the F Clef

Study the names of the lines and spaces in the F clef.
*Letter names of the **lines**:*

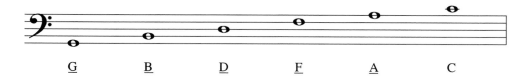

| G | B | D | F | A | C |

The names of the five lines of the bass clef can be remembered by the mnemonic: "**G**ood **B**oys **D**o **F**ine **A**lways." The ledger line above the staff is **middle C**.
*Letter names of the **spaces**:*

| A | C | E | G |

A mnemonic for these space notes is: "**A**ll **C**ows **E**at **G**rass."

Exercise 20

Name the line notes below.

18

Name the space notes below.

1.   2.   3.   4.   5.   6.   7.   8.   9.

Name the bass clef notes below.

1.   2.   3.   4.   5.   6.   7.   8.   9.

Exercise 21

The following examples are songs from different countries. Write the name of the pitch below each note and then sing the exercise. Which of the following melodies are pentatonic?

1.   "All Through the Night," Welsh song

- Brackets are placed around the notes in the first four measures. Locate and bracket four other measures that are exactly the same as the opening ones.

7

Vocabulary note

REPEAT SIGN

:‖ A sign telling the performer to repeat from the beginning.

2.   "Zum Gali Gali," Israeli song

3.   "Amazing Grace," American traditional song

4.   Piano Sonata, K.284 (W.A. Mozart) (originally in D)

🔊 **TRACKS 18–21**

Listen, then sing the musical excerpts from Exercise 21.

18. *"All Through the Night," Welsh song*
19. *"Zum Gali Gali," Israeli song*
20. *"Amazing Grace," American traditional song*
21. *Piano Sonata, K.284 (W.A. Mozart)*

Exercise 22

Draw the following notes (use 𝅝) being careful to place the notes precisely through the lines or in the spaces. There will be two notes for G, A, B, and C in different octaves.

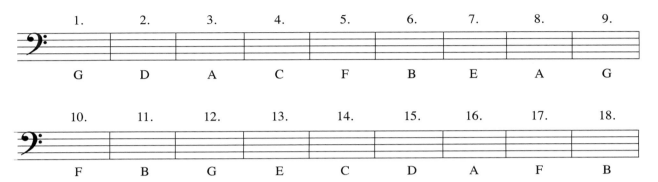

1.	2.	3.	4.	5.	6.	7.	8.	9.
G	D	A	C	F	B	E	A	G

10.	11.	12.	13.	14.	15.	16.	17.	18.
F	B	G	E	C	D	A	F	B

Relating the Bass Clef to the Keyboard

The F clef at the beginning of the staff determines which specific keys of the keyboard represent the notes of that staff. In the F clef, middle C is written on the ledger line above the staff.

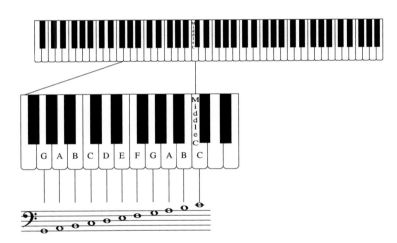

Study the relationship between each note of the bass clef with the corresponding key on the keyboard.

Exercise 23

Draw each pitch on the staff (𝐨). Then write the letter name below each note.

Example

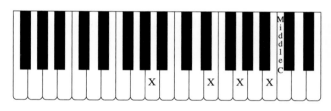

C   E   F   C

1.

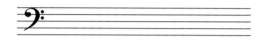

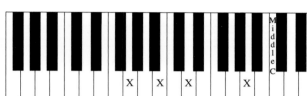

2.

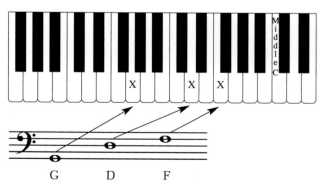

3.

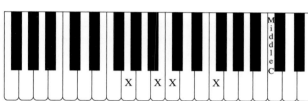

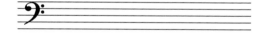

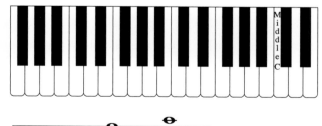

Exercise 24

Write the letter name of the note below the staff. Place an **X** on the corresponding key above and draw an arrow connecting the two.

Example

G   D   F

1.

2.

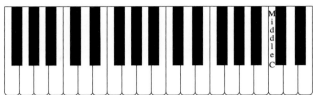

3.

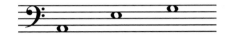

Workbook Exercises 1.6–1.11

 Theory Trainer

(Your instructor will assign the number of exercises to complete.)

Exercise 1a Find white keys on the staff (bass clef).
Exercise 1b Find white keys on the keyboard (bass clef).

Singing in the Bass Clef

Exercise 25 Class Exercise

Sing the following exercises with solfège or numbers. (*Students:* If you have a keyboard outside of the classroom, first accompany yourself as you sing; i.e. play and sing along. Then sing without the keyboard accompaniment. Repeat all exercises several times.)

1. Track 22

Do	Re	Mi	Fa	Sol	La	Ti	Do	Do	Ti	La	Sol	Fa	Mi	Re	Do
1	2	3	4	5	6	7	8	8	7	6	5	4	3	2	1

2. Track 23

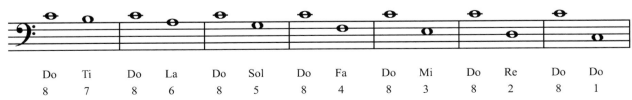

Do	Ti	Do	La	Do	Sol	Do	Fa	Do	Mi	Do	Re	Do	Do
8	7	8	6	8	5	8	4	8	3	8	2	8	1

3. Track 24

4. Track 25

5. Track 26

6. Track 27

🔊 **TRACKS 22–27**

> *Listen, then sing the above exercise; each exercise will be played twice. Listen the first time, then sing the second time, matching your pitch with the audio accompaniment.*

Exercise 26 Class Exercise—Ear Training

Your instructor will play or sing three notes. Place a check in the appropriate blanks below, indicating whether the notes are ascending (up) or descending (down). You will hear each example twice.

- Try to match the pitches by singing to yourself.
- If you are unsure of the answer, check the first answer that comes to mind. (First impressions are frequently correct.)

	Ascending	Descending
1.	_____	_____
2.	_____	_____
3.	_____	_____
4.	_____	_____
5.	_____	_____
6.	_____	_____

 Theory Trainer

(Your instructor will assign the number of exercises to complete.)

Exercise 1c Listen to three notes and identify ascending or descending steps or skips.

Workbook Exercise 1.12

The Grand Staff

The Grand Staff combines both the treble and bass clefs.

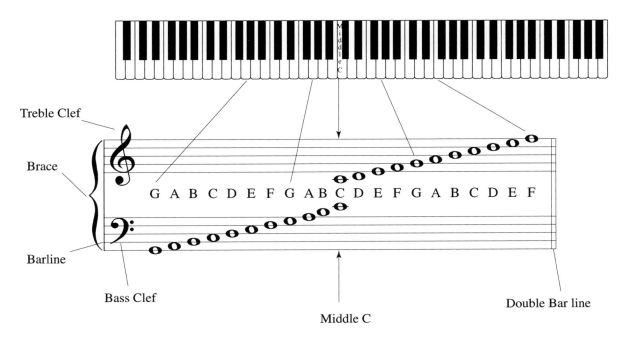

Treble Clef

Brace

Barline

Bass Clef

Middle C

Double Bar line

Notice that:

* Middle C names the ledger line just below the treble clef and the ledger line just above the bass clef.
* In music written for the keyboard, the right hand usually plays middle C when it is written in the treble clef, and the left hand usually plays middle C when it is written in the bass clef. In "Sonata X" by Georg Benda, middle C is first played by the left hand before being switched to the right hand and so on.

Sonata X (Georg Antonin Benda)

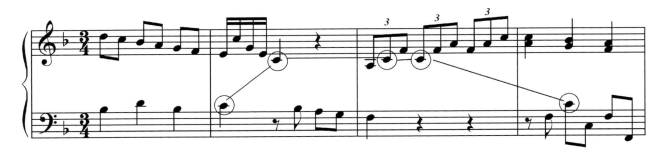

Vocabulary note

GRAND STAFF

the combination of the treble and bass staves (with middle C placed on a ledger line between the two staves)

BRACE

a sign at the beginning of the grand staff joining the treble and bass staves

BAR LINE

a vertical line drawn at the beginning of the grand staff before the clef signs, and in the music to assist with counting. (Bar lines separate the music into **measures**; this is discussed in Module 2.)

DOUBLE BAR LINE

two bar lines at the end of the staff used to signify the end of a section of music

TREBLE CLEF, ALSO CALLED G CLEF

indicates that the G above Middle C is on the second line

BASS CLEF, ALSO CALLED THE F CLEF

indicates that the F below Middle C is on the fourth line

Exercise 27 Class Exercise

1. Draw the **Grand Staff** below. Include the following:

    - Brace
    - Bar line
    - Treble clef and bass clef
    - Double bar line

2. **Ascend**, notating all notes from the first line (G) in the bass clef to the fifth line (F) in the treble clef. (Use **o**.)
3. Notate two middle Cs, one in the treble clef and one in the bass clef.
4. Write the letter name below each note.

Workbook Exercises 1.13–1.14

Exercise 28 Class Exercise

Name the notes written on the Grand Staves below.

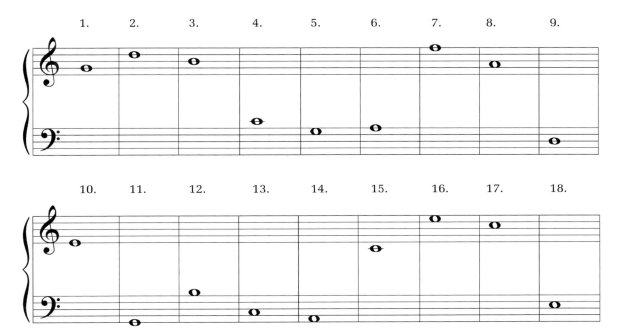

Exercise 29 Singing—Class Exercise

"Sansa Kroma," Akan Mmoguo song (African playground song)

This song is a duet written for two voices (or two groups of voices). As a class, first sing the letter names of the notes in the top lines from beginning to end, followed by those of the lower lines. Then sing the lines together, with half the group singing the top lines and the other half singing the bottom lines. Sing this again with the performers switching parts.

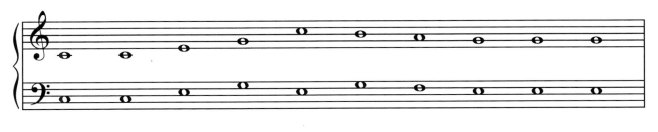

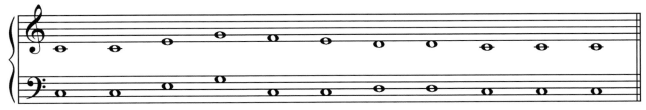

Further Study of Ledger Lines

Ledger lines can extend the range of the grand staff higher than the F line of the treble clef, lower than the G line of the bass clef, and can accommodate notes between the treble and bass clefs. Middle C can be written both as a ledger line *below* the treble staff *and* as a ledger line *above* the bass staff.

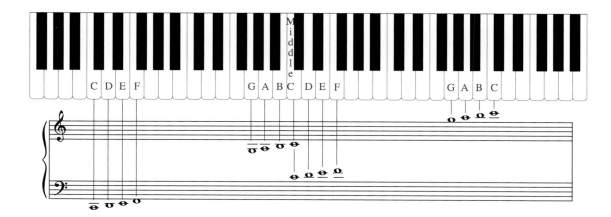

Pitches normally written in the treble clef may also be written in the bass clef using ledger lines. Likewise, pitches normally written in the bass clef may also be written in the treble clef using ledger lines.

Exercise 30 Class Exercise

Name the notes written on the Grand Staff below.

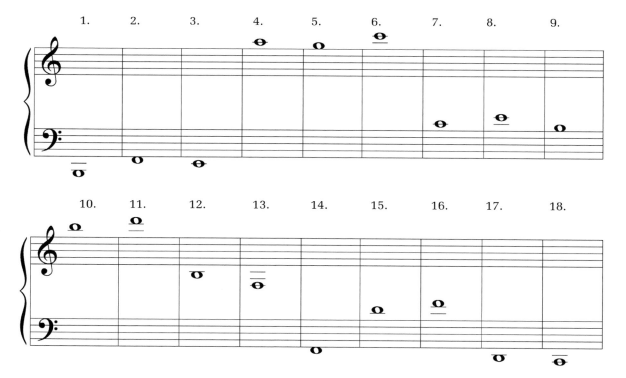

Exercise 31

Draw the following **treble clef** notes as the same pitch in the *bass clef* using **ledger lines** as needed.

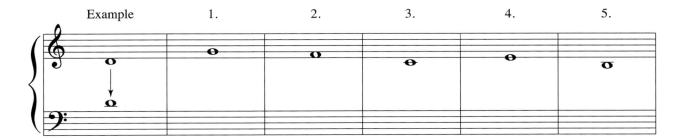

Exercise 32

Draw the following **bass clef** notes as the same pitch in the *treble clef* using **ledger lines** as needed.

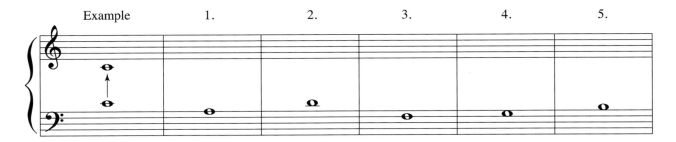

Exercise 33

Draw the following notes *above* the staff using ledger lines as needed.

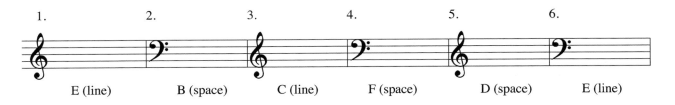

Draw the following notes *below* the staff using ledger lines as needed.

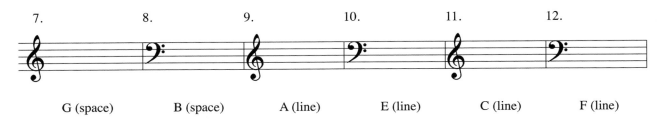

Workbook Exercises 1.15–1.19

Theory Trainer

(Your instructor will assign the number of exercises to complete.)

Exercise 1a Find white keys on the staff (both clefs).
Exercise 1b Find white keys on the keyboard (both clefs).

Octave Higher (8va) or Octave Lower (8vb)

The symbols 8va and 8vb are used when too many ledger lines are needed to notate a note and it becomes difficult to read. The sign **8va** (Italian: *all' ottava,* or "at the octave") tells you to play a note or a series of notes an octave higher than written. The 8va is notated **above** the note or notes to be played an octave higher and is followed by a dotted line ending with a downstroke.

When **8vb** (Italian: *ottava bassa,* or "at the octave below") is notated **below** the note or notes to be played an octave lower, it is followed by a dotted line ending with an upstroke. The sign 8va may be used in place of 8vb; it will be placed below the note or notes and will be followed by the dotted line ending with the upstroke. Your instructor will tell you which sign to use.

The examples below show three notes on the left, which are to be played an octave higher than written. Their sounding pitches are drawn on the right.

On the keyboard below, the sounding pitches (S) are an octave **higher** than the written pitches (W).

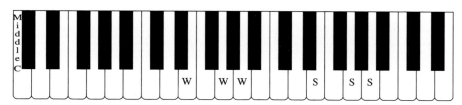

W = Written pitches
S = Sounding pitches

The example below shows three notes on the left, which are to be played an octave lower than written. Their sounding pitches are drawn on the right.

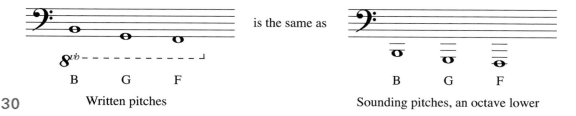

On the keyboard below, the sounding pitches (S) are an octave **lower** than the written pitches (W).

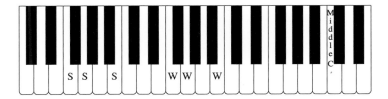

W = Written pitches
S = Sounding pitches

Exercise 34 Class Exercise

Following is a musical example by Frederic Chopin using 8va in order to reduce the need for more than two ledger lines above the treble staff.

Chopin, Etude Op. 10 No. 1, mm. 77-79

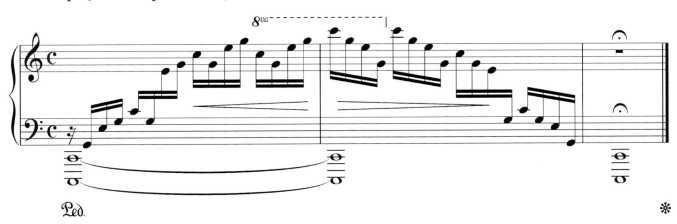

- In the music above, circle the highest note used in the excerpt.
- On the keyboard below, write "W" for the written pitch, and "S" for its sounding pitch.

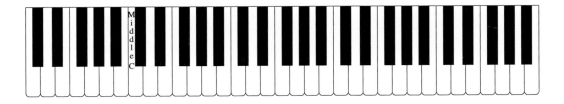

Exercise 35 Class Exercise

Following is a musical example by Claude Debussy using 8vb in order to reduce the need for more than two ledger lines below the bass staff.

Debussy, *La Cathédrale engloutie*, mm. 72-76

- In the music above, circle the lowest note used in the excerpt.
- On the keyboard below, write "W" for the written pitch, and "S" for its sounding pitch.

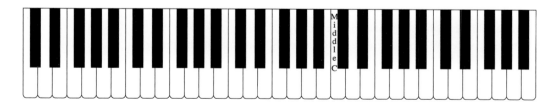

🔊)) **TRACKS 28–29**

28. Etude in C, Op. 10, No. 1 (F. Chopin)
29. La Cathédrale engloutie *(C. Debussy)*

Exercise 36

1. Draw the following pitches an octave higher or lower as indicated, using ledger lines. (The first answer is given.)
2. If you have a keyboard, play both notes (the written and sounding pitches).

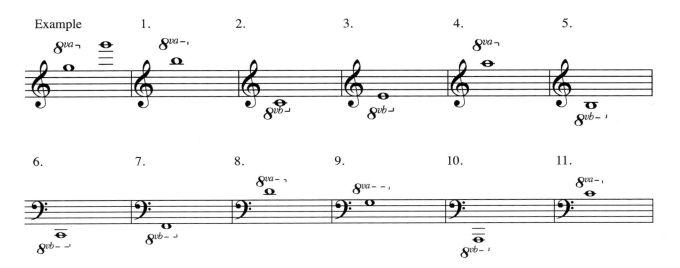

Workbook Exercise 1.20

Name _____

Exercise 1.1

On the staff below, draw a **treble clef** and all the **ascending** notes on the staff from the **ledger line middle C**, up to the **fifth line F**. Then **descend**, returning to middle C. Use whole notes (**𝅝**). Label the letter names below each note.

Exercise 1.2

Name the notes below.

Exercise 1.3

Write the name of the pitch below each note and then sing the melodies.

1. "Cielito Lindo" ("My Pretty Darling") (Q. F. Mendoza Cortes)

2.   Sonatina, Op. 36, No. 4 (Third Movement) (M. Clementi)

Exercise 1.4

Label the letter name of the note below the staff. Above, place an X on the corresponding key and draw an arrow connecting the two. The first letter is done for you.

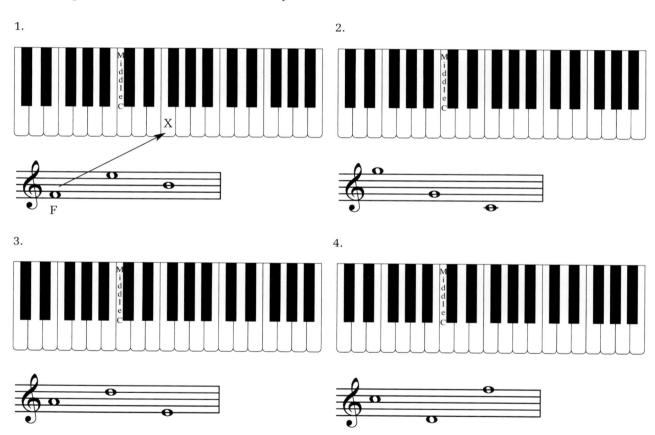

1.

2.

3.

4.

NAME:

Exercise 1.5

Notate each pitch on the staff (**O**). Then write the letter name below each note.

1.

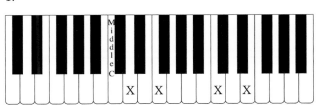

2.

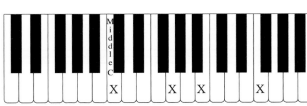

3.

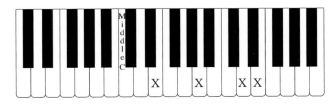

4.

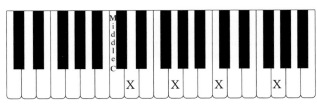

Exercise 1.6

Draw an **F**, or **bass clef** and the **ascending** notes on the staff from the **first line (G)** to the **middle C ledger line**. Then **descend**, returning to G. Use whole notes (**O**). Write the letter names below each note.

Exercise 1.7

Name the notes below.

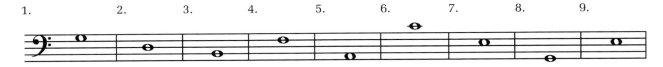

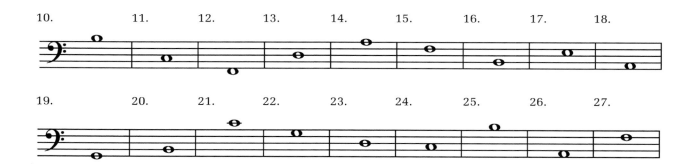

Exercise 1.8

Write the name of the pitch below each note and then sing the melodies.

1. Toccatina, Op. 27, No. 8 (D. Kabalevsky)

   Note: A bracket is placed around a musical figure, called a motive. Find another example of the same motive and bracket it.

2. "Hong Cai Mei Mei" ("A Girl Named Red Rainbow"), Chinese folk melody

   Which measures are identical? _____

3. "Toreador Song" from *Carmen* (originally in F) (G. Bizet)

   Which measures are similar? _____ Explain their similarities and differences. _____

   _____

   _____

To - re - a-dor, en gar - de! To - re - a-dor! To - re - a-dor!

NAME:

Exercise 1.9

Draw the following notes (use 𝅝) being careful to place the notes precisely through the lines or in the spaces.

1.	2.	3.	4.	5.	6.	7.	8.

| B | D | F | A | E | G | C | A |

9.	10.	11.	12.	13.	14.	15.	16.

| C | F | D | G | B | E | A | F |

17.	18.	19.	20.	21.	22.	23.	24.

| D | A | C | G | F | B | E | C |

Exercise 1.10

Label the letter name of the note below the staff. Above, place an **X** on the corresponding key and draw an arrow connecting the two.

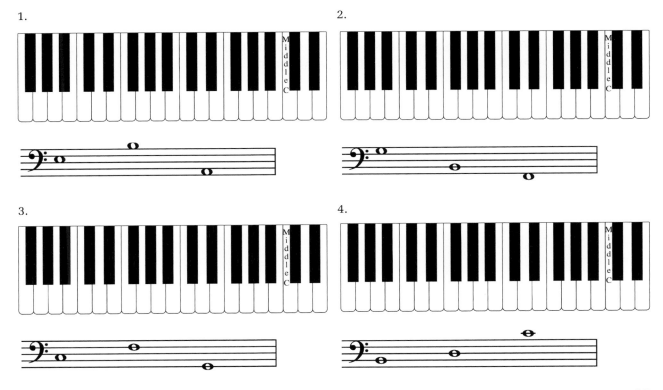

Exercise 1.11

Notate each pitch on the staff (𝅝). Then write the letter name below each note.

1.

2.

3.

4.

Exercise 1.12 Ear Training

Your instructor will play or sing three notes. Place a check in the appropriate blanks below, indicating whether the notes are ascending (going up) or descending (going down), and whether the notes are moving by step or by skip. You will hear each example twice.

•   Match the pitches by singing quietly to yourself.
•   If you are unsure of the answer, write the first answer that comes to mind. (First impressions are frequently correct.)

	Ascending	Descending	Step	Skip
1.	_____	_____	_____	_____
2.	_____	_____	_____	_____
3.	_____	_____	_____	_____
4.	_____	_____	_____	_____
5.	_____	_____	_____	_____
6.	_____	_____	_____	_____

 Theory Trainer

Exercise 1c Listen to three notes and identify ascending or descending steps or skips.

Exercise 1.13

1. Draw the **Grand Staff** below. Include the following:

   - Brace
   - Bar line
   - Treble clef and bass clef
   - Double bar line

2. **Descend**, notating all notes from the fifth line (F) in the treble clef to the first line (G) in the bass clef. (Use 𝅝.)
3. Notate two middle Cs, one in the treble clef and one in the bass clef.
4. Write the letter name below each note.

On your own staff paper, repeat this exercise.

Exercise 1.14

The Menuet en Rondeau by Jean-Philippe Rameau was written for the harpsichord; the notes in the treble staff are played by the right hand, and the notes in the bass staff are played by the left hand. Write the name of the pitch below each note for the treble and bass staves.

Menuet en Rondeau (J.-P. Rameau)

Exercise 1.15

Draw the appropriate treble or bass clef before each note to create the given pitch. The first answer is given.

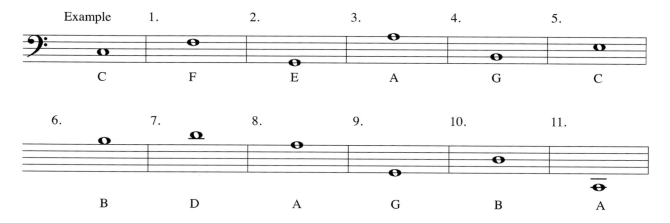

Exercise 1.16

Define the following words:

1. Musical alphabet
2. Grand Staff
3. Bar line
4. Brace
5. Double bar line
6. Treble G clef
7. Bass F clef
8. Ledger line
9. Octave
10. 8va, 8vb
11. Solfège
12. Pentatonic

NAME:

Exercise 1.17 Further Study of Ledger Lines

Label the letter name of the note below the staff. Place an **X** on the corresponding key above and draw an arrow connecting the two. (Keep track of middle C!)

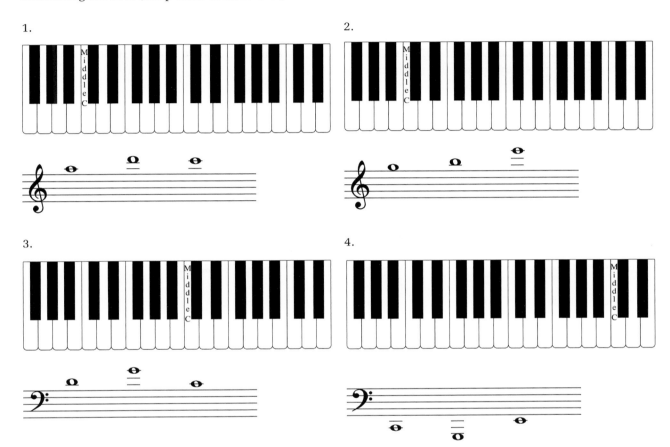

Exercise 1.18

Draw at least four octave notes for each letter. Use ledger lines when needed.

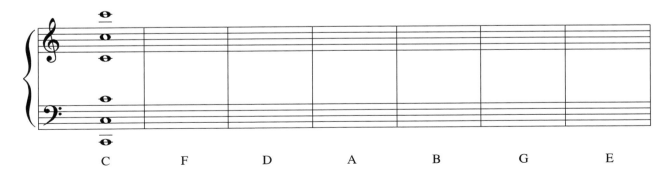

C   F   D   A   B   G   E

Exercise 1.19

Write the letter name of the pitch below each note and then sing the melodies.

1. A Pleasant Morning, Op. 63, No. 1 (L. Streabbog)

Note: Brackets are placed around two different motives. Find other examples of the motives, bracket and label them. (Some examples may be varied from the original motives.)

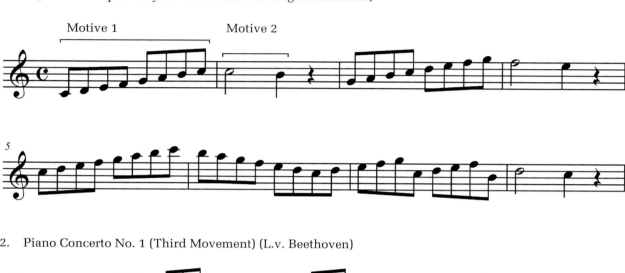

2. Piano Concerto No. 1 (Third Movement) (L.v. Beethoven)

3. "Over the Rainbow" (H. Arlen)

NAME:

Exercise 1.20 | 8va and 8vb

Write the letter name of the note below the staff. Place an **X** on the corresponding key above and draw an arrow connecting the two. (Keep track of middle C!)

Example

F   A   D

1.

2.

3.

MODULE 2

BASICS OF RHYTHM

Pulse: Feeling the Beat

We have been studying music as the organization of sound. In this module, we will add the important dimension of **time**, which is the duration of sounds or silences. This organization of sound in time is called **rhythm**.

Rhythm plays an organizing role in dance, poetry, and theatre—even comedy routines. Our bodies experience rhythm with our heartbeats, breathing, and locomotion. In music, when you tap your foot to a song, you are responding to its rhythm, or "feeling the beat."

Beat is the regularity of a **pulse**. This can be shown as equidistant lines:

| | | | | | | |

Tempo is the rate of speed of the beat. Many composers use Italian words to indicate the tempo of a piece. For example, *Allegro* (happy or cheerful in Italian) is used for a fast tempo, *Moderato* means medium speed, and *Adagio* is used for a slow tempo. If musicians who are performing together do not agree on the same tempo, to maintain a steady beat, and to accelerate or decelerate at the same time, they will not play together and the result will be cacophony (from the Greek language meaning "bad sounds").

🔊 **TRACKS 30–34**

> 30. *"Hong Cai Mei Mei," Chinese folk song*
> 31. *Intermezzo, Op. 116, No. 4 (J. Brahms)*
> 32. *Italian Concerto (First movement) (J.S. Bach)*
> 33. *"Nautilus," Sea Pieces (E. MacDowell)*
> 34. *Riff in C (S. Takesue)*

Exercise 1 Class Exercise

Using Tracks 30–34 or examples played by your instructor, determine the tempo and place a check on the appropriate blank below. As you are listening, feel the pulse of the piece and clap it. Is the tempo fast, medium, or slow?

	Fast (*Allegro*)	Medium (*Moderato*)	Slow (*Adagio*)
30.	_____	_____	_____
31.	_____	_____	_____
32.	_____	_____	_____
33.	_____	_____	_____
34.	_____	_____	_____

Types of Rhythmic Values

Rhythmic values are the duration of pitches. When we study rhythmic values, we are studying their mathematical relationships, which are not affected by the tempo.

Beginning with the whole note, each note divides into two smaller parts.

- Notice that each note is **one-half** the value of the note in the line immediately above it. For example, the half note (♩) is half the value of the whole note (o):

$$ \text{𝅗𝅥} \; + \; \text{𝅗𝅥} \; = \; \text{o} $$

Likewise, the quarter note (♩) is one half the value of the half note (𝅗𝅥):

$$ \text{♩} \; + \; \text{♩} \; = \; \text{𝅗𝅥} $$

- Notice that each note is **one-fourth** the value of the note two lines above it. For example, the quarter note (♩) is one-fourth the value of the whole note (o):

$$ \text{♩} \; + \; \text{♩} \; + \; \text{♩} \; + \; \text{♩} \; = \; \text{o} $$

Likewise, the eighth note (♪) is one-eighth the value of the whole note.

- Any note may be used to represent the beat; we sometimes call this note the **pulse note**. When the quarter note represents one beat, then the note values named below on the left receive the corresponding number of beats written to the right.

Whole	𝅝	=	4 beats
Half	𝅗𝅥	=	2 beats
Quarter	♩	=	1 beat
Eighth	♪	=	½ beat
Sixteenth	𝅘𝅥𝅯	=	¼ beat

Exercise 2 Class Exercise

Give *one* note value to make the equation correct.

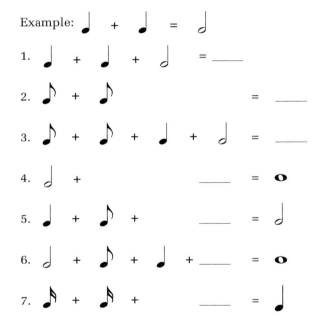

Example: ♩ + ♩ = 𝅗𝅥

1. ♩ + ♩ + 𝅗𝅥 = ___

2. ♪ + ♪ = ___

3. ♪ + ♪ + ♩ + 𝅗𝅥 = ___

4. 𝅗𝅥 + ___ = 𝅝

5. ♩ + ♪ + ___ = 𝅗𝅥

6. 𝅗𝅥 + ♪ + ♩ + ___ = 𝅝

7. 𝅘𝅥𝅯 + 𝅘𝅥𝅯 + ___ = ♩

Stems and Flags

Notes may consist of the following parts:

Stem ↘ 𝅘𝅥𝅮 ↙ Flag

Note head   or   Note head filled in   Stem   Stems with flags   Note head

Exercise 3

1. Begin drawing notes with the note head, which is elliptical in shape. This is similar to the **whole note** $\mathbf{o}$ which is round rather than elliptical.

2. Add stems to the following note heads to change whole notes to **half notes**. Alternate stemming notes on the right and above the note head, and on the left and below the note head as shown.

3. Fill in the note heads and add stems to change whole notes to **quarter notes**, alternating stems up and down.

4. Fill in the note heads, add stems and flags to change whole notes to **eighth notes**. Notice that flags are always drawn to the right of the stem.

> Adjacent eighth notes may be connected with **beams** (♩♩ or ♩♩) instead of using flags for each note. This will be discussed later in the module.

5. Fill in the note heads, add stems and two flags to change whole notes to **sixteenth notes**. As with eighth notes shown earlier, flags are always drawn to the right of the stem.

Additional flags may be added to note heads, resulting in thirty-second notes (♬) and sixty-fourth notes (♬) and others.

The **direction of the stem** is determined by the placement of the note on the staff, regardless of the clef. Notes that are drawn through the third line of the staff usually stem down, but they can stem in either direction, regardless of the clef.

Notes that are drawn below the third line of the staff stem **up** on the right. Notes above the third line stem **down** on the left of the notes, regardless of the clef.

Exercise 4

Add stems to these note heads to change them to half notes. Write the letter name below each note. The first one is done for you.

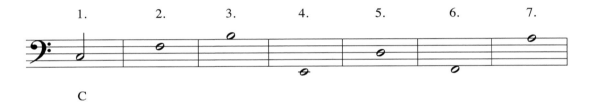

Fill in the note heads and add stems to these note heads to change them to quarter notes. Write the letter name below each note.

Rhythmic Patterns with Beams

Stems with flags can be added only to note heads that are filled in: single eighth notes are drawn with a stem and one flag (♪) and single sixteenth notes have a stem and two flags. Several adjacent eighth or sixteenth notes frequently are linked together with thick, straight lines called **beams**. Because beams replace flags, eighth notes have one beam and sixteenth notes are drawn with two beams.

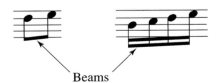

Beams

Beams facilitate note reading and counting by grouping notes into units reflecting the beat. In older editions of vocal music it was common to use individual notes with flags, instead of beams, to match each syllable of the lyrics with a specific pitch; this practice is not in use today.

Difficult to read   Easier to read

When beaming groups of notes together, the direction of the stems will be determined by the placement on the staff of the majority of the notes.

If a majority does not exist, one usually stems the notes away from the note that is farthest from the middle line of the staff.

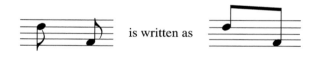   is written as

Workbook Exercises 2.1 and 2.2

Exercise 5

In the following exercises, rewrite the single eighth notes by using beams. Group notes by two as needed.

1. "Pentatonic Tune" from *For Children Vol. 1* (B. Bartók)

    Notice the clef change from bass clef at the beginning to the treble clef in the middle of the line.

2. "The Bonny Lass" (English dance tune from "The Dancing Master")

3. "Tarong, Kamatis, Parya" ("Eggplant, Tomato, and Bitter Melon"), Filipino folk ballad, Iloko dialect

Cultural note: Filipino folk ballads

Filipino folk ballads frequently include animals and plants in their narrative. In this song, the eggplant, tomato, and bitter melon argue: which vegetable is the most delicious?

("Early in the morning, we looked out of the window, and the eggplant, tomato, and amargoso were there, I heard them talking. . .")

I - ti big - bi - gat nga ag - sa - pa ag - ta - tam - dag kam man i - diay ta -

wa ad - da da ta - rong, ka - ma - tis, par ya nang - ngeg ko i - da nga'g - sa - sa - ri - ta.

In our longer music examples the measures are numbered for convenience—see the small figure 5 at the beginning of the second line of music.

Time Signature, Bar Line, Double Bar Line

The **time signature** indicates the recurrent grouping of accented and unaccented beats. The time signature is found at the beginning of a piece of music just after the clef sign (*not* at the beginning of every staff of music). Vertical lines called **bar lines** are placed at the end of each grouping of beats and separate the groups into **measures**. A **double bar** (‖) is placed at the end of a section of music (*not* at the end of every staff). The end of a piece is indicated by a final double bar (𝄂).

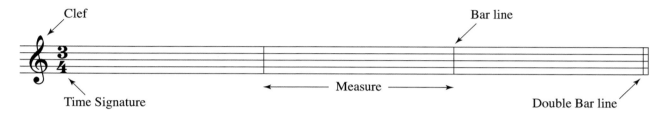

The *upper* number of the time signature indicates the number of beats or counts in each measure. In this module, the upper number will be 2, 3, or 4.

The *lower* number of the time signature indicates the type of note that receives one beat (sometimes called the **pulse note**), and subsequently determines the number of beats that each note receives. When the lower number of the time signature is 4, as in the example above, the quarter note is the pulse note and receives one count. We will be using 4 as the lower number of the time signature in this module. The lower number will change in subsequent modules.

Exercise 6 Class Exercise

Clap and say the counts for the following rhythmic patterns:

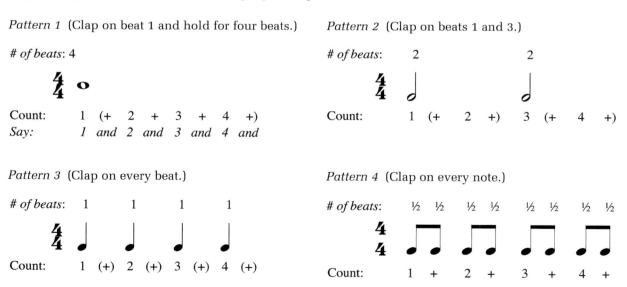

Pattern 5 (Clap on every note.)

Count: 1 e + a   2 e + a   3 e + a   4 e + a
Say: 1 ee and uh 2 ee and uh 3 ee and uh 4 ee and uh

Workbook Exercise 2.3

Meter

Meter refers to the stresses of strong and weak beats. An example of the stressing of accented words may be heard in the opening line of Edgar Allan Poe's narrative poem "The Raven":

/   /   /   /   /   /   /   /
Once u**pon** a **mid**night **drear**y, **while** I **pon**dered, **weak** and **wear**y,

In music, the first beat of each measure is normally the strongest and is given an accent (>). The repeating pattern of strong beats followed by weaker beats is called the metric accent.

Simple Meter

When the top number of the time signature is a 2, 3, or 4, this is called **simple meter**. In simple meter, the pulse note is divided into two or four equal parts.

Exercise 7 Class Exercise

Count and clap the following rhythms in simple meter, stressing beat one.

Meter: Simple duple

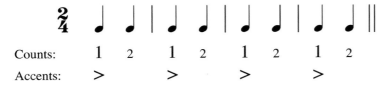

Counts: 1   2   1   2   1   2   1   2
Accents: >   >   >   >

Meter: Simple triple

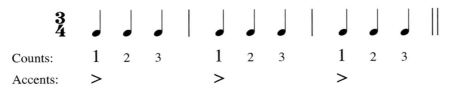

Counts: 1   2   3   1   2   3   1   2   3
Accents: >   >   >

Meter: Simple quadruple

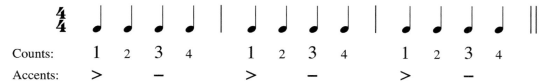

Counts: 1   2   3   4   1   2   3   4   1   2   3   4

Accents: >   –   >   –   >   –

In simple quadruple meter, the first beat is the strongest and is given an accent; the third beat is slightly stressed (–). The second and fourth beats are the weakest beats.

The time signature $\frac{4}{4}$ can also be written as **C** which stands for "common time."

For example: "Qing Hai Min Ge" ("Boys and Girls Working Together to Plant Rice") Chinese folk song

Counts: 1   2   3   4   1   2   3   4   1   2   3   4   1   2   3   4

Accents: >   –   >   –   >   –   >   –

Comparing a Melody in Different Meters

The pitches of a melodic line will sound differently when they are written in different meters. Each of the melodies below consists of the same pitches; however, each is written in a different meter.

Exercise 8 **Class Exercise**

Clap the examples below, emphasizing the indicated strong beats. Discuss how meter may affect the tempo you select. How does the change in meter affect the melody even though identical pitches are used for each melody?

Melody in simple duple meter

Melody in simple triple meter

Melody in simple quadruple meter

Theory Trainer

Exercise 2a Simple rhythm tapping: Start the metronome, then press key "a", "s", "j", or "k" to the notated rhythm.

Conducting Patterns

Conducting patterns can help to demonstrate meter. Notice that the strong beat (beat one) is always a downward motion, also known as the **downbeat**. The last beat of each pattern is always an upward motion, also known as the **upbeat**.

Sing and conduct these songs, feeling the accent on the first beat of each measure.

Simple Duple Meter   Sing and conduct: "Jingle Bells."

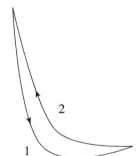

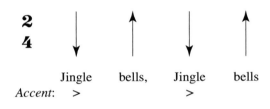

Simple Triple Meter   Sing and conduct: "My Favorite Things" (R. Rodgers, O. Hammerstein II)

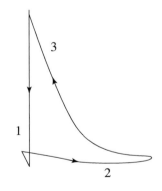

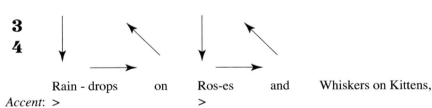

Simple Quadruple   Sing and conduct: "Love Me Tender" (E. Presley, V. Matson)

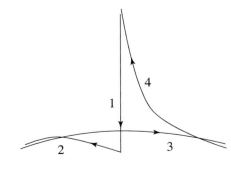

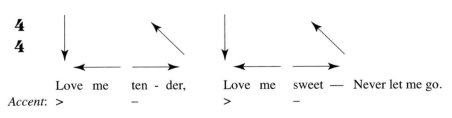

57

🔊 **TRACKS 35–37**

35. *"Jingle Bells"*
36. *"My Favorite Things"* (R. Rodgers, O. Hammerstein II)
37. *"Love Me Tender"* (E. Presley, V. Matson)

Conducting Exercises

You will hear taps for two measures to establish the tempo; beat one will be emphasized. Conduct each piece listed above, feeling the strong downbeat. Can you sing the words or the syllable "La" and conduct at the same time?

Workbook Exercises 2.4–2.6

Exercise 9

Identify the meter for the following exercises. Write the number of beats for each note value above the note and place the counts and accents below. Be sure that:

- Above the exercise, the total number of beats in each measure should equal the **upper** number of the time signature.
- When counting, all numbers should be consecutive; begin every measure with 1. For example: 1 2 3 4.
- While clapping the rhythm, count out loud, emphasizing the beat that gets the accent.

Example:

Meter: <u>Simple Duple</u>

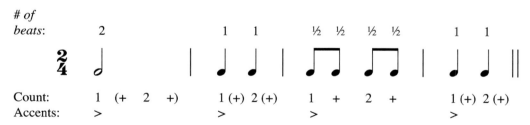

 # of
beats: 2   1   1   ½ ½   ½ ½   1   1

Count: 1 (+ 2 +)   1 (+) 2 (+)   1   +   2   +   1 (+) 2 (+)
Accents: >   >   >   >

1. Meter: _____

 # of
beats: 2   2

Count: 1 (+ 2 +) 3 (+ 4 +)
Accents: >   —

2. Meter: _____

# of beats: 1   1   1

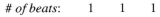

Count: 1 (+) 2 (+) 3 (+)
Accents: >

3. Meter: _____

# of beats: 2

Count: 1 (+ 2 +)
Accents: >

4. Meter: _____

# of beats: ½ ½ 1 1 1

Count: 1 + 2 (+) 3 (+) 4 (+)
Accents: >

5. Meter: _____

# of beats: ¼ ¼ ¼ ¼   ¼ ¼ ¼ ¼

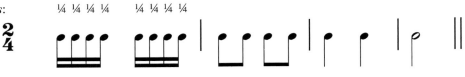

Count: 1 e + a   2 e + a
>

6. Meter: _____

# of beats: 2   1

Count: 1 (+ 2 +) 3 (+)
>

Exercise 10 Class Exercise

Add the missing barlines and double barlines according to the time signature given at the beginning of each line.

 Theory Trainer

Exercise 2b Draw missing bar lines in simple rhythms.

Exercise 11

Identify the meter for the following melodies. Write the number of beats above the melody and the consecutive counts and accents below. Then clap and sing each exercise.

Vocabulary note

MOTIVE

A motive is a short musical idea consisting of a melodic contour in a particular rhythmic pattern. A composer uses motives to give unity to a piece of music through repetition of the motive, and to create variety by varying the motive in pitch and/or rhythm. (See "Sakura" and "Sliding Around the Block.")

PHRASE

A phrase is the musical equivalent of a sentence, usually between four and eight measures long. (See "Zum Gali Gali.")

GLISSANDO

The glissando instructs the performer to "slide," singing all pitches between the two notes. This technique is used by guitarists in rock bands to timpani players in symphony orchestras, as well as jazz, blues and Chinese opera singers. (See "Sliding Around the Block.")

---

1. "Sakura," Japanese **pentatonic** folk song

    Meter _____

    The first three notes of this piece form a motive; a bracket is placed above these notes. Locate and bracket repetitions of the motive. Find a different motive; bracket and label each occurrence "Motive 2."

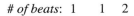

Count: 1   2   3   (4)
Accents: >   –

2. "Zum Gali Gali," Israeli Folk Song

    Meter _____

    Do you hear one or two phrases in this melody? _____

Count: 1   ½ ½
Accents: >

3.   "Sliding Around the Block" (R. Dorin)

Meter _____

Bracket the rhythmic motive that is used throughout this piece. Does this constant repetition render the piece uninteresting? _____ If not, why not?

_____

Counts:

Exercise 12 Class Exercise—One and Two Hand Exercises

Tap the notes above the line with your right hand; tap the notes below the line with your left hand. Tap both hands for two-hand exercises. Counting out loud, practice slowly at first, then faster. (If you tap a pencil in one hand and tap on the desk with your other hand, you will hear two different sounds for the parts. Bring a drum and snare to class for even greater variety.)

1.

2.

3.

4.

5.

Exercise 13 Three-Part Rhythm Exercises

Tap or clap each line separately. Then divide the class into three, each section performing a different line. For greater interest, each line may be produced in a different manner: tapping on a table top, clapping, snapping fingers.

Alternatively, each student may tap two lines at once: lines 1 and 2, lines 2 and 3, or lines 1 and 3.

1.

2.

Exercise 14 Vocabulary

Define the following words:

1. Rhythm
2. Pulse note
3. Stem
4. Note head
5. Flag
6. Beam
7. Tempo:
    Allegro
    Moderato
    Andante
8. Rhythmic values:
    Whole note
    Half note
    Quarter note
    Eighth note
    Sixteenth note
9. Measure
10. Time signature
11. Bar line
12. Meter:
    Simple meter
    Duple
    Triple
    Quadruple
13. Metric accent
14. Motive
15. Phrase
16. Conducting patterns
17. Upbeat
18. Downbeat

 Theory Trainer

Exercise 2a   Simple rhythm tapping: Start the metronome, then press the "a," "s," "j," or "k" key to the notated rhythm.

Exercise 2c   Listening to rhythms.
Reproduce rhythms you hear by clicking on the boxed rhythms (stamps). Can you complete the exercise in one hearing?

Workbook Exercises 2.7–2.11

Name _____

Exercise 2.1

Draw two notes an octave apart in the rhythmic values that are indicated.

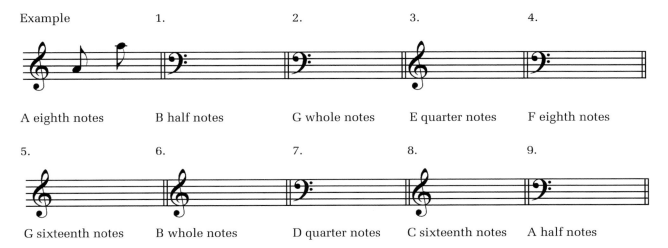

Example   1.   2.   3.   4.

A eighth notes   B half notes   G whole notes   E quarter notes   F eighth notes

5.   6.   7.   8.   9.

G sixteenth notes   B whole notes   D quarter notes   C sixteenth notes   A half notes

Exercise 2.2

Add beams and stems, and fill in the note heads to change these whole notes into groups of two eighth notes or four sixteenth notes as shown below. Alternate stemming above and below the note head as shown.

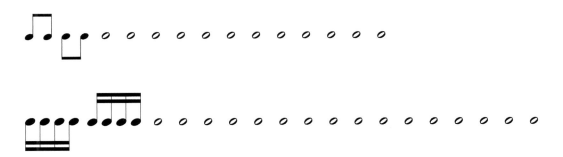

Exercise 2.3

Add stems and beams to the following melodies so that the total number of beats in every measure corresponds to the top number of the time signature. The number of beats is given above each note. (Review pages 49–51 for rules on stemming.)

1. *# of beats*: 1 1 1 1 1 1 2 1 2 ½ ½ 1 1 2

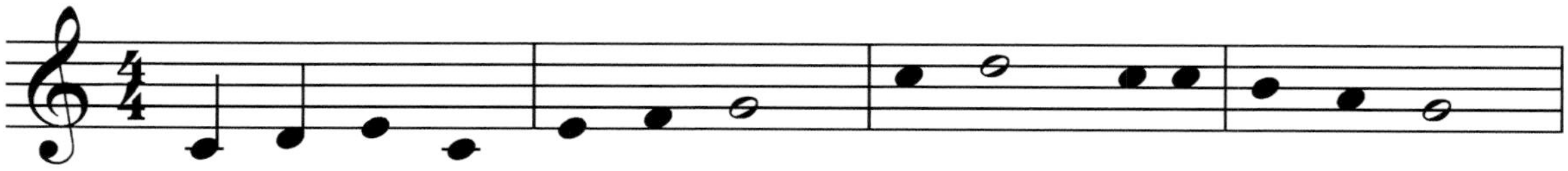

2. "Diu Diu Tong Zai" (Y. Z. Zhen), Chinese **pentatonic** folk melody whose lyrics mimic the sound of raindrops.

# of beats: 1 1 ½ ½ ½ ½ ½ ½ ½ ½ 1 ½ ½ 1 ½ ½ 2 1 1

# of beats:

8 ½ 1 ½ 1 ½ ½ ½ ½ ½ ½ ½ ½ ½ ½ ½ ½ ½ ½ 1 1 2

3. "Knecht Ruprecht," Op. 69, No. 12 (R. Schumann)
   Notice the clef change in measure 3, which does not affect the counting.

# of beats: ¼ ¼ ¼ ¼ ¼ ¼ ¼ ¼ ½ ½ ½ ½ ½ ½ ½ ½ ½ ½ 1

Exercise 2.4 | Ear Training

Place a check on the appropriate blank below, indicating the meter. Tips to remember:

- Find the basic pulse.
- Determine the strong beat.
- Count the number of beats from strong beat to strong beat.
- If you are unsure of the answer, check the first answer that comes to mind. (First impressions are frequently correct.)

🔊 **TRACKS 38–43**

Determine the meter of the pieces: duple, triple, or quadruple. Each exercise will be played twice.

	Duple	Triple	Quadruple
38. *Waltz in A Minor (F. Chopin)*	_____	_____	_____
39. *Anglaise (Anon.)*	_____	_____	_____
40. *Dance of Slovaks (B. Bartók)*	_____	_____	_____
41. *"Toryanse," Japanese folk song*	_____	_____	_____
42. *Menuet in G Major (J.S. Bach)*	_____	_____	_____
43. *"Lady Sant' Ana," Mexican-American folk song*	_____	_____	_____

Exercise 2.5

In the following exercises, write the number of beats above the notes. Write the consecutive counts and accents below. Then clap and sing each exercise.

1. Menuet (J.S. Bach)

    A bracket is placed above a musical motive at the beginning of the piece. Examine how the motive is varied in the following two measures.

# of beats: ½ ½ 1   1

Count: 1 + 2   3
Accents: >

2. Symphony No. 94 (Second Movement) (F.J. Haydn)

# of beats: 2   2

Count: 1 (2) 3 (4)
Accents: >   —

# of beats:

Count:
Accents:

3. Allegro moderato (L. Schytte)

    Locate and bracket a motive that is used twice in the excerpt below. Is the motive repeated exactly, or is it varied?

# of beats: 1   ½ ½   1   1

Count: 1   2 + 3   4
Accents: >   —

Exercise 2.6

Write the counts below each exercise. Clap and count, emphasizing the beat that gets the accent.

NAME: _____

Exercise 2.7

Match the word with the definition.

1. Allegro   _____   Part of the note that is oval; its placement on the staff indicates the pitch of the note

2. Bar line   _____   Eighth notes

3. Beam   _____   Recurring division of the pulse into a pattern of strong and weak beats

4. Downbeat   _____   Note that represents the beat; note that receives one count

5. Flag   _____   Quarter notes

6. Measure   _____   Vertical line through the horizontal lines of a staff or staves separating music into measures

7. Meter   _____   Horizontal line connecting the end of note stems of rhythmic values smaller than a quarter note; replaces the flag on individual notes

8. Motive   _____   Musical sentence, frequently four to eight measures long

9. Note head   _____   The two numbers placed at the beginning of a piece that indicate the number of beats in a measure (top number) and the note value of the basic pulse (lower number); sometimes called Meter signature

10. Phrase   _____   Short curved line attached to the stem on the right at the opposite end of the note head that changes the note's value by half

11. Pulse note   _____   Grouping of metered beats (strong and weak beats) separated by lines called bar lines

12. Tempo   _____   Italian. Fast tempo

13. Time signature   _____   Short rhythmic and melodic idea used in a phrase

14. 🎵   _____   Rate of speed of the pulse

15. 🎵   _____   First beat of the measure, named for the conductor's downward motion used to indicate the first beat

Exercise 2.8

Add the missing barlines and double barlines according to the time signatures given at the beginning of each line. Write the consecutive counts below the rhythms.

Exercise 2.9

Compose rhythms to fill measures that are left blank.

- Use combinations of notes that are similar to those in the surrounding measures.
- Be sure that the number of counts in each measure equals the upper number of the time signature.
- Count and clap the completed exercise.

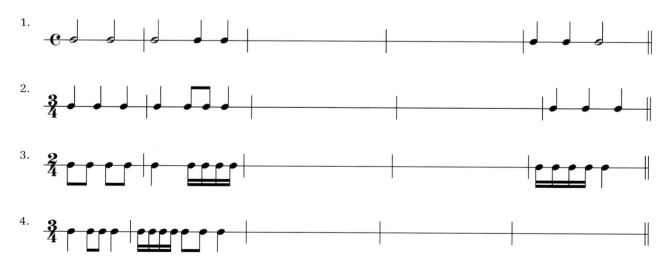

Exercise 2.10

Rewrite the following melodies below each exercise. Add the missing bar lines and double bar lines according to the time signature given at the beginning of each line. Write the consecutive counts below the rhythms; clap. The first two beats for each melody are given.

1.

a. Notate the melody in 2/4.

b. Notate the melody in 3/4.

c. Notate the melody in 4/4.

2.

a. Notate the melody in 2/4.

b. Notate the melody in 3/4.

c. Notate the melody in 4/4.

Exercise 2.11

Correct the counting errors in each measure for the following exercises.

1.

Incorrect counting: 1   2   3 4   1 2 3 4   1   2   3 (4) 4

Correct counting: 1   (2)   3 + 4   1 (2) 3 (4)

2.

Incorrect counting: 2   1   2   +   1   + 2   1   +   2   3   4

Correct counting: 1   (2)   1   2

MODULE 3

BASICS OF RHYTHM: EXTENDING DURATION, ANACRUSIS, RESTS

Tied Notes: Extending Duration

Note values may be extended through the use of a **tie:** ⌣ or ⌢. Ties connect two or more notes of the same pitch by adding together the note values of each tied note. Ties must be drawn from note head to note head and must connect each note.

Correct notation

Incorrect notation

Tied notes are played only once and continue to sustain for the duration of all tied note values. For example:

 = Half note

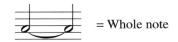 = Whole note

Ties may be used to hold a note into the next measure. For example:

Incorrect

Beats: 4   1   1

Correct

Beats: 2   +   2   1   1

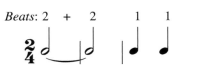

Here, a whole note in the first measure exceeds the number of beats allowed in a 2/4 time signature. In order to hold the first note for four beats, a half note would be tied to another half note.

Exercise 1

In the following exercises, write the number of beats above the tied notes and give the total note value below.

Example:
Symphony No. 7 (Third Movement) (A. Bruckner)

1. "Ma Che Fu Chi Lian" ("Love Story of the Wagon Driver"), Chinese folk song

2. Suite in C for Orchestra (J.S. Bach)

3. "My Cherie Amour" (Stevie Wonder, S. Moy, H. Cosby)

4. Evening in the Country (*from Ten Easy Pieces*, No. 5) (B. Bartók)

   Note the time signature change in measure 4.

5. "Honeysuckle Rose" (Thomas "Fats" Waller, A. Razaf)

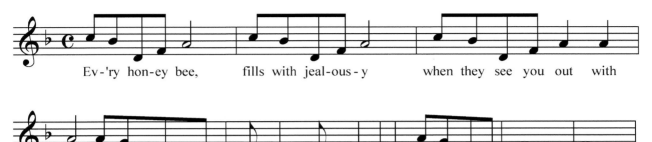

Ev-'ry hon-ey bee,   fills with jeal-ous-y   when they see you out with

me. I don't blame them, good-ness knows, -   Hon-ey-suck-le Rose.

Slurs

Slurs should not be confused with **ties**. Ties connect notes of the same pitch while slurs connect two or more notes of different pitches. Slurs should be played smoothly and connected. Following are some examples of ties and slurs:

Ties

Slurs

Dotted Notes: Extending Duration

Dots placed after a note extend the duration of that note by adding one-half of its value.

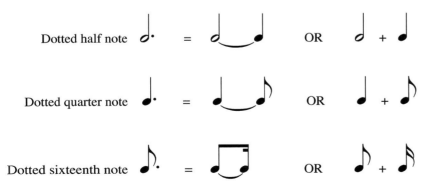

Vocabulary note

A dotted note should not be confused with the staccato, which is a dot that is placed above or below a note. Staccato notes are played in a disconnected or unconnected manner.

Exercise 2

Listen to your instructor play the following excerpt from "I Believe" which uses both dotted notes and tied notes. The values of the dotted notes are written above the measures with dots; consecutive counts are written below those measures. Notice that the value of the dot is half the value of the preceding note. Count and clap.

"I Believe" (E. Drake, I. Graham et. al.)

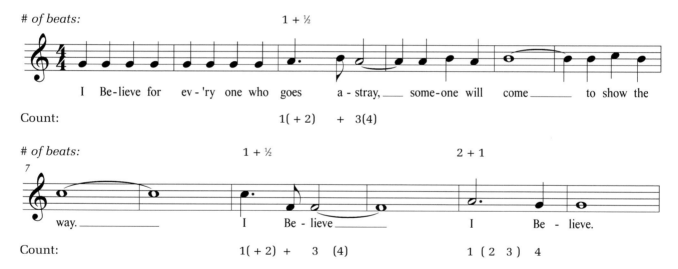

- Notice that the dotted quarter notes in mm. 3 and 9 are equivalent to 1½ beats.
- Notice that the dotted half note in m. 11 is equivalent to 3 beats.
- Locate the four pairs of tied notes. How many total counts does each of the pairs of tied notes receive? _____ _____ _____ _____.

Below, "I Believe" is rewritten using ties to replace the dots in mm. 3, 9, and 11. Consecutive counts are written below those measures.

"I Believe" rewritten with ties to replace dots.

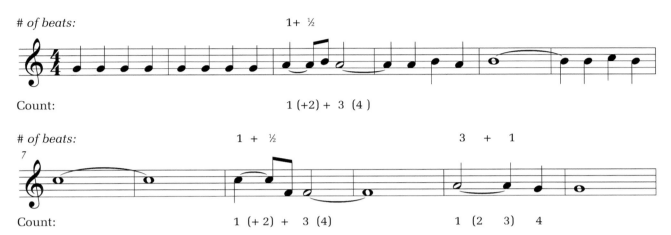

# of beats: 1+ ½

Count: 1 (+2) + 3 (4)

# of beats: 1 + ½   3   +   1

Count: 1 (+ 2) +   3 (4)   1 (2   3)   4

- Discuss why some of the tied notes in the second version may be replaced with dots in the first version, and why others may not.
- Count and clap both versions of "I Believe." They should sound exactly the same.

Exercise 3 Class Exercise

Write the meter in the following exercises. Then write the number of beats for each note value above the note, and write the counts below. Count and clap the exercises.

Be sure that:

- The total number of beats in each measure equals the top number of the time signature.
- The number beneath the note is placed directly under the note that gets the count.

Example:
Meter: <u>Simple duple</u>

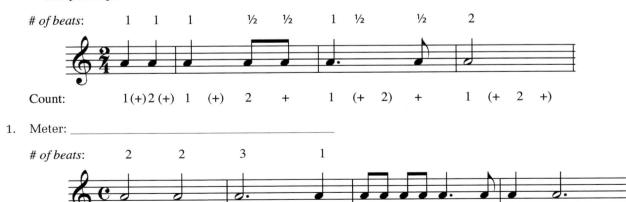

# of beats: 1   1   1   ½   ½   1   ½   ½   2

Count: 1(+)2 (+) 1   (+)   2   +   1   (+ 2)   +   1   (+   2   +)

1.   Meter: _____

# of beats: 2   2   3   1

Count: 1 (+ 2 +) 3 (+ 4 +) 1 (+ 2 + 3 +) 4 (+)

2. Meter: _____

# of beats: 2

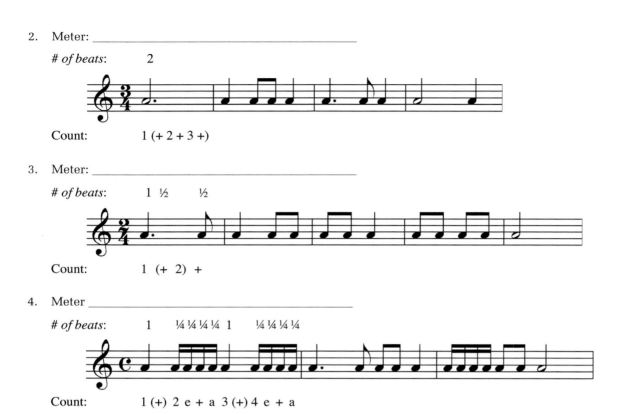

3. Meter: _____

# of beats: 1 ½   ½

4. Meter _____

# of beats: 1   ¼ ¼ ¼ ¼ 1   ¼ ¼ ¼ ¼

Count: 1 (+) 2 e + a 3 (+) 4 e + a

Exercise 4

Add the missing bar lines according to the time signatures given at the beginning of each rhythm. Write the number of beats above each note.

@ Theory Trainer

Exercise 3b Simple rhythm tapping with two hands.

Begin by tapping each hand separately: right hand on key "j" or "k" and left hand on the key "a" or "s". Then tap two hands together.

Exercise 3c Listening to rhythms.

Reproduce rhythms you hear by clicking on the boxed rhythms (stamps). Can you complete the exercise after hearing the exercise no more than three times?

Exercise 5 Class Exercise—Singing

In the following songs, the solfège syllables and numbers are given above each note. Write consecutive counts below.

- First, count and clap the exercise.
- Then sing with solfège, numbers, or letter names.

1. Track 44

Numbers 1 2 3 1 2 3 4 2 3 4 5 6 5 6 7 8
Solfège Do Re Mi Do Re Mi Fa Re Mi Fa Sol La So La Ti Do

Count: 1 2 3 1 (2 3)

2. Track 45

Numbers 1 3 2 4 3 5 4 6 5 4 3 2 1
Solfège Do Mi Re Fa Mi Sol Fa La Sol Fa Mi Re Do

Count: 1 (2 3) 4

3. Track 46

Numbers 8 7 8 7 6
Solfège Do Ti Do Ti La

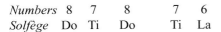

Count: 1 2 1 (2) 1 2

79

4. Track 47

Numbers 1 1 3 5
Solfège Do Do Mi Sol

Count: 1 + 2   3   (1)

🔊 **TRACKS 44–47**

> *Each of the exercises above will be played twice without pause, at a slow tempo. Listen the first time, then sing the second time, matching your pitch with the audio track. Repeat the exercise.*

Fermata

The **fermata** (🎵) extends the duration of a note by extending the count of a pitch (or pitches that sound simultaneously). The exact length of the count is determined by the performer's musical taste or interpretation.

Exercise 6

1. Sing "Happy Birthday to You" (M. J. Hill, P.S. Hill)
    In the second line, sustain the note with the fermata written above it.

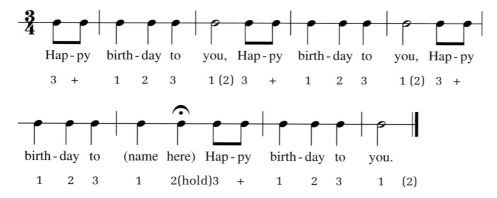

2. Chorale, Op. 68, No. 4 (originally 2/2) (R. Schumann)

*   Count and clap.
*   Then sing the letter name of each note, sustaining the notes with fermatas longer than their written note values.

Anacrusis

Music compositions do not always begin on the first beat of the measure. An incomplete measure at the beginning of a piece is called an **anacrusis** (from the Greek word, *anákrousis*, meaning "to strike, push back"). An incomplete measure at the end of the piece together with the anacrusis measure at the beginning will usually total the correct number of beats signified by the top number of the time signature.

The anacrusis is sometimes called a **pick-up** or **upbeat**. Do you recall that the conducting pattern for the first beat is always a downbeat, and that the last beat of the measure is always an upward motion? The term "upbeat" is derived from this upward motion. In "Oh, Susanna," the first two notes form an anacrusis measure:

"Oh, Susanna" (S. Foster)

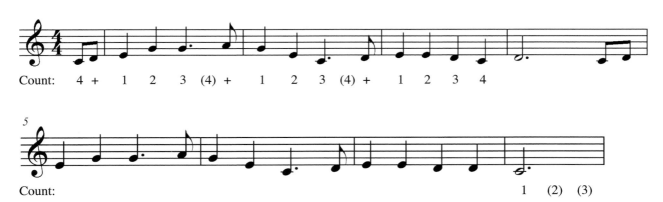

MODULE 3

Exercise 7

The following examples begin with anacrusis measures. Write the note value above each note and the count below. The number of beats in the anacrusis measure added to those in the last measure should equal the upper number of the time signature.

1. Viennese Sonatina No. 1 in C, K.439b (Second Movement) (W.A. Mozart)

# of beats: 1   1   1   1

Count: 3   1   2   3

2. Melody (R. Schumann)

# of beats:

Count:

3. Allegro, Op. 38, No. 3 (J.W. Hässler)

# of beats:

Count:

4. "There's No Business Like Show Business" (I. Berlin)
How many total counts do the tied notes receive? _____

# of beats:

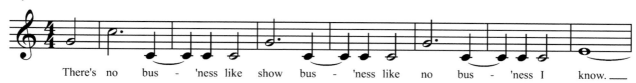

Count:

82

# of beats:

Ev-'ry thing a - bout it is ap - peal - ing.   Ev-'ry-thing the traf-fic will al - low.

Count:

5.   "Oboro Zukiyo" ("Hazy Moonlit Night") (O. Teiichi), Japanese folk song

# of beats:

Count:

# of beats:

Count:

Workbook Exercises 3.1–3.3

Rests

Rests are symbols for silence; for every note value there is a corresponding symbol to rest.

Whole rest	Half rest	Quarter rest	Eighth rest	Sixteenth rest

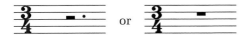

Rests may be dotted, but they may not be tied. For example, a complete measure of silence in 3/4 may be written as a dotted half rest; it also may be written as a whole rest.

Exercise 8

1. Draw whole rests, which are always written below the fourth line.

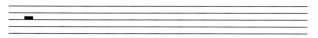

2. Draw half rests, which are always written above the third line.

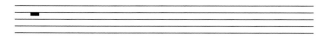

3. Draw quarter rests.

4. Draw eighth rests.

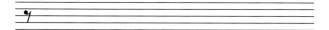

5. Draw sixteenth rests.

Exercise 9

Write in the beats above and the counts below each note or rest. Then clap the exercise and count out loud.

1. Tracks 48 and 49—The **whole rest**, unlike the whole note, extends through the **entire** measure; the number of counts it receives is dependent on the upper number of the time signature.

   In the first example below, you will find an assymetrical time signature where there are five beats in every measure. (For example, the jazz piece "Take Five," made famous by Dave Brubeck, is in 5/4.)

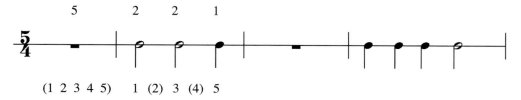

In the next example, the whole rest instructs you to be silent for the entire measure, which is three beats.

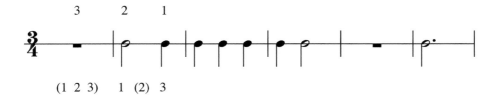

2. Track 50 – The **half rest** is equivalent to the half note.

3. Track 51 – The **quarter rest** is equivalent to the quarter note.

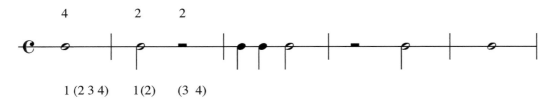

4. Track 52 – The **eighth rest** is equivalent to the eighth note.

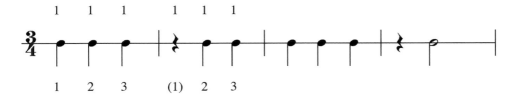

5. Track 53 – The **sixteenth rest** is equivalent to the sixteenth note.

🔊 **TRACKS 48–53**

Each rhythm in Exercise 9 will be played twice. If necessary, first listen, then clap on the repeat.

Exercise 10

Draw **one** rest that is equivalent to the given notes; draw a second option where indicated.

Example:

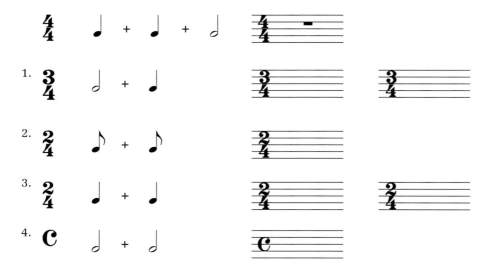

Exercise 11

Draw one rest below each arrow to complete the measure according to the given time signature. Write the note values above the notes and the consecutive counts below. The first measure is done for you. Count and clap.

3.

# of beats:

Count:

4.

# of beats:

Count:

5.

# of beats:

Count:

Workbook Exercises 3.4–3.6

Exercise 12

Write the note values above the note or rest and the consecutive counts below.

1. "El Mexico Que Se Nos Fue" ("The Mexico That We Were") (J. Gabriel)

# of beats: 1   1   1

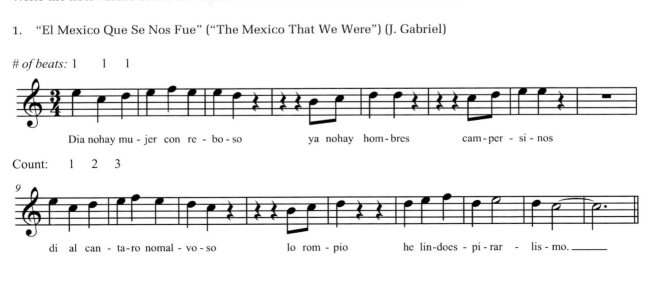

Dia nohay mu - jer con re - bo - so   ya nohay hom - bres   cam - per - si - nos

Count: 1   2   3

di al can - ta-ro nomal - vo - so   lo rom - pio   he lin-does - pi - rar - lis - mo. _____

Cultural note: Juan Gabriel

Born Alberto Aguilera Valadez (1950–), Juan Gabriel is one of the most popular Mexican singer/songwriters. Naming himself "Juan" in honor of the man who was his first music teacher and mentor, and "Gabriel" for his father, a field laborer who died tragically, Gabriel has written and recorded over a thousand songs in a variety of genres: Latin-Mexican pop, mariachi, and ranchera.

In this song, Gabriel sadly mourns the Mexico that he knew and loved, but is no longer. "There are no women with shawls, men are no longer farmers, and the pitcher does not go to the well. Industrialism broke it."

2.   Quintet in C, K.515 (First Movement) (W.A. Mozart)

# of beats: 1   ½ ½

Count: 3 (+) 4 (+)

3.   Prelude No. 1 in C, BWV 933 (J.S. Bach)

# of beats: 1 ½ ½ 1 ½ ½

Count: 1   (2) +   3 (4)+

4.   "Ah! vous dirai-je, Maman," Variation 2 (W.A. Mozart)

# of beats:1   ½   ½

Count: 1   (2) +

5.   "Ma Che Fu Chi Lian" ("Love Story of the Wagon Driver"), Chinese folk song
     Tap the treble clef rhythm with the right hand and the bass clef rhythm with the left hand.

Count: (1) + 2 +

 Theory Trainer

Exercise 3a Simple rhythm tapping with rests.

Exercise 3b Simple rhythm tapping with two hands.

Exercise 3c Listening to rhythms and pitch.

Reproduce rhythms you hear by clicking on the boxed rhythms (stamps). Can you complete the exercise in three hearings?

Exercise 13 Class Exercise—Two-Hand Exercises

These exercises are for coordination and for improving your reading and counting skills. On your desk or your knees, tap hands separately; tap the notes above the line with your right hand; tap the notes below the line with your left hand. Then tap hands together. Counting out loud, practice slowly at first, then faster.

Exercise 14 Class Exercise

Tap or clap each line separately. Then divide the class into three, each section performing a different line. For greater interest, each line may be produced in a different manner: tapping on a table top, clapping, snapping fingers.

Alternatively, each student may tap two lines at once: lines 1 and 2, lines 2 and 3, or lines1 and 3.

1.

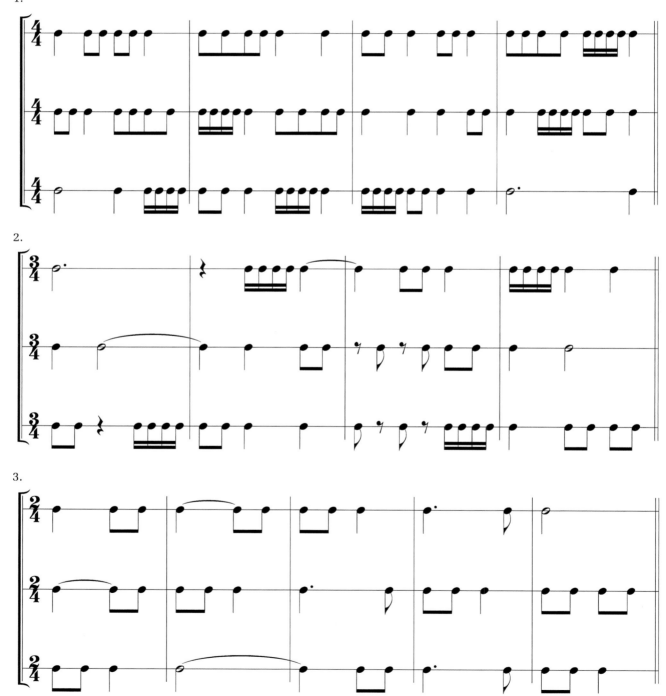

2.

3.

Exercise 15 Singing

In the following songs, the solfège syllables and numbers are given above each note. Write the counts below the notes.

- First, count and clap the exercise.
- Then sing with solfège or numbers.
- If you are familiar with the song, sing the words.

1. "Deck the Halls with Boughs of Holly," Traditional

| *Numbers* | 5 | | 4 | 3 | 2 | | 1 | 2 | 3 | 1 | | 2 | 3 | 4 | 2 | 3 | | 2 | 1 | 7 | 1 |
| *Solfège* | Sol | | Fa | Mi | Re | | Do | Re | Mi | Do | | Re | Mi | Fa | Re | Mi | | Re | Do | Ti | Do |

Count: 1 (2) +   3   4   1   2   3   4
Words: Deck   the halls with boughs of   hol - ly   Fa   La   La   La   La   La   La   La   La

2. "Do Re Mi" from *The Sound of Music* (R. Rodgers, O. Hammerstein II)

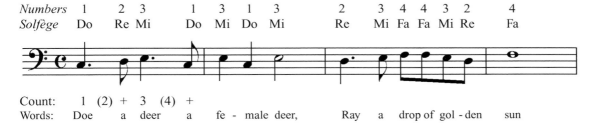

| *Numbers* | 1 | | 2 | 3 | | 1 | 3 | 1 | 3 | | 2 | | 3 | 4 | 4 | 3 | 2 | | 4 |
| *Solfège* | Do | | Re | Mi | | Do | Mi | Do | Mi | | Re | | Mi | Fa | Fa | Mi | Re | | Fa |

Count: 1 (2) +   3 (4) +
Words: Doe   a   deer   a   fe - male deer,   Ray   a   drop of gol - den   sun

Exercise 16

Define the following words:

1. Bar line
2. Measure
3. Time signature
4. Meter
5. Rest:
     Whole rest
     Half rest
     Quarter rest
     Eighth rest
     Sixteenth rest
6. Tie
7. Articulation marks:
     Staccato
     Slur

8. Double bar line
9. Dotted note
10. Fermata
11. Anacrusis
12. Pulse

Workbook Exercises 3.7–3.10

Name _____

Exercise 3.1

Draw one note that is equivalent to the tied notes.

Example

1.
2.
3.
4.
5.
6.
7.
8.

Exercise 3.2

Add the missing bar lines and double bar lines according to the time signature given at the beginning of each rhythm. Write the number of beats above each note. The first measure is done for you.

Exercise 3.3

Identify the meter. Write the number of beats above each melody and the consecutive counts below. Which examples begin with an anacrusis ("pick-up")? _____ Sing, using the letter names of the notes, the counts, or the words if provided.

1. "Auld Lang Syne" (R. Burns)
    Meter: _____

# of beats

Should auld ac-quaint-ance be for-got, And nev-er brought to mind?

Count:

2. How many slurs are used in the following exercise? ___ How many counts will the tied notes receive? ___

    Nocturne, Op. 15, No. 3 (originally in G minor) (F. Chopin)

# of beats:

Count:

3. How many counts do the tied notes receive?

    "Cielito Lindo" ("My Pretty Darling") (Q. Mendoza y Cortés)

# of beats

Ay, ay, ay, ay! _____ can - tay no llo - res, _____ por -

Count:

# of beats

que can - tan - do sea - le-gran, cie - li-to lin-do, los - co-pa - zo - nes.

Count:

94

Exercise 3.4

Match the word with the definition.

1. Anacrusis   _____   Dotted half note

2. Articulation   _____   Sign (◠) to hold longer or to pause

3. Bar line   _____   Whole rest

4. Double bar line   _____   Recurring division of the pulse into a pattern of strong and weak beats

5. Fermata   _____   Curved line above or below two or more different pitches indicating to play those notes smoothly or connected

6. Measure   _____   Half rest

7. Meter   _____   Vertical line through the horizontal lines of a staff or staves separating music into measures

8. Rest   _____   Dotted quarter note

9. Slur   _____   Eighth rest

10. [dotted half note symbol]   _____   Tie. A curved line connecting two or more consecutive notes of the same pitch. The first note is sounded and held for the combined value of all notes connected by the curved line(s).

11. [dotted half note symbol]   _____   Note or notes of an incomplete measure at the beginning of a piece of music (also called "pick-up")

12. [whole rest symbol]   _____   Two vertical lines on a staff or staves used to indicate the end of a section of music

13. [half rest symbol]   _____   Symbol to represent a specific duration of silence

14. [eighth rest symbol]   _____   Grouping of metered beats (strong and weak beats) separated by lines called bar lines

15. [tied notes symbol]   _____   An indication of how smoothly or detached written notes are to be sounded; words or symbols may be used

Exercise 3.5

Compose rhythms to fill measures that are left blank. Write counts below each exercise; clap.

- Use combinations of notes or rests that are similar to those in the surrounding measures.
- The total number of counts in each measure should equal the top number of the time signature.

1.

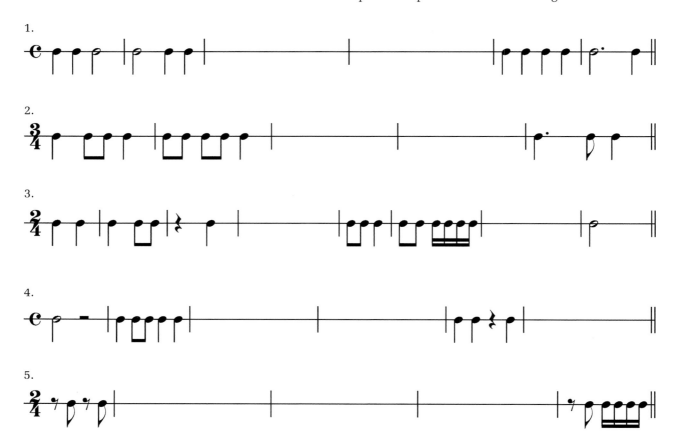

2.

3.

4.

5.

NAME: _____

Exercise 3.6

Rewrite the following measures using ties and changing the placement of the bar lines when necessary. Give the number of beats above each note.

Example

# of beats: 4   1   1   3   1

Rewrite answer:

# of beats: 2   2   1   1   2   1   1

1. *# of beats:*   1   1   2

Rewrite answer:

# of beats:

2. *# of beats:*   4   3   2

Rewrite answer:

# of beats:

3. *# of beats:*   2

Rewrite answer:

# of beats:

Exercise 3.7

Analyze the following melodies. Identify the meter. Do the examples begin with anacrusis measures? _____
Above the tied notes and rests, write the number of counts they receive; below the notes, write the consecutive
counts. The first measure is done for you.

1. "Your Song" (Elton John, B. Taupin)
    Meter: _____

My gift is my song   and___   this one's   for   you.   And you can tell   ev-'ry-bod   -   y

Count: (1)   2   3   +   4

this is your   song.___   It may be   quite   sim-ple, but   now that it's   done.___

Count:

2. "Guántanamera" (J. Fernandez)
    Meter: _____

Yo soy un hom-bre sin-cer-o,   de don-de   cre-ce la   -   pal-ma.   -   Yo soy un   hom-bre sin-cer-o,

Count:

de don-de   cre   -   ce la   pal-ma.   -   Yan-tes de mor-rir me quie-ro,   E-chat mis   ver-sos del al   -   ma.

Count:

Cultural note: "Guantánamera"

"Guantánamera" ("Woman from Guantanamo") is a popular Cuban anthem sung in many countries. In the United States it was popularized by folk singers such as Pete Seeger and Celia Cruz. Because words were frequently improvised, there are many versions of the lyrics. The composer, Joseito Fernandez, sang "Guantanamera" on his Cuban radio show, adding lyrics discussing the news of the day.

NAME: _____

Exercise 3.8 Class Exercise—Rhythmic Dictation

Various combinations of the following rhythms will be played. Each example will be three measures long. Your instructor will tell you the time signature to write at the beginning of the line and will count one measure out loud to establish the tempo immediately before beginning the exercise. Can you notate the exercise after hearing the exercise three times?

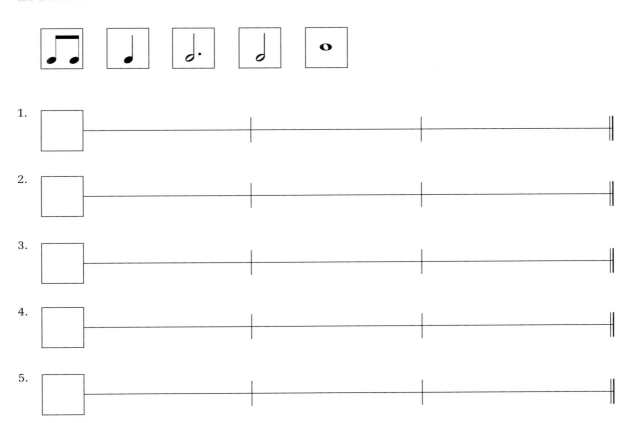

Exercise 3.9 Class Exercise

Complete each melody below using the two-measure motives, time signatures, and rhythms provided.

- Compose two phrases, each four or five measures long; the second phrase may be similar or contrasting to the first. Use rhythms that are similar to those of the given motive.
- Add additional bar lines as needed and end with a double bar line.
- To give your melody a sense of finality, end on a strong beat with a longer note value or a rest.
- Sing or play your compositions, or ask your instructor to play them for you.

1. Title: _____

Complete the melody below using the notes in the order given; any of the notes may be repeated. The original motive is characterized by repeated notes; consider repeating the rhythmic pattern of the motive to give the melody cohesion.

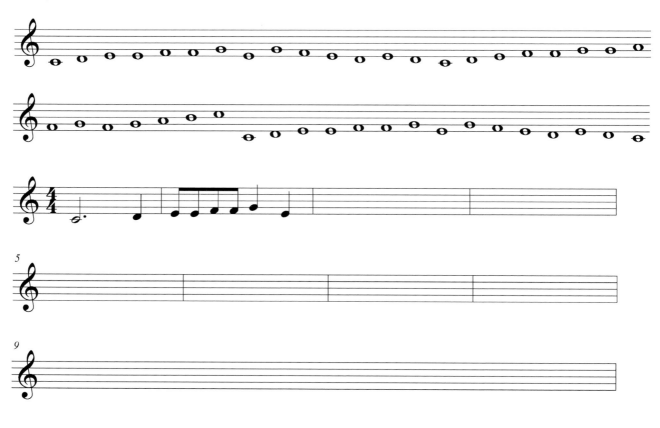

2. Title: _____

Complete the melody below using the rhythms given in the beginning instructions and the notes in the order given below. Any of the notes may be repeated. The original motive is characterized by skips; locate the sequence of the motive beginning on C. Consider repeating the rhythmic pattern of the motive to give the melody cohesion.

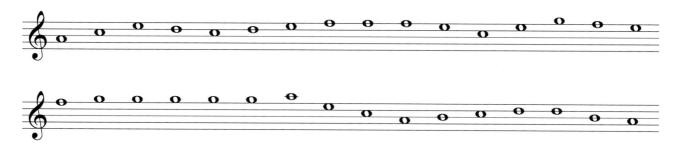

NAME: _____

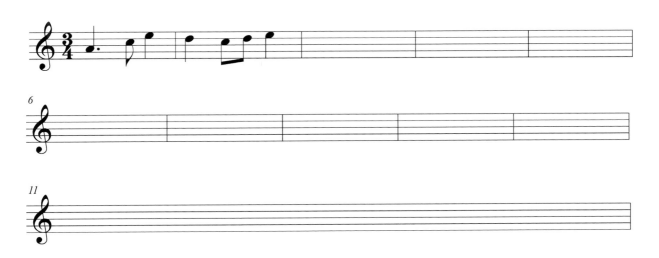

Exercise 3.10 | Class Exercise—One-, Two- and Three-Part Exercises

Tap or clap the following rhythms using tied notes. Your instructor may ask you to write the consecutive counts below each line.

1.

2.

3.

Tap or clap the following rhythms using dotted notes. Your instructor may ask you to write the consecutive counts below each line.

4.

5.

6.

Tap or clap the following rhythms beginning with an anacrusis measure. Your instructor may ask you to write the consecutive counts below each line.

7.

8.

Tap or clap the following rhythms using rests. Your instructor may ask you to write the consecutive counts below each line.

9.

10.

11.

NAME:

Tap the two-part rhythm. Begin by tapping or clapping each line separately. Then divide the class into two, each section performing a different line. For greater interest, each line may be produced in a different manner: for example, tapping on a table top, clapping, snapping fingers.

Alternatively, each student may tap the two lines at once.

12.

Tap the three-part rhythm. Begin by tapping or clapping each line separately. Then divide the class into three, each section performing a different line. For greater interest, each line may be produced in a different manner: for example, tapping on a tabletop, clapping, snapping fingers.

Alternatively, each student may tap two lines at once: lines 1 and 2, lines 2 and 3, or lines 1 and 3.

13.

MODULE 4

ACCIDENTALS

Sharp, Flat, Natural

In music of the West, the octave is divided into 12 equal parts called **half steps**, or **semitones**. In non-Western music (for example, as in Middle Eastern music), the octave may be divided into 24 units (**quartertones**). In some more modern Western music, it may be divided into even smaller units (**microtones**), as in the 43-unit music by American composer Harry Partch.

🔊 **TRACK 54**

>   *Listening: Hindustani jor improvisation on a zither accompanied by a tambura, a drone lute*

In Module 1 we discussed the white keys of the piano; in this module we will discuss the black keys. On the keyboard below, each key is numbered from 1 to 12. Notice that the white keys are separated by black keys except for E to F (5–6) and B to C (12–1). All *adjacent* numbered keys are called **half steps (HS)**. Half steps are paired white to black keys, or black to white keys, like steps 1–2 or 9–10, except for the two adjacent pairs of white keys (E to F and B to C).

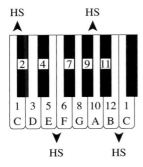

Five symbols called **accidentals** may be used to name all of the keys. We will begin our study with the first three accidentals shown in the box below; the last two will be discussed beginning on page 119.

♯	Sharp	– Raises a note a half step
♭	Flat	– Lowers a note half a step
♮	Natural	– Cancels a previous accidental
𝄪	Double sharp	– Raises a note two half steps
♭♭	Double flat	– Lowers a note two half steps

♯ The sharp **raises** a note a half step; the letter name of the note remains the same. On the keyboard, move to the nearest note to the **right**.

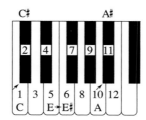

Notice that:

- The black key C sharp (key 2) is a half step **higher** in pitch than the white key C (key 1).
- The white key E sharp (key 6) is a half step **higher** in pitch than the white key E (key 5).
- The black key A sharp (key 11) is a half step **higher** in pitch than the white key A (key 10).
- There are two notes with sharps that are white keys: E sharp (E♯) and B sharp (B♯). Note that B♯ corresponds to C, and E♯ corresponds to F. When a note has more than one spelling, this is called an **enharmonic spelling**. (See page 110 for further discussion on enharmonic spellings.)

Exercise 1

Using sharps to name the note, write the letter name of the keys in the boxes below. The first answer is given.

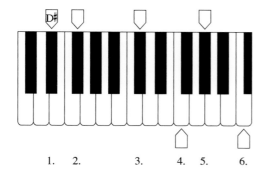

1.   2.   3.   4.   5.   6.

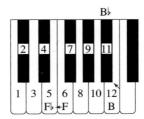

> ♭ The flat **lowers** a note a half step; the letter name of the note remains the same. On the keyboard, move to the nearest note to the **left**.

Notice that:

- The white key F flat (key 5) is a half step **lower** in pitch than the white key F (key 6).
- The black key B flat (key 11) is a half step **lower** in pitch than the white key B (key 12).
- There are two notes with flats that are white keys: F flat (F♭) and C flat (C♭). Note the enharmonic spellings: F flat is the enharmonic equivalent to E, and C flat is the enharmonic equivalent to B.

Exercise 2

Using flats to name the note, write the letter name of the keys in the boxes below. The first answer is given.

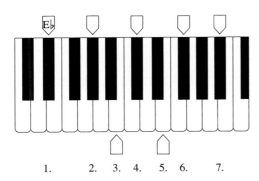

1.   2. 3. 4. 5. 6.   7.

> ♮ The natural **cancels** a previous accidental. All naturals are white keys.

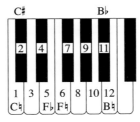

Notice that:

- The white key C natural (key 1) is a half step lower than C sharp (key 2).
- The white key F natural (key 6) is a half step higher than F flat (key 5).
- The white key B natural (key 12) is a half step higher than B flat (key 11).

Historical note: The natural

During the Middle Ages (approximately AD 475 to 1450) a squared shaped "♮" was used to raise the B flat to B natural. Eventually, the shape for any natural was altered to its modern-day design and now cancels a previous accidental. To draw a natural, combine an "L" with a "⌐".

 Theory Trainer

Exercise 4a Find white/black keys on the staff.

Drawing Accidentals on the Staff

Accidentals are used within the body of a piece of music to raise or lower the pitch of a note.

* Accidentals drawn on the staff are placed precisely on the same line or in the same space as the note being modified and directly in front of the note. However, when labeling a note, accidentals **follow** the letter name: we draw "sharp F" and say "F sharp."

Correctly placed accidentals

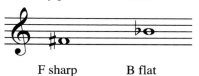

F sharp   B flat

Incorrectly placed accidentals

* An accidental lasts for one complete measure or until another accidental cancels it. In both measures below, the first and second E's are flatted, but the third E is not.

E♭ E♭ E G C   E♭ E♭ E G C

* Bar lines cancel previous accidentals. In the example below, the sharps must be drawn in mm. 1, 2 and 4 to raise the D to D sharp; in the third measure, the D returns to D natural.

* An accidental applies only to a note on **one** line or space; notes an octave higher or lower are not affected by previous accidentals. For example, the third C is a natural but the last C is sharped.

C♯ C♯ C   C♯

- A "courtesy" accidental may be placed in front of a note as a reminder. For example, in "Call Me Irresponsible," the natural in front of the last D is a courtesy accidental, reminding the musician that the bar line had cancelled the D flat in the previous measure.

B   C D   D♭ C   D natural

Relating Accidentals on the Staff to the Keyboard

Exercise 3

On the keyboard, label the notes drawn on the staff above. Draw an arrow connecting each note on the staff with its corresponding key as shown.

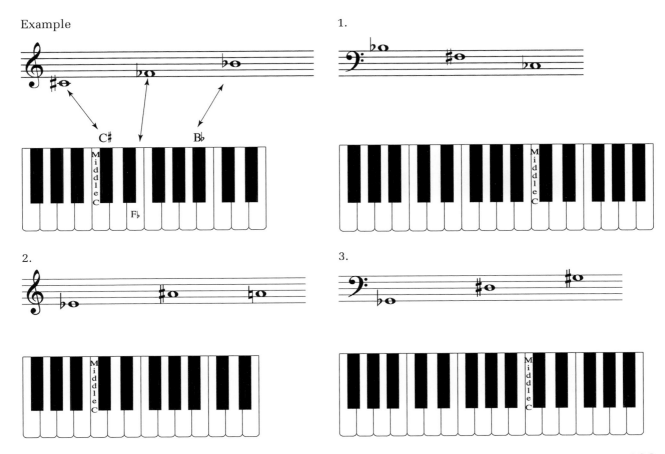

Enharmonic Spellings

All notes have at least two letter names called **enharmonic spellings**. Enharmonic pitches sound the same but have different names. Enharmonics may be compared to homonyms in English, words that sound the same, but have different meaning and spelling. For example, the words "ate" and "eight" are homonyms: the two words are pronounced the same, but have different meaning and spelling.

Two examples of enharmonic pitches are given below.

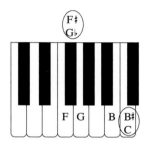

- F sharp and G flat are enharmonic names for the same black key.
- B sharp and C are enharmonic names for the same white key.
- Later in this module we will discuss all possible "spellings" and their uses.

 Theory Trainer

Exercise 4b Find white/black keys on the keyboard.

Exercise 4

Write the enharmonic spellings for the keys in the boxes below. The first answer is given.

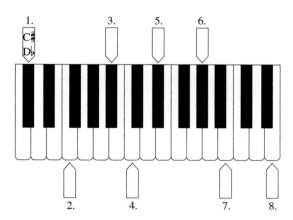

Exercise 5

On the staff below each keyboard, write the enharmonic spellings for the keys marked with an **X**. Identify the letter name below each note.

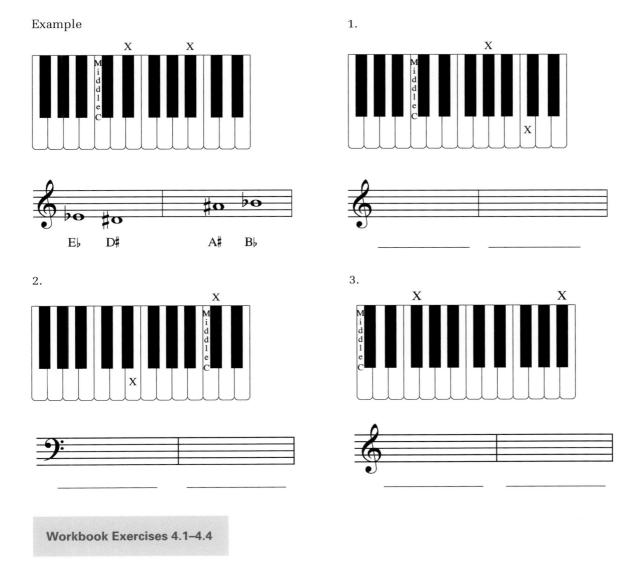

Example

Eb   D#   A#   Bb

1.

2.

3.

Workbook Exercises 4.1–4.4

Diatonic and Chromatic Half Steps

Notes forming a half step may be written in two ways: both notes may be written using the same letter name or the notes may be written with two consecutive letter names. For example, the half step F to F# may also be written F to Gb. If the letter names are *different* consecutive letters, the half step is called a **diatonic** half step (*di* = two). If the letter names are the *same*, this is called a **chromatic** half step (*chroma* = color).

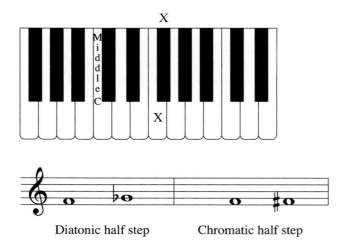

Diatonic half step   Chromatic half step

Exercise 6

On the staff below, notate the diatonic and chromatic half steps **above** the given pitch and identify the note.

Example   1.   2.   3.

Diatonic: D♭
Chromatic: C♯

On the staff below, write the diatonic and chromatic half step **below** the given pitch and identify the note.

4.   5.   6.   7.

Diatonic:
Chromatic:

Theory Trainer

Exercise 4c   Draw diatonic or chromatic half steps above or below a given note.

Chromatic Scales

A **scale** is a pattern of notes. When a scale consists only of notes that are half steps apart, this is called a **chromatic scale**.

Properties of a chromatic scale:

- All pitches are a half step apart.
- When notating an ascending chromatic scale, sharps are usually used to identify black keys. When descending, flats are usually used.
- There are 12 **different** pitches in a chromatic scale; the thirteenth pitch is the octave note.
- Although this is called a *chromatic* scale, both *chromatic* half steps (C–C♯) and *diatonic* half steps (C♯–D) are used. Note that diatonic spellings usually are used for the two pairs of white key half steps, E–F and B–C.

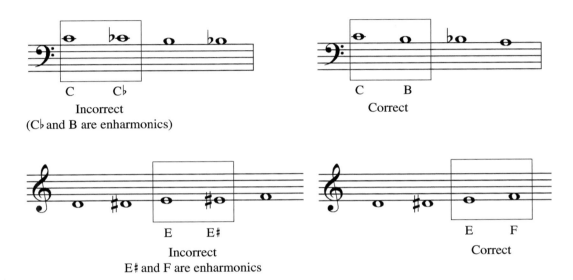

Exercise 7

1. Ascending chromatic scale

   Ascending and descending chromatic scales are drawn below. Note that ascending scales use sharps, descending scales use flats.

   Identify which half steps are chromatic (Ch) and which half steps are diatonic (Dia). The first four are given.

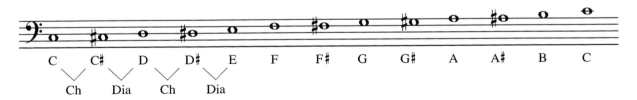

2. Descending chromatic scale

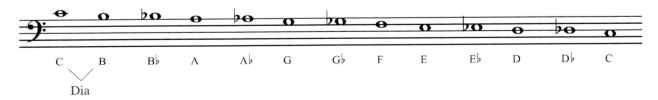

TRACKS 55–56

55. Ascending chromatic scale.
56. Descending chromatic scale.

The ascending and descending chromatic scales from C will be played twice. Listen first, then sing the note names the second time.

Exercise 8

Draw the following chromatic scales using whole notes. Identify each note below the staff. Make sure that:

- There are 12 different notes, each a half step apart. A thirteenth note at the end is an octave higher or lower than the beginning note.
- Accidentals on the staff are placed **in front** of the note and on the same line or space as the note.
- When identifying the letter name, the accidental is written **following** the letter (for example, F♯ or D♭).
- When ascending, use sharps; when descending, use flats.

1. Ascending chromatic scale from C♯ to C♯.

2. Ascending chromatic scale from B to B.

3. Descending chromatic scale from F to F.

Exercise 9 Class Exercise—Singing

Sing using solfège, numbers, note names or the syllable "La."

1. Track 57—To review, sing C to C, ascending and descending.

| Do | Re | Mi | Fa | Sol | La | Ti | Do | Do | Ti | La | Sol | Fa | Mi | Re | Do |

2. Track 58—Sing the ascending chromatic scale. Use the second line as a pronunciation guide.

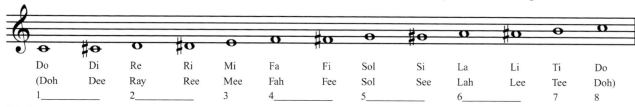

Do	Di	Re	Ri	Mi	Fa	Fi	Sol	Si	La	Li	Ti	Do
(Doh	Dee	Ray	Ree	Mee	Fah	Fee	Sol	See	Lah	Lee	Tee	Doh)
1___		2___		3	4___		5___		6___		7	8

3. Track 59—Sing the descending chromatic scale. Use the second line as a pronunciation guide.

Do	Ti	Te	La	Le	Sol	Se	Fa	Mi	Me	Re	Ra	Do
(Doh	Tee	Tay	La	Lay	Sol	Say	Fa	Mee	May	Ray	Rah	Doh)
8	7_____		6_____		5_____		4	3_____		2_____		1

4. Track 60—Sing the blues.

Do Me Mi Sol Do Me Mi Sol Do Me Sol La Te La Sol

5. Track 61—Sing two Japanese pentatonic scales.

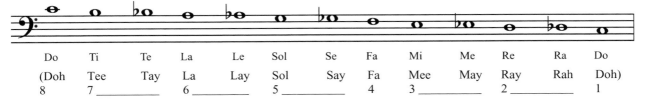

Do Re Mi Sol La Do Do La Sol Mi Re Do Do Me Fa Se Te Do Do Te Se Fa Me Do

 TRACKS 57–61

Listen, then sing: each of the exercises above will be played twice at a slow tempo. Listen first, then sing the second time.

Whole Steps

Two adjacent half steps comprise a **whole step**. On the keyboard, skip one key between two notes to create a whole step. Whole steps may be illustrated on the keyboard as a white key to a white key (W–W), black key to a black key (B–B), white to black (W–B), or black to white (B–W). For example:

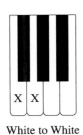
White to White   Black to Black   White to Black or Black to White

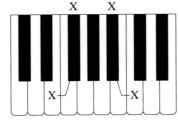

Diatonic whole steps consist of two half steps with adjacent letter names. For example, the whole step shown below can be written diatonically in two ways.

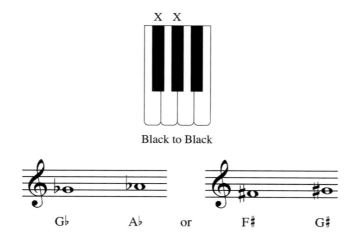

The following example is *not* a diatonic whole step because the letter names F and A are not adjacent letters of the alphabet.

Exercise 10

Below the keyboard, label each pair of keys marked with an **X** either "WS" for whole step or "HS" for half step.

1.

2.

3.

4.

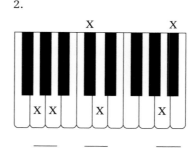

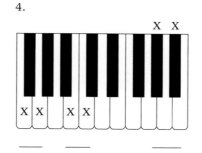

 Theory Trainer

Exercise 4c Draw half steps and whole steps above or below a given note.

Exercise 11 Class Exercise

Label the bracketed notes: whole step (WS) or half step (HS). The first two are done for you.

1. "Weeping Willow" (S. Joplin)

2. "Sha Lee Hung Ba," Chinese pentatonic folk melody from Xinjiang Province (pronounced "Shin-jee-ang")

Vocabulary note

CHINESE PENTATONIC MELODIES

Below are the notes used in "Sha Lee Hung Ba." Label the bracketed pairs of notes as whole steps (WS) or half steps (HS). What is unusal about this pentatonic scale? Notice the relatively wide range of this piece, which is not uncommon in Chinese folk songs.

The words of the title are nonsensical; the lyrics describe the market places along the Silk Road, an important trading route dating back thousands of years.

A few students may accompany the song with the following rhythm using drums (stems down in the music) and clapping (stems up). *Or* students may improvise their own rhythms.

Na li - lai de luo tuo - ke ya, Sha lee hung - ba, - Hay - yee, hay! Sha li - lai de

luo - tuo - ke ya, Sha lee hung - ba, Hay - yee, hay! Hay - yee, hay!

3. "Dark Eyes," Russian folk melody

Vocabulary note

NAME THESE SIGNS. WHAT DO THEY TELL YOU TO DO?

4. "Hava Nagila," Hebrew folk song

Workbook Exercises 4.5–4.7

Double Sharp, Double Flat

Vocabulary note

ACCIDENTALS

There are five accidentals: sharp, flat, natural, double sharp, and double flat. Although the sharp, flat, and natural were used as early as the Middle Ages, the double sharp and double flat began to be used later in the Baroque period (1600–1750) to accommodate the harmonic demands created by music using a greater number of sharps and flats.

✖   The **double sharp** raises a note a **whole step**; the letter name of the note remains the same.

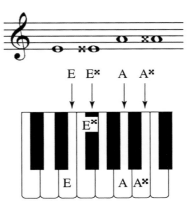

♭♭   The **double flat** lowers a note a **whole step**; the letter name of the note remains the same.

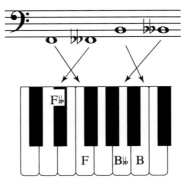

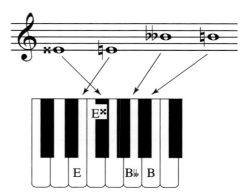

The natural **cancels** a previous accidental.

There are two ways to **lower** a double sharp a **half step**; the first example is preferred in modern practice.

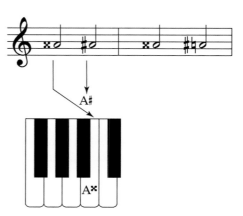

There are two ways to **raise** a double flat a **half step**; the first example is preferred in modern practice.

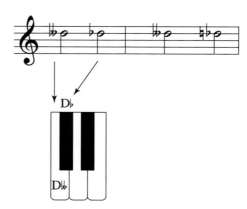

 Theory Trainer

Exercise 4a Find white/black keys on the staff using double accidentals.

Exercise 4b Find white/black keys on the keyboard using double accidentals.

Exercice 12 Class Exercise

Historical note: Étude

The étude (French for "study") is an instrumental composition that addresses one or more technical difficulties. Études achieved heightened popularity in the nineteenth century with compositions such as those by Chopin and Liszt; twentieth-century composers including György Ligeti and John Cage continued to expand the range of technical demands.

Chopin composed two sets of études for piano that required both technical and musical mastery: Opp. 10 and 25. In the excerpt below, Chopin begins the first measure without a time signature and creates a rhapsodic, improvisatory melody.

Étude, Op. 25, No. 7 (F. Chopin)

Write the names of underscored notes. Circle the 13 notes that are played on the black keys. Reminder: Accidentals continue to affect pitches until the double bar lines.

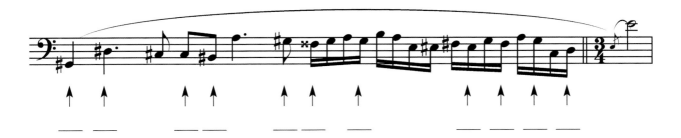

Exercice 13

Draw the chromatic half step above and below the given pitch.

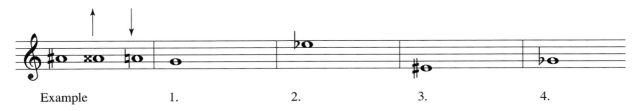

Example   1.   2.   3.   4.

Draw the diatonic half step above and below the given pitch.

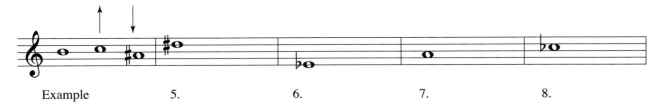

Example   5.   6.   7.   8.

Workbook Exercises 4.8–4.11

Theory Trainer

Exercise 4c Draw half steps and whole steps using double accidentals.

Vocabulary note

ACCIDENTALS

A sign used to alter a pitch

Sharp	An accidental (♯) used to raise a note a half step
Flat	An accidental (♭) used to lower a note a half step
Natural	An accidental (♮) used to cancel a previous sharp, flat, natural, double sharp, double flat for that note
Double sharp	An accidental (𝄪) used to raise a note a whole step
Double flat	An accidental (𝄫) used to lower a note a whole step

DIATONIC

Pitches, either a whole step or half step apart, that are identified using consecutive letter names; for example A–B, or E–F.

CHROMATIC HALF STEP

Pitches a half step apart that are identified using the same letter names, but with different accidentals; for example, A(natural)–A♯, or B♭–B(natural).

CHROMATIC SCALE

A scale consisting only of half steps.

ENHARMONIC

Different letter names for the same pitch; for example, F♯ and G♭

INTERVAL

The numeric distance between two notes

Half step	On the keyboard, two adjacent keys. In Western tonal music, the half step is the smallest interval. Half steps may be diatonic or chromatic; also called the *semitone*.
Whole step	On the keyboard, skip one key between two notes; two adjacent half steps. All whole steps are diatonic.

SCALE

A pattern of notes consisting of a variety of intervals, usually whole steps and half steps. Examples include the pentatonic, chromatic, whole tone, major, and the three forms of the minor scales.

Name _____

Exercise 4.1

Draw the following notes, being careful to place the accidental directly in front of each note. Indicate whether the note on the keyboard is white or black.

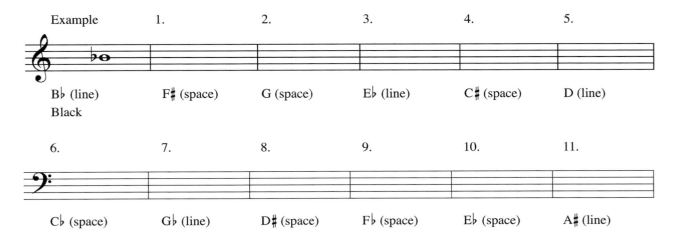

Example	1.	2.	3.	4.	5.
B♭ (line) Black	F♯ (space)	G (space)	E♭ (line)	C♯ (space)	D (line)

6.	7.	8.	9.	10.	11.
C♭ (space)	G♭ (line)	D♯ (space)	F♭ (space)	E♭ (space)	A♯ (line)

Exercise 4.2

On the keyboard, write the letter name of the notes drawn below. Draw an arrow connecting the note on the staff with its corresponding key as shown.

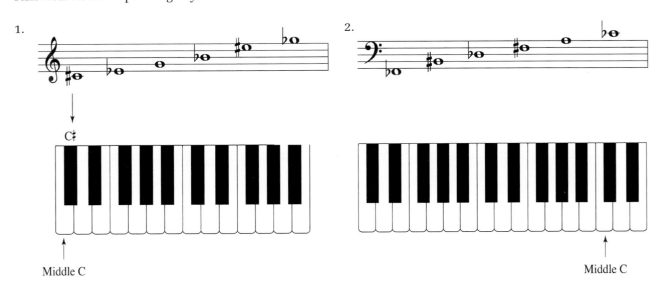

1.

C♯

Middle C

2.

Middle C

Exercise 4.3

To the right of each given pitch, draw a note that is an enharmonic equivalent.

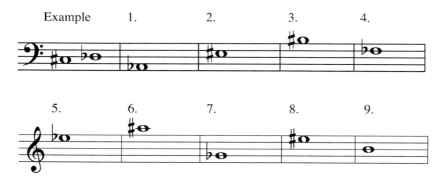

Exercise 4.4

Write the letter name for each indicated pitch.

1. Fugue No. 17 from *The Well Tempered Clavier*, Bk. II (J.S. Bach)

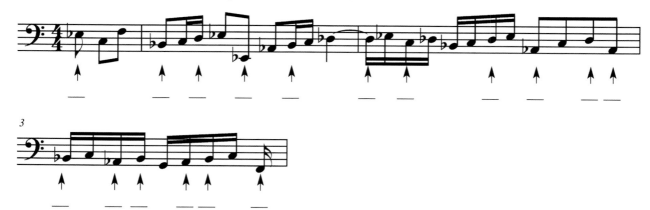

2. Sonata in A, K.331 (Third Movement: "Rondo Alla Turca") (W.A. Mozart)

First name the pitches. Then circle the notes below that are played on the black keys of the keyboard.

Exercise 4.5

Draw the following chromatic scales using whole notes. Identify each note below the staff.

1. Ascending chromatic scale from E to E.

2. Descending chromatic scale from E♭ to E♭.

3. Ascending chromatic scale from B to B.

Exercise 4.6

Label the bracketed notes: whole step (WS) or half step (HS). The first answer is given.

1. "Se Ji Ge" ("Song to the Seasons"), Chinese folk melody

2. Symphony No. 5 (Third Movement) (L.v. Beethoven)

3. Dona Nobis Pacem ("Give Us Peace"), Latin Mass

4. "Moon River" (H. Mancini) (Originally in C)

5. "Cabaret" (F. Ebb)

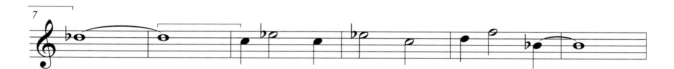

Exercise 4.7 | Listening

Your instructor will play two notes, either ascending or descending. Check whether the notes you hear are half steps or whole steps.

	Half Step	Whole Step
1.	_____	_____
2.	_____	_____
3.	_____	_____
4.	_____	_____

Exercise 4.8

Match the word or symbol with the definition.

1. Accidental   _____   Two adjacent half steps

2. Chromatic   _____   Symbol to lower a note two half steps

3. Chromatic scale   _____   Symbol used to alter a pitch

4. Diatonic   _____   Adjacent note on the keyboard

5. Double flat   _____   Symbol to raise a note a half step: sharp

6. Double sharp   _____   Symbol to lower a note a half step: flat

7. Enharmonic   _____   Pattern of notes that are half steps apart

8. Half step   _____   Spelling for two notes using the same letter name, but with different accidentals

9. Interval   _____   Symbol to cancel a previous accidental for that note: natural

10. Whole step   _____   Symbol to raise a note two half steps

11. ♯   _____   Spelling using consecutive letter names

12. ♮   _____   Different spellings to identify the same pitch

13. ♭   _____   Distance between two notes

Exercise 4.9

On the keyboard, write the letter name of the notes drawn below. Draw an arrow connecting the note on the staff with its corresponding key.

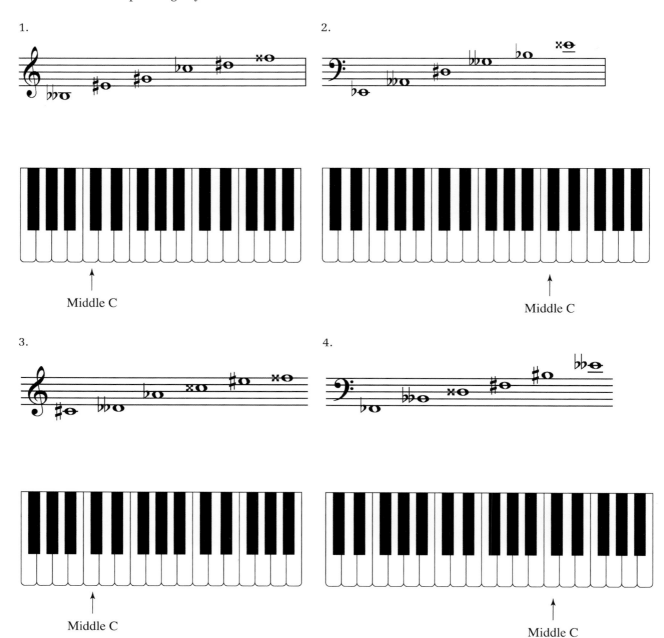

NAME: _____

Exercise 4.10

To the right of each given note, draw an enharmonic equivalent pitch.

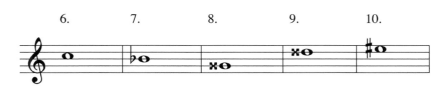

Exercise 4.11

Write the letter name below each note that is underscored; circle the half steps. The first half step has been circled.

Nocturne, BI 49 (F. Chopin)

MODULE 5

RHYTHM: SIMPLE METER EXPANDED

Subdividing the Quarter Note

In the musical example below, eighth notes and sixteenth notes are beamed together to form unit beats. Notice that the counts written below the notes are placed at the beginning of each new beam that connects the notes. As we discussed in Module 2, a **beam** is a thick line that connects the stems of two or more notes and substitutes for individual flags.

"James Bond Theme" (M. Norman)

Count:　　1　　　　2　　　　3　　　　4　　　　1　　　　2　　　　3　　　　4

The "James Bond Theme" has been rewritten below without beams connecting the eighth or sixteen notes. The counts are written below the same pitches as in the example above.

Count:　　1　　　　2　　　　3　　　　4　　　　1　　　　2　　　　3　　　　4

Notice in the first "James Bond" example how beams have replaced flags to indicate the four main beats in each measure. When the quarter note is subdivided into smaller units, notes with flags may be connected with beams.

• Beaming notes indicates the beat.

- When combining note values smaller than a quarter note, each beat is indicated by a new beam.

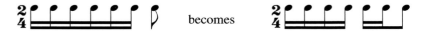

becomes

- Use beams connecting values smaller than a quarter note to form one beat.

becomes

Counting Sixteenth Note Patterns

When reading music, we read rhythms as a combination of long and short notes that form patterns. Similarly when you are reading this book, words are read as a *combination* of letters, not individual letters.

When the lower number of the time signature is four (2/4, 3/4, 4/4, or C) the quarter note is the pulse note (♩ = 1). The quarter note may be divided into a combination of eighth or sixteenth notes as shown in the following exercise.

Exercise 1

Use the chart below to count and clap the following patterns. Before you begin clapping, count three beats aloud to establish the tempo.

Quarter note as pulse note

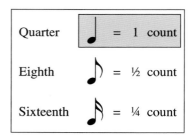

Practice each pattern separately. Then tap Pattern 1 with your foot. While continuing to tap, clap patterns 1 through 6. Be sure to count aloud.

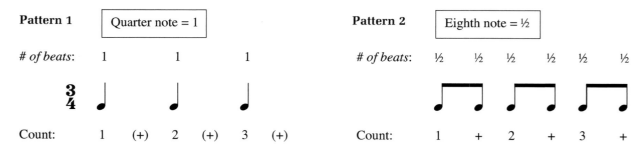

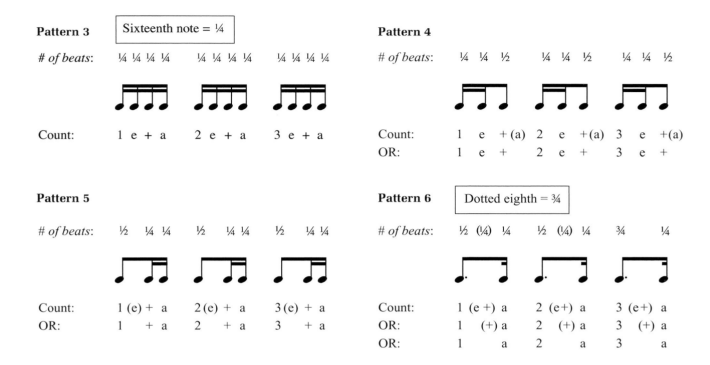

Pattern 3 | Sixteenth note = ¼

# of beats: ¼ ¼ ¼ ¼   ¼ ¼ ¼ ¼   ¼ ¼ ¼ ¼

Count: 1 e + a   2 e + a   3 e + a

Pattern 4

# of beats: ¼ ¼ ½   ¼ ¼ ½   ¼ ¼ ½

Count: 1   e   + (a)   2   e   +(a)   3   e   +(a)
OR: 1   e   +   2   e   +   3   e   +

Pattern 5

# of beats: ½   ¼ ¼   ½   ¼ ¼   ½   ¼ ¼

Count: 1 (e) + a   2 (e) + a   3 (e) + a
OR: 1   + a   2   + a   3   + a

Pattern 6 | Dotted eighth = ¾

# of beats: ½ (¼) ¼   ½ (¼) ¼   ¾   ¼

Count: 1 (e +) a   2 (e+) a   3 (e+) a
OR: 1   (+) a   2   (+) a   3   (+) a
OR: 1   a   2   a   3   a

Exercise 2   Class Exercise

The musical examples below use the six patterns of Exercise 1. Above each note write the number of beats for each note value (1, ½, or ¼) and notate the counts below.

1. "Ali Shan Zi Ge" ("The Song of Ali Mountain") (You-Li Huang), Chinese folk song

# of beats: ½¼¼ ½¼¼ 2   ½½

Count: 1 + a 2 + a   1 (2)   1 +

2. *Jurassic Park Theme* (J. Williams)

# of beats   ½   1   ½ ¼ ¼ 1   ½ ¼ ¼

Count: +   1   (2) + a 3   (4)+ a

3. "Non piu andrai" ("From now on") from *The Marriage of Figaro* (W.A. Mozart)

In this comic opera, Count Almaviva's personal valet, Figaro, sarcastically scolds the flirtatious servant, Cherubino. Figaro sings:

"You won't go any more, amorous butterfly,
Fluttering around inside night and day,
Disturbing the sleep of beauties,
A little Narcissus and Adonis of love."

4. Kundiman in 1800 (Tagalog dialect), Filipino **Kundiman** song

Vocabulary note

KUNDIMAN SONGS

Kundiman songs are traditional Filipino serenades in the Tagalog (pronounced "Ta-ga'log") dialect. Rhythms are gentle and flowing, and the melody is characterized by big leaps.

This particular song is humorous; the first line of the song translates, "They killed a mosquito once in our poor town."

5.   **Polonaise** from French Suite, BWV 817 (originally in E) (J.S. Bach)

Vocabulary note

POLONAISE

The **polonaise** is a dance originally from Poland. Bach uses it occasionally in his collections of dances called suites. The rhythm used in measure 7 (♩ ♫) is characteristic of the polonaise.

REPEAT SIGN :‖

Repeat back to the beginning; play the section twice.

 # beats ¼ ¼ ½ 1   1

Count: 1 e + 2   3

6

Count:

Exercise 3

On the staves below, rewrite the melodies using beams to replace flags. (Review stemming rules in Module 2.)

1.   Sonatina in G (First Movement) (L.v. Beethoven)

2.   "Weggis Zue" (Swiss Hiking Song) (J. Luthi)

Exercise 4 Two-Hand Exercises

- To set the tempo, count out loud for one measure before you begin. Practice slowly at first, then faster.
- Practice each hand separately. Tap the notes above the line with your right hand; tap the notes below the line with your left hand. (To achieve two different timbres, tap a pencil with your right hand and tap on a desk with your left hand.)
- Tap hands together after mastering the hands separately.

1.

2.

3.

Syncopation

Syncopation occurs when a rhythmic stress or accent is on a weak beat. For example, we normally emphasize beats one and three in a 4/4 time signature. Clap and count the rhythm below, playing the first and third beats louder.

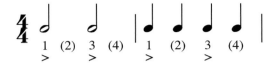

1 (2) 3 (4) | 1 (2) 3 (4)

When the weaker beats (2 and 4) are emphasized, this is called syncopation. Clap and count the rhythm below, feeling the "missing" beats one and three.

(1) 2 (3) 4 | (1) 2 (3) 4   OR   1 2 (3) 4 (1) 2 (3) 4

Exercise 5   Class Exercise

Using the instructions given in Exercise 4, tap the following rhythms.

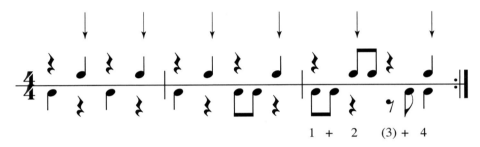

1 + 2 (3) + 4

Notice:

- The lower voice establishes the regularity of the strong beats on 1 and 3—until the end of the third measure.
- The upper syncopated voice (indicated with arrows) taps on the weak beats 2 and 4.
- In the third measure, the regularity of the two voices is affected when a rest occurs in the lower voice on the first half of beat 3. This creates a further push or "drive" to the fourth beat that normally is the weakest beat of the measure.

Tap another two-hand syncopated rhythm. Be sure to accent beats 2 and 4 by tapping and counting louder on those beats. Can you feel the "drive" to the fourth beat in the second measure?

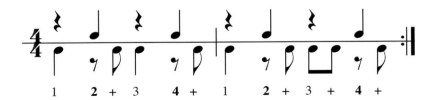

1   2 + 3   4 +   1   2 + 3 + 4 +

Composers of rags, blues, gospel songs, and jazz are known for their use of syncopation. The following are examples of syncopated rhythms:

- The second eighth note may be emphasized:

Count: (1) + (2) +

- The second and fourth sixteenth notes of a group of four sixteenths may be accented:

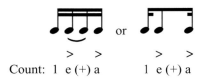

Count: 1 e (+) a   1 e (+) a

Exercise 6 | Class Exercise

Count and clap the following rhythms.

1. "I'll Always Be in Love with You" (B. Green, H. Ruby, S. H. Stept)

- The counts for the first two measures are given below the treble clef; complete the counts for the remaining measures.
- Using your right hand, first tap the treble clef rhythms; then tap the bass clef rhythms using your left hand.
- Tap hands together while your instructor plays the excerpt below.

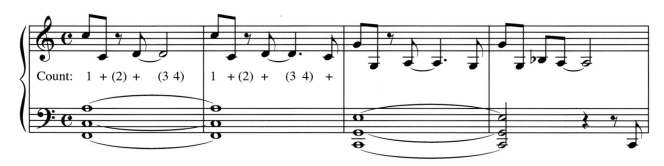

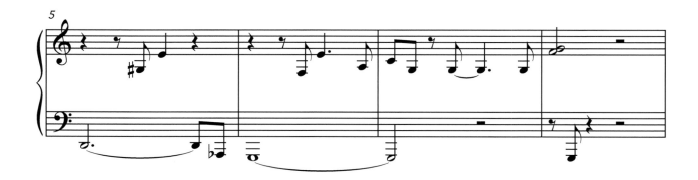

2. "Maple Leaf Rag" (S. Joplin)

Count: 1 + 2 + a   (1) e + a 2 e (+) a

3. "He's Got the Whole World," Gospel song

In the first example, ties are used to show the quarter note subdivision into eighth notes.

Counts: +   4   a   1   (2)   3   +   (4)

Count:

The second example does *not* use ties. Although both examples will sound the same and either notation is correct, using ties as in the example above may make it easier to see the main beat.

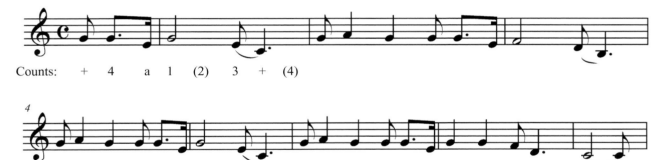

Counts: +   4   a   1   (2)   3   +   (4)

Count:

Western Classical composers also used syncopated rhythms, although not as extensively as jazz and blues musicians.

4.   Fugue in D minor, BWV 875 (J.S. Bach)

In the first example, ties are *not* used.

Count: 1   +   2   +   3   +   (4) +

In the second example below, the composer's original notation of the syncopated quarter note rhythms is changed to pairs of tied eighth notes. Complete the counts below each example and tap the rhythms; both examples should sound the same. Which notation is easier for you to read?

Count: 1   +   2   + 3 + (4) +

Although the notation with ties may make it easier for one to see the main beat, composers usually notate syncopated rhythms *without* ties, necessitating the importance of "feeling the beat." Return to the earlier examples without ties and clap the rhythms; count the main beats out loud with heightened emphasis.

5.   Piano Sonata in C, Hob. XVI/50 (F.J. Haydn)

Count: (1) +   (2) + (3) + (4) +

Count:

In the empty staff below, rewrite the selection using ties to show the quarter note subdivision into eighth notes. (Reminder: Notes with accidentals tied across bar lines continue to be altered.)

Count: (1) + (2) + (3) + (4) +

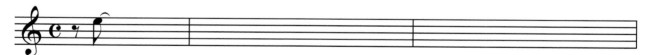

Workbook Exercises 5.1–5.4

Theory Trainer

Exercise 5a Rhythm tapping with quarter note as pulse note.

Changing the Pulse Note in Simple Meter: The Half Note

When the lower number of the time signature is 2 (**2/2** or **¢**, **3/2** or **4/2**), the half note becomes the pulse note (𝅗𝅥 = 1).

Exercise 7 Class Exercise

Compare the two charts below; the one on the left uses the half note as the pulse note, the one on the right uses the quarter note as the pulse note. Notice in both charts, two quarter notes equal one half note (𝅘𝅥 + 𝅘𝅥 = 𝅗𝅥); the difference between the charts is the value of the quarter note and all subsequent notes.

Use the chart on the left below to count and clap the six patterns that follow. Before you begin clapping, count three beats out loud to establish the tempo.

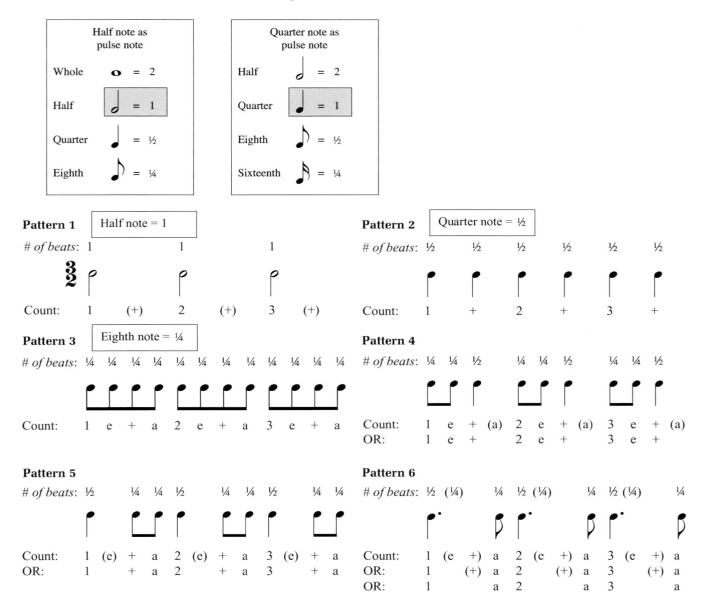

Exercise 8

Two rhythms are given below. Clap rhythm 1, then 2, keeping the tempo constant. Notice that:

- The meter for the examples is the same: simple duple.
- The pulse note for these two examples is *not* the same; therefore, the time values are not the same.
- **2/2** can be written as **¢**; it can also be called "cut time." (Italian: *Alla breve*).

1. Meter: Simple duple

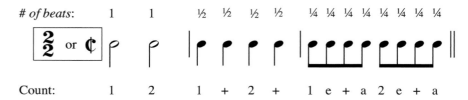

2. Meter: Simple duple

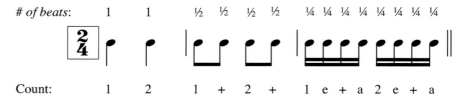

Exercise 9

In the following examples, state the meter. Then write the number of beats for each note value above the note, and write the counts below. Count and clap. (Reminder: rests are counted like their corresponding note values.)

1. Liebster Jesu (J.S. Bach)
    Meter _____

2. "On the Street Where You Live" from *My Fair Lady* (F. Loewe, A.J. Lerner)
   Meter _____

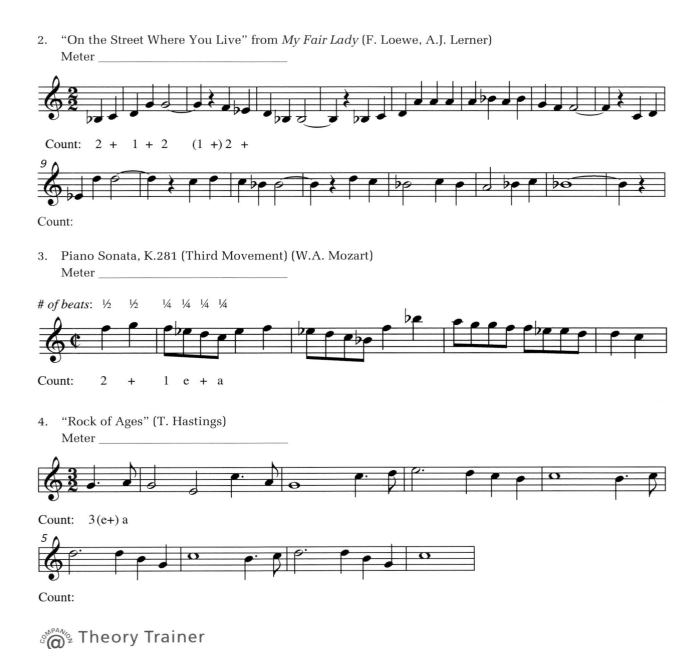

Count: 2 +   1 + 2   (1 +) 2 +

Count:

3. Piano Sonata, K.281 (Third Movement) (W.A. Mozart)
   Meter _____

# of beats: ½   ½   ¼ ¼ ¼ ¼

Count: 2   +   1 e + a

4. "Rock of Ages" (T. Hastings)
   Meter _____

Count: 3 (e+) a

Count:

Theory Trainer

Exercise 5b Rhythm tapping with half note as pulse note.

Changing the Pulse Note in Simple Meter: The Eighth Note

When the lower number of the time signature is 8 (**2/8, 3/8,** or **4/8**), the eighth note becomes the pulse note
(♪ = 1).

Exercise 10 Class Exercise

Draw the note values to complete the charts below. The first chart, where the eighth note is the pulse, is done for you.

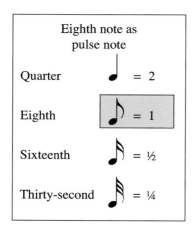

Eighth note as pulse note		
Quarter	♩	= 2
Eighth	♪	= 1
Sixteenth	♬	= ½
Thirty-second	♬	= ¼

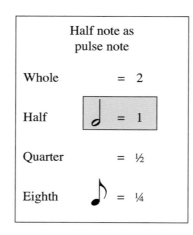

Half note as pulse note		
Whole		= 2
Half	𝅗𝅥	= 1
Quarter		= ½
Eighth	♪	= ¼

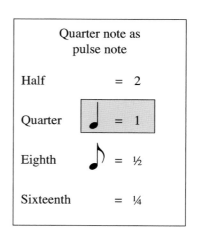

Quarter note as pulse note		
Half		= 2
Quarter	♩	= 1
Eighth	♪	= ½
Sixteenth		= ¼

Exercise 11 Class Exercise

Use the chart in Exercise 10 to count and clap the following patterns. Before you begin clapping, count four beats aloud to establish the tempo.

Pattern 1

# of beats: 1   1   1   1

⁴⁄₈ ♪ ♪ ♪ ♪   ♪ = 1

Count: 1 (+) 2 (+) 3 (+) 4 (+)

Pattern 2

# of beats: ½ ½ ½ ½ ½ ½ ½ ½

⁴⁄₈ ♬ ♬ ♬ ♬   ♬ = ½

Count: 1 + 2 + 3 + 4 +

Pattern 3

# of beats: ¼ ¼ ¼ ¼ ¼ ¼ ¼ ¼ ¼ ¼ ¼ ¼ ¼ ¼ ¼ ¼

⁴⁄₈ ♬ ♬ ♬ ♬   ♬ = ¼

Count: 1 e + a 2 e + a 3 e + a 4 e + a

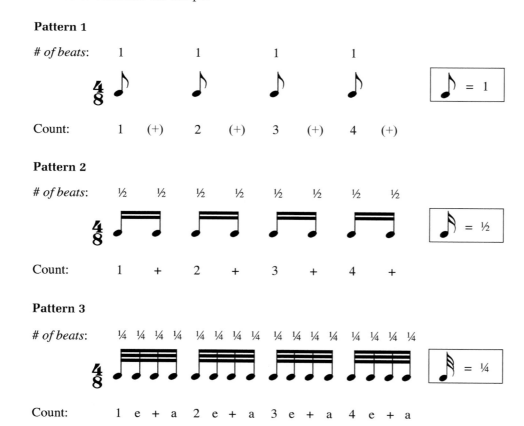

Exercise 12

In the following examples, identify the meter and the pulse note. Then write the number of beats for each note value above the note, and write the counts below. Count and clap. (Note: count rests like their corresponding note values.)

Vocabulary note

 The treble clef sign with an "8" directly below is sometimes used for songs written for tenor voices. All notes are to be sung an octave lower than written.

APPOGGIATURA (GRACE NOTE)

The small sixteenth notes in the seventh and eighth measures are called appoggiaturas, also commonly known as grace notes. These are embellishments and do not affect the counting.

---

1. "Libiamo ne' lieti calici" ("Drinking Song") from *La Traviata* (G. Verdi)
    Meter _____ Pulse note _____

# of beats: 1   3

Count: 3   1 (2 3 1)

2. Allegro (W.A. Mozart)
    Meter _____

# of beats: ¼ ¼   ¼ ¼   1   1   1

Count: 3   e   +   a   1   2   3

Vocabulary note

CHANGING METER, POLYMETER, COMPLEX METER

When the time signature in a piece changes, the meter is called **CHANGING METER, POLYMETER,** or **COMPLEX METER.**

In this piece, the time signature changes from 4/8 to 3/8. When performing this, be sure to keep the eighth note pulse constant.

3. "Cai Diau" ("I Spy," a children's game of guessing the object), Chinese folk song from Un Nan Province
   Meter _____

# of beats: 1   1   1   ½   ½

Count: 1   2   3   4   +

Count:

4. Sonata, K. 119 (D. Scarlatti)
   Meter _____   Pulse note _____

Count: 1   2   + 3   +

Workbook Exercises 5.5–5.6

 **Theory Trainer**

    Exercise 5c Rhythm tapping with eighth note as pulse note.

Composing Rhythms

Exercise 13

Compose rhythms to fill measures that are left blank.

- Use combinations of notes or rests that are similar to those in the surrounding measures.
- Count and clap the completed exercise.

1.

2.

3.

Exercise 14 Class Exercise—Rhythm Review

Clap or tap the following rhythms.

- Count one measure before beginning.
- Practice slowly at first, then faster.

Pulse Note in Simple Meter: Quarter Note

1.

2.

3.

4.

5.

6.

Pulse Note in Simple Meter: Half Note

Pulse note in Simple Meter: Eighth Note

Vocabulary note

ALLA BREVE

The time signature ₵ or 2/2 time, simple duple meter with the half note as the pulse note; also called cut time

APPOGGIATURA (GRACE NOTE) ( )

Embellishment also commonly known as a grace note; note that does not belong to the prevailing harmony (non-harmonic or non-chord tone) that subsequently resolves

CHANGING METER, POLYMETER, COMPLEX METER

Meters that change within a piece of music; for example, when the beginning time signature is 3/4 and changes to 4/4

COMMON TIME

Time signature C or 4/4 time; simple quadruple meter with the quarter note as the pulse note

CUT TIME (SEE ALLA BREVE)

FIRST ENDING, SECOND ENDING | 1. | 2.

The first time, play the ending indicated by the first bracket; the second time, play the ending indicated by the second bracket; also called "multiple endings"

NOTE VALUES, RHYTHMIC VALUE

The duration of pitches or rests (silence); is determined by the lower number of a time signature. Includes the duration of the following:

    Whole note

    Dotted half, dotted quarter, dotted eighth

    Half note

    Quarter note

    Eighth note

    Sixteenth note

    Thirty-second note

PULSE NOTE

Rhythmic value that gets one beat; indicated by the bottom number of a time signature

REPEAT SIGN

Indicates an instruction to repeat a section of music

SIMPLE METER

The recurring division of the pulse into a pattern of strong and weak beats; when the top number of a time signature is a 2, 3, or 4

SYNCOPATION

Rhythmic stress or accent on a weak beat

Workbook Exercises 5.7–5.9

Name _____

Exercise 5.1

Add the missing bar lines and double bar lines according to the time signature given at the beginning of each rhythm. Write the number of beats above each note. Note: One exercise begins with an anacrusis measure.

Exercise 5.2

Rewrite the rhythms below according to the given time signature, correcting the beaming as necessary. Write the number of beats above each note value, and notate counts below. The first one is done for you.

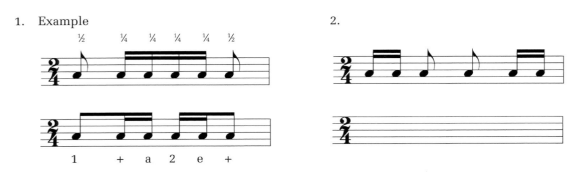

3.

4.

5.

6.

7.

8.

Exercise 5.3

Identify the meter and the pulse note. Write the counts below the melodies.

1. Scene from *Faust* (C. Gounod) (The heroine, Marguerite, is singing; an English translation is given below the French lyrics.)

   What is unusual about the pitches of this melody? _____ How do the pitches contribute to the mood of the piece? _____

   Meter _____ Pulse note _____

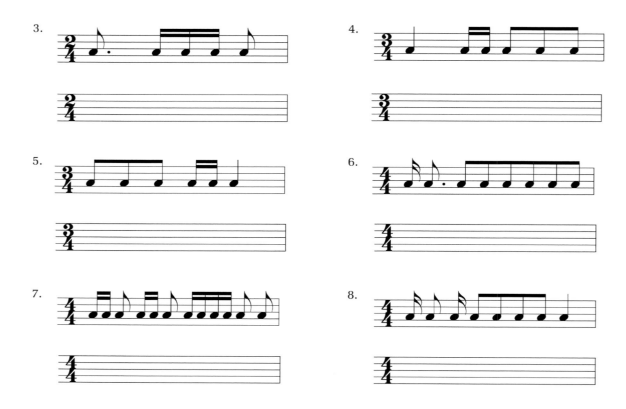

Je   voud - rais bien sa - voir - quel e - tait - ce jeune hom - me
I   wish I could but know - who was he - that ad - dressed me;

Count: +   4   e   +   a

Si c'est un grand sei - gneur, ___   et com - ment il se nom - me?
of no - ble he of birth.   -   what's his name and his sta - tion?

NAME: _____

2. Serenade (F.J. Haydn)
    Meter _____ Pulse note _____

Count:

Count:

Vocabulary note

1. ⌐——— First ending and second ending signs instruct the performer to repeat the beginning of a section, but to play the
          endings differently. In "Serenade," play measures A, 1–6, 1–3, 7–9; notice that the last two notes in the first
2. ⌐——— ending are identical to those in the anacrusis measure. Reminder: the anacrusis measure is labeled "A."

Exercise 5.4

Identify the meter and the pulse note. Write the counts below the melodies. Which of the pieces begins with an anacrusis measure?_____

1. "Can You Feel the Love Tonight?" (Elton John and T. Rice)

And can you feel___ the love___ to - night   It is where we are.___

It's e-nough for this wide-eyed wan-der er___   That we got this far. ___

2. "Original Rag" (S. Joplin)
    Meter _____ Pulse note _____

Count:

Count:

3. "Là ci darem le mano" ("There we will entwine our hands") from *Don Giovanni* (W.A. Mozart)
    A bracket has been placed around notes forming a motive. Locate and bracket a repetition of this motive.

    Meter _____ Pulse note _____

La   ci da - rem   le   ma - no,   la   mi di - re - te   si;
Count:

ve - di, non e   lon - ta - no,   par - tiam, - ben - mio,   da - qui.
Count:

NAME: _____

4. "You've Got a Friend" (C. King)

Meter _____ Pulse note _____

How many ties are found below?_____ How many slurs are found below? _____

You   just   call   -   out   my __ name   -   -   and   you   know   -   where-ev - er   I   am

Count:

__   I'll   come   run   -   nin' _____   to   see   you   a - gain.

Count:

Exercises continue on next page.

Exercise 5.5

Identify the meter and the pulse note. Write the counts below the melodies. Which pieces begin with an anacrusis?_____ Which of the melodies use syncopation? _____ In each excerpt, a bracket is placed over notes that form a motive; locate and bracket the same motive used in repetition, or with slight changes.

1. "Simple Gifts," Shaker melody
    Meter _____ Pulse note _____

Count:

Count:

2. "Wayfaring Stranger," Spiritual
    Meter _____ Pulse note _____

Count:

Count:

3. Symphony No. 40, K. 550 (W.A. Mozart)
    Meter _____ Pulse note _____

Count:

Count:

Exercise 5.6

Identify the meter and the pulse note. Write the counts below the melodies. Which of the pieces begin with an anacrusis? _____ Is syncopation used? _____

1. "L'Éléphant" from *Le Carnaval des Animaux* (C. Saint-Saëns)

Discuss how the composer's tempo marking and low melodic range reflect the title of the piece.

a. Tempo_____
b. Range _____
    Meter _____ Pulse note _____

Allegretto pomposo *(A little slower than Allegro and played with an exaggerated sense of importance.)*

# of beats: 2   1

Count: 1 (2) 3

Count:

2. "Makiba no asa" ("Morning Ranch") (E. Funabashi), Japanese song
    Meter _____ Pulse note _____

beats: 1 ½ ½ 1 1   ½ ½

Count: 1(2)+ 3 4   1+

3. Symphony No. 5 in C minor (Second Movement) (L.v. Beethoven)
    Meter _____ Pulse note _____

Adagio

Count:

NAME: _____

Exercise 5.7

Complete the melodies, using the motive and time signature provided. Compose two phrases, each four or five measures long; the second phrase may be similar or contrasting to the first.

- Add bar lines and end with a double bar line.
- To provide musical cohesion, use rhythms and a melodic contour similar to those of the given motive. To give the melody a stronger ending, end on a strong beat.
- Perform the completed melodies yourself, or have them performed by another class member or by your instructor.

1.   Title: _____

Using the notes in the order given below, complete the melody. (Any of the notes provided may be repeated; notice that the original motive is characterized by repeated notes.) Locate the repetition of the motive that begins on G; to give the melody cohesion, consider repeating the rhythmic pattern of the motive.

2. Title: _____

Using any of the pitches of the pentatonic scale provided below, complete the melody; end on a C.

4

3. Title: _____

Using the notes in the order given below, complete the melody; end on an F. Locate repetitions of the melodic contour that are used in the opening motive; consider giving your melody cohesion by repeating the rhythm of the motive. Note: 1) any of the given pitches may be repeated; 2) the melody begins with an anacrusis, or "upbeat."

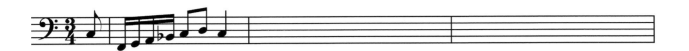

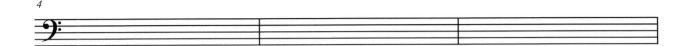

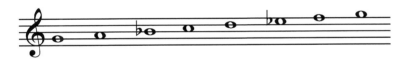

4. Title: _____

Using any of the pitches drawn below, complete the melody. Incorporate syncopated rhythms elsewhere in your melody; end on a G.

5. Create your own motive and compose a melody. Draw the clef at the beginning of each line; in the first line, draw the time signature directly after the clef. Bracket your motive drawn at the beginning of the melody.

Title: _____

NAME:

Exercise 5.8 Class Exercise Rhythmic Dictation

Various combinations of the following rhythms will be played. Each example will be three measures long. Your instructor will tell you the time signature to write at the beginning of the line and will count one measure out loud to establish the tempo immediately before beginning the exercise. Notate the rhythm. Each exercise will be played three times.

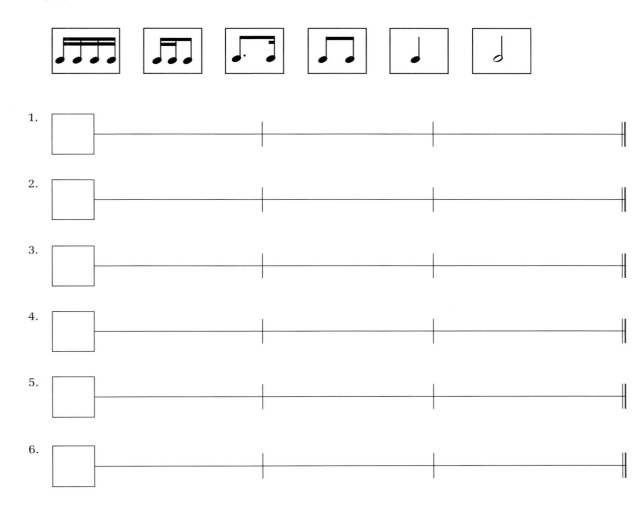

Exercise 5.9

Match the word or symbol with the definition.

1. Beam   _____ Multiple endings

2. Changing meter, polymeter, complex meter   _____ Repeat a section of music

3. Pulse note   _____ Horizontal line(s) connecting the stems of two or more notes, replacing individual flags

4. Simple meter   _____ Appoggiatura (grace note); an embellishment

5. Simple duple meter   _____ Rhythmic stress or accent on a weak beat

6. Syncopation   _____ Two numbers placed at the beginning of a piece that indicate the number of beats in a measure (top number) and the note value of the basic pulse (lower number)

7. Time signature   _____ Alla breve or 2/2, simple duple meter with the half note as the pulse note; also called cut time

8.   _____ Refers to the stresses of strong and weak beats, when the top number of the time signature is a 2, 3, or 4

9.   _____ Clef sign sometimes used for tenor voices; all notes sung an octave lower

10.   _____ Rhythmic value that gets one beat indicated by the bottom number of the time signature

11.   _____ Meter with two beats per measure, where the first beat is stressed, and the top number in a time signature is 2

12.   _____ Name of meter for a piece with changing time signatures

MODULE 6

MAJOR SCALE

What Is a Major Scale?

The major scale (from *scala*, Italian for "ladder") developed from the modal system of the Middle Ages and Renaissance (see Appendix 4). Along with the minor scale (Module 9), these scales are the foundation for Western harmony and our study of intervals (Module 10) and chords (Modules 11, 13, 14).

Historical note: The scale

As early as 500 BCE, understanding about how pitches may be organized developed in Greece and subsequently influenced the development of Western scales, perhaps through Roman or Arabic scholars. Greek ideas included:

- Acoustical theory (the science of sound), which is founded on mathematical principles of physics.
- Scales formed by joining two four-note groups of notes called **tetrachords**. (See page 166 for a further discussion on tetrachords.)

Greek words were used to name the seven medieval modes. The medieval Ionian mode has the same construction as the present-day major scale, and the Aeolian mode has the same construction as the minor scale.

Other scales were created in countries around the world, varying the number of notes in the scale and the distance between adjacent notes of the scale. These include:

- Indian ragas (from Sanskrit for "color" or "aura'), which are sometimes defined as melodic modes;
- The six-note hexatonal or whole tone scale (comprising only whole steps);
- The five-note pentatonic scales of Japan, China, and early American blues.

The pattern for the Western major scale can be shown by the white keys from C to C. Notice the arrangement of whole steps (W) and half steps (H) between each pair of keys.

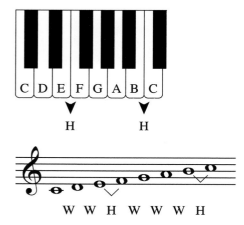

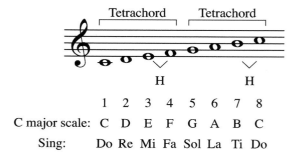

Elements of the major scale:

- Has eight diatonic notes (adjacent letter names)
- Spans one octave, beginning and ending with the same letter name
- Lowest note gives the scale its name
- Consists of two tetrachords
- Has adjacent notes which are whole steps except for half steps between 3 and 4 and between 7 and 8.

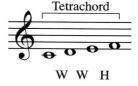

1	2	3	4	5	6	7	8

C major scale: C D E F G A B C

Sing: Do Re Mi Fa Sol La Ti Do

- This pattern may begin on any note; when one changes the starting pitch while keeping the same arrangement of whole and half steps, this is called **transposition.** Each resulting scale will sound similar because the interval distance between each of the notes remains the same. All major scales except C major will need at least one accidental.
- Use sharps or flats exclusively in a major scale

Writing Major Scales: Using Tetrachords

The word "tetrachord" comes from the Greek words *tetra* (meaning "four") and *chord* (from the Greek word *chordē* meaning "string"). There are several kinds of tetrachords, but we will study the tetrachord pattern that is used in the major scale, that of a whole step, whole step, followed by a half step.

Exercise 1

Draw a tetrachord from the given note using accidentals as needed. Place an **X** on the corresponding keys below.

Example

1.

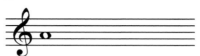

2.

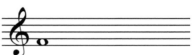

3.

4.

5.

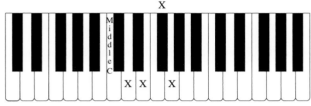

6.

7.

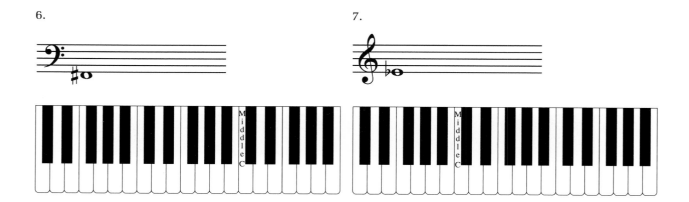

To construct a major scale, join together two tetrachords with a whole step connecting them. The resulting major scale pattern is: W W H W W W H.

Exercise 2

Draw major scales from the given note. Place an **X** on the keys below.

- Begin by drawing a tetrachord from the given note. Place a bracket above it.
- Add a fifth note a whole step above the fourth note.
- Draw another tetrachord from the fifth note. Place a bracket above it.
- Indicate half steps as shown below.

Play these major scales on a keyboard. For example, you may use four fingers of the left hand to play the first tetrachord and four fingers of the right hand to play the second tetrachord. (Traditional fingerings are given in Appendix 7 on the website.) If you do not have access to a keyboard, play them on a guitar or place your fingers on the paper keyboard included in your textbook.

Example:

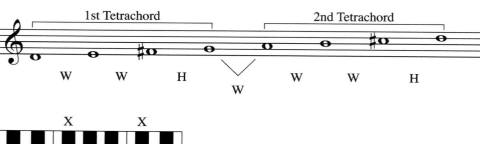

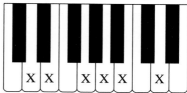

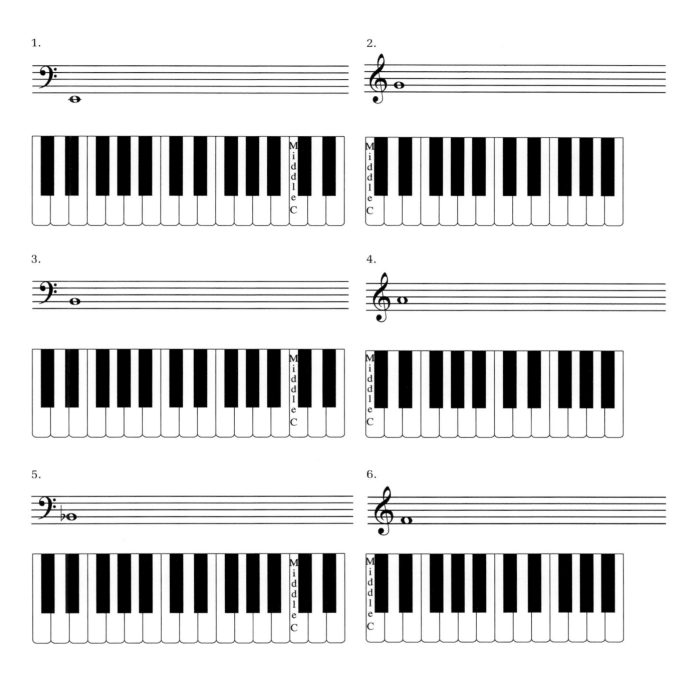

Writing Major Scales: Using Whole and Half Steps

Major scales may also be written by following the pattern of whole steps (W) and half steps (H):

W W H W W W H

Exercise 3

- Draw eight **diatonic** notes, beginning and ending with the same pitch.
- Add accidentals as needed to create the correct series of whole and half steps:

  1 1 ½ 1 1 1 ½

- Draw an **X** on the keys below.

Example:

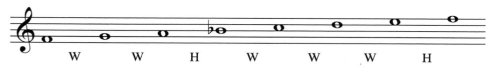

1.

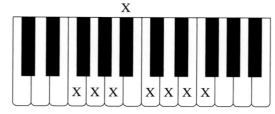

2.

3.

4.

5.   6.

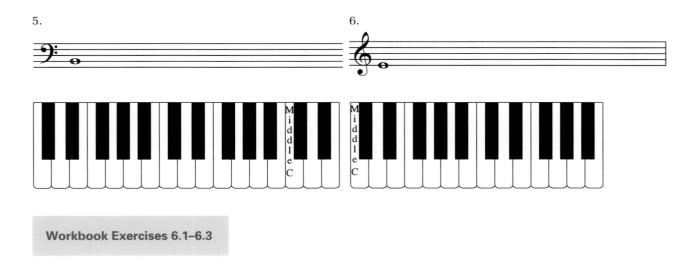

Workbook Exercises 6.1–6.3

Theory Trainer

Exercise 6a Input major scales.

Scale Degree Names—Major Keys

Each of the seven notes of a scale is given a name called a scale degree name. These names are the same for every scale regardless of the letter name of the scale or the octave placement of the notes.

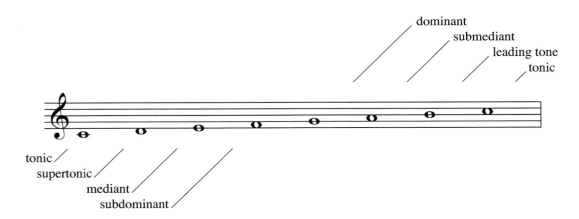

Notice how these names have been derived:

Dominant – five notes UP from the tonic,
counting the tonic as 1.
Second note in importance after the tonic.

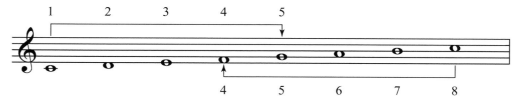

Subdominant – note below the dominant.
(Also five notes DOWN from the tonic.)

Submediant – three notes DOWN from the tonic,
counting the tonic as the eighth note of the scale.

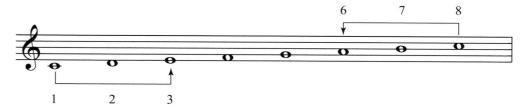

Mediant – three notes UP from the tonic,
midway between the tonic and dominant

Leading tone – the seventh note of the
scale, LEADS to the tonic; may be
referred to as a tendency tone.

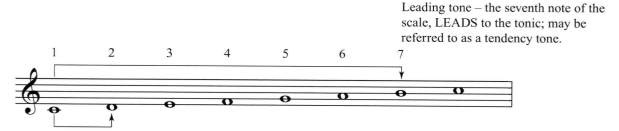

Supertonic – note ABOVE the tonic.

Changing the Tonic—Singing

Let's compare the letter name, scale degree name, and solfège syllable of each note in the D major scale.

Number	Letter name	Scale degree name	Solfège syllable
1	D	Tonic	Do
2	E	Supertonic	Re
3	F♯	Mediant	Mi
4	G	Subdominant	Fa
5	A	Dominant	Sol
6	B	Submediant	La
7	C♯	Leading tone	Ti
8	D	Tonic	Do

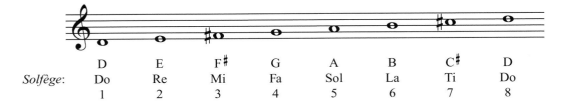

When we sing in the key of D, our tonic note is D, which becomes "Do."

In "Jingle Bells" below, the scale of this piece is D major; therefore the tonic is D, and D becomes "Do," E becomes "Re" and so forth. The piece begins on F sharp which is the third degree of the D major scale, or "Mi." We call this singing "in D major" or singing "in D".

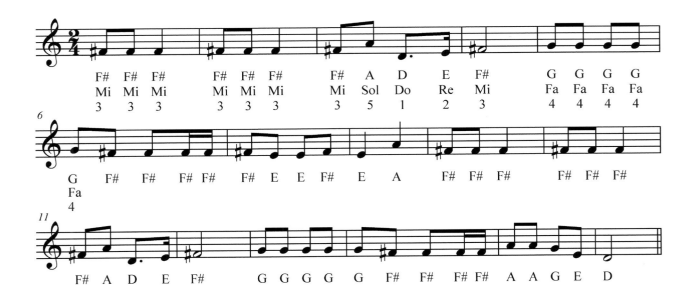

173

🔊 **TRACKS 62–69**

Each exercise below will be played twice. Listen the first time, then sing along, trying to match the pitches.

Exercise 4

Sing with scale numbers, solfège syllables, or letter names.

1. Track 62—Scale: F Major

1	3	2	4	3	5	4	2	1
Do	Mi	Re	Fa	Mi	Sol	Fa	Re	Do

2. Track 63—Scale: E Major

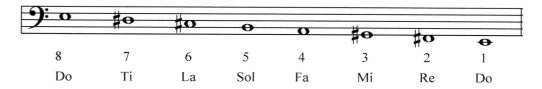

8	7	6	5	4	3	2	1
Do	Ti	La	Sol	Fa	Mi	Re	Do

3. Track 64—Scale: D Major

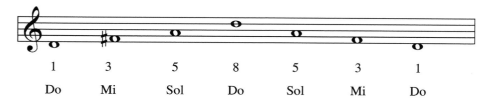

1	3	5	8	5	3	1
Do	Mi	Sol	Do	Sol	Mi	Do

4. Track 65—Scale: Pentatonic

1	1	2	3	5	6	8	5	3	2	1
Do	Do	Re	Mi	Sol	La	Do	Sol	Mi	Re	Do

5. Track 66—Scale: Pentatonic

| | 1 | 1 | 1 | 2 | 3 | 5 | 3 | 2 | 1 | 3 | 5 | 6 | 6 | 5 | 5 | 8 | 5 | 5 |
| Do | DoDo | Re | Mi | Sol | Mi | Re | Do | Mi | Sol | La | La | Sol | Sol | Do | Sol | Sol |

6

6

La

6. Track 67—Scale: Chromatic ascending

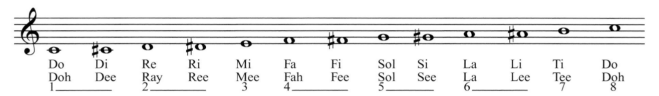

Do	Di	Re	Ri	Mi	Fa	Fi	Sol	Si	La	Li	Ti	Do
Doh	Dee	Ray	Ree	Mee	Fah	Fee	Sol	See	La	Lee	Tee	Doh
1___		2___		3	4___		5___		6___		7	8

7. Track 68—Scale: Chromatic descending

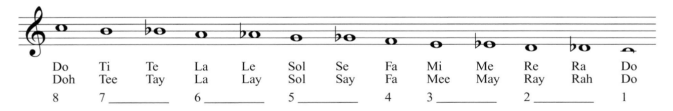

Do	Ti	Te	La	Le	Sol	Se	Fa	Mi	Me	Re	Ra	Do
Doh	Tee	Tay	La	Lay	Sol	Say	Fa	Mee	May	Ray	Rah	Do
8	7___		6___		5___		4	3___		2___		1

8. Track 69—Scale: Whole tone

| Do | Re | Mi | Fi | Si | Li | Do | Do | Te | Le | Se | Mi | Re | Do |
| Doh | Ray | Mee | Fee | See | Lee | Do | Do | Tay | Lay | Say | Mee | Ray | Doh |

Exercise 5 Class Exercise

If your instructor prefers to equate "C" with "Do," then you will be singing in the "fixed Do" system. If your instructor moves "Do" to correspond with a scale's tonic note, you will be singing in the "movable Do" system. If this is the case, write the letter name, solfège syllable and corresponding scale number for the remainder of "Jingle Bells." Then sing with letter names, solfège syllables and/or scale degree numbers.

Then sing "Someone to Watch Over Me" by George Gershwin. Draw the A major scale. Label the solfège syllable and/or scale degree number below each scale note and in the music below. Sing with syllables or numbers, then with the lyrics.

Vocabulary note

SOLFÈGE (or solfeggio)

The system of singing with syllables devised by an 11th-century medieval monk, Guido d'Arezzo, who used the first syllable of each line of a Latin hymn to name consecutive ascending pitches. At first, only six syllables were used; a seventh was added in the 17th century. Today, the syllables are as follows: Do Re Mi Fa Sol La Ti (or Si).

SOLFÈGE—"FIXED DO"

When "Do" is equated with "C", "Re" is "D," and so forth.

SOLFÈGE—"MOVABLE DO"

When "Do" is equated with the tonic (the first note of the scale), "Re" is the supertonic, and so forth.

10

I know __ I could,   al - ways __ be good   to one who'll watch   o - ver me. _____

Transposition

Transposition in music occurs when a melody or piece is played or sung higher or lower than the original. We see this at the beginning of Module 7 on page 193 when "You Are the Sunshine of My Life" is written first in C major and then transposed to E major. The transposed melody will sound "the same" as the original because the relationship between the pitches is the same. Transposition may be accomplished by using the scale degree number or solfège symbol of the original scale of the melody.

Exercise 6 | Class Exercise

The piece "Galop" by Jacques Offenbach was originally composed in G major. Below the original version in G major, transpose the melody to E major.

- Begin by drawing the G and E major scales.
- Write the solfège symbols and/or numbers below each scale note and in the music below.
- Then transpose "Galop" from G to E major; be sure to maintain the rhythms of the original. The first notes of the melody in E major are given. Locate the entire descending major scale in both melodies.
- Sing the original and transposed melody using solfège or numbers. Does it sound "the same"?

G major scale   E major scale

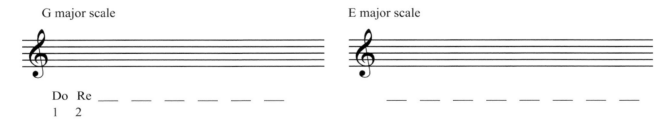

Do Re __ __ __ __ __ __ __
1   2

"Galop" by Offenbach in the original key of G major

Sol Do
5   1

"Galop" by Offenbach transposed to E major

Sol Do
5   1

 Theory Trainer

Exercise 6b Identify tonic or dominant by ear after hearing a major scale.

Enharmonic Scales—Major Keys

Six scales form three pairs of **enharmonic** scales, scales that sound the same but are written either with sharps or with flats (never both sharps and flats.) The six enharmonic keys are B and C♭, F♯ and G♭, and C♯ and D♭.

Exercise 7

Draw an **X** on the keys corresponding to the pitches of the scales drawn below.

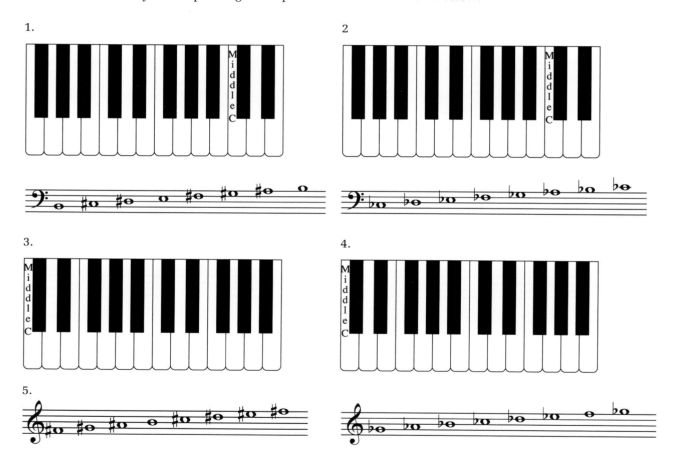

6.

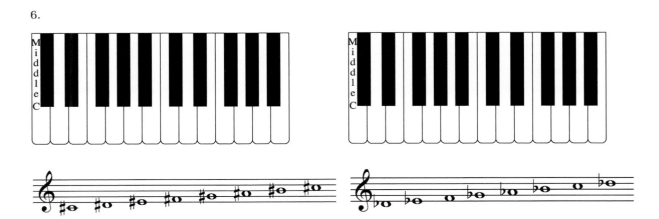

There are a total of 15 major scales: a scale beginning on each of the seven white keys, a scale beginning on each of the five black keys, and three enharmonic scales.

Workbook Exercises 6.4–6.9

Vocabulary note

ENHARMONIC SCALES

Scales that sound the same pitches but are notated differently, using different letter names and accidentals. Note: Scales must be notated with either sharps or flats, never a combination of the two. There are three pairs of enharmonic scales: B and C♭, F♯ and G♭, and C♯ and D♭.

SCALE

A pattern of notes consisting of a variety of intervals, usually whole steps and half steps

Chromatic scale	A scale consisting only of half steps
Major scale	A pattern of eight diatonic notes, including the octave, made of whole and half steps with the half steps occurring between 3 and 4, and between 7 and 8
Pentatonic scale	A pattern of five notes within the octave; for example, the five black keys comprise a pentatonic scale
Whole tone scale	A six-note scale consisting only of whole steps; also called a *hexatonal* scale

SCALE DEGREE NAME

Names given to specific notes of a major scale

Tonic	The first note of a scale; also names the key of a piece
Supertonic	The second note of a scale; the prefix, "super," meaning "above" the tonic
Mediant	The third note of a scale, midway between the tonic and dominant
Subdominant	The fourth note of a scale; the prefix "sub" meaning "below" the dominant as well as five notes below the tonic
Dominant	The fifth note of a scale; the second note of importance after the tonic
Submediant	The sixth note of a scale, also three notes below the tonic
Leading tone	The seventh note of a scale, also a half step below the tonic; the leading tone "leads" up to the tonic and is sometimes called a *tendency tone*.

SOLFÈGE

Singing with syllables; "solfège" is a combination of the two syllables, Sol and Fa.

Fixed Do	When "Do" is equated with "C," "Re" is "D," and so forth
Movable Do	When "Do" is equated with the tonic note of a scale, "Re" is the supertonic, and so forth

TENDENCY TONE

Notes in a scale or chord that "tend" to lead to up or down to another note; for example, the leading tone "leads" up to the tonic.

TETRACHORD

Four diatonic notes consisting of two whole steps followed by a half step (WS WS HS); from the Greek word *tetra* ("four") and *chordē* ("string"). Two tetrachords connected by a whole step form a major scale.

TRANSPOSE

Changing a piece or section of music from one key to another. All pitches retain the same intervallic relationship throughout.

Name _____

Exercise 6.1

Beginning with C major, draw the 15 major scales in both clefs using tetrachords. Indicate tetrachords with a bracket.

Note:

- A major scale consists of two tetrachords.
- Each tetrachord pattern consists of: whole step, whole step, half step. The second tetrachord of a scale begins a diatonic whole step above the last note of the first tetrachord.
- As shown below, the second tetrachord of C major becomes the first tetrachord of the following scale, G major. The same principle applies to each subsequent scale.

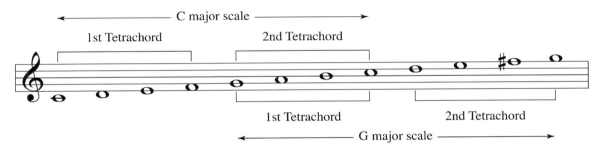

- The three pairs of enharmonic scales are C♯–D♭, F♯–G♭ and B–C♭.
- There are at most seven different sharps or seven different flats in a major scale.
- The number of sharps increases from one sharp in G major up to seven sharps in C♯ major.
- The number of flats decreases from seven flats in C♭ major to one flat in F major.

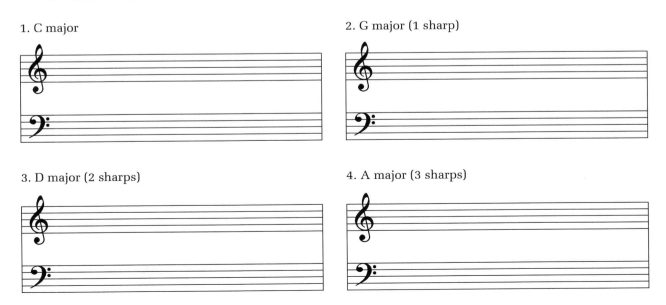

1. C major

2. G major (1 sharp)

3. D major (2 sharps)

4. A major (3 sharps)

5. E major (4 sharps)

6. B major (5 sharps)

7. F# major (6 sharps)

8. C# major (7 sharps)

9. C♭ major (7 flats)

10. G♭ major (6 flats)

11. D♭ major (5 flats)

12. A♭ major (4 flats)

13. E♭ major (3 flats)

14. B♭ major (2 flats)

15. F major (1 flat)

Exercise 6.2

Circle the errors in the scales drawn below. Rewrite the scales on the right, correcting the errors.

1.

2.

3.

4.

Exercise 6.3

Above each musical example, draw the scale that is used in the piece. Then insert accidentals in front of the appropriate notes in the music according to the sharps or flats used in the scale. (Remember not to mix sharps and flats.) The first accidental is given. Below each line of music, write in the counts. Sing and clap the exercise.

1. Menuet in B♭ (J.S. Bach)

Draw the B♭ major scale in both clefs.

2. "Just the Way You Are" (B. Joel)

Draw the E major scale.

NAME:

Exercise 6.4

Beginning with C major, draw the 15 major scales moving the tonic note up chromatically. Note the three pairs of enharmonic scales: C♯–D♭, F♯–G♭ and B–C♭.

1. C major

2. C♯ major

3. D♭ major

4. D major

5. E♭ major

6. E major

7. F major

8. F♯ major

9. G♭ major

10. G major

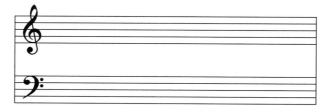

11. A♭ major

12. A major

13. B♭ major

14. B major

15. C♭ major

NAME: _____

Exercise 6.5 | Class Exercise

Complete the melody using any of the rhythms shown in boxes above each exercise. A motive and the scale of the piece are provided. To give the piece a sense of finality, end with the tonic note on a strong beat. Compose two phrases, four or five measures in length. Sing or play your compositions, or ask your instructor to play them for you.

Example: The completed melody is written on the lower staff.
Scale: G major

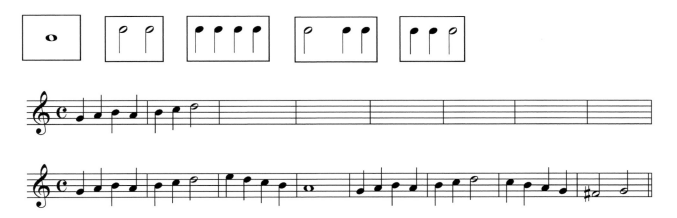

Note how the music repeats: each four-measure phrase begins identically. Notice how this repetition helps to give the music cohesion.

1.   Scale: F major

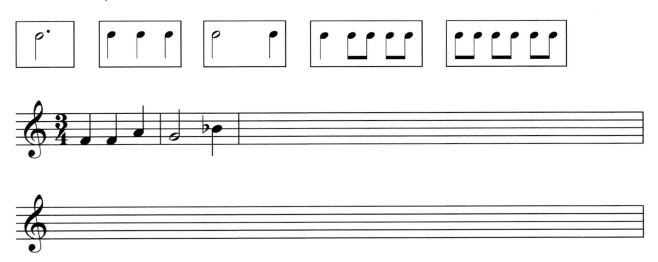

2. Scale: A major

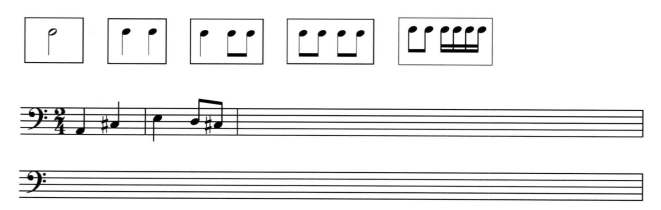

Exercise 6.6

1. Draw the D major scale. Then identify the letter name of each scale degree for D major.

Example:

Tonic note   D̲

1.	Subdominant _____	5.	Supertonic _____
2.	Dominant _____	6.	Leading tone _____
3.	Supertonic _____	7.	Tonic _____
4.	Mediant _____	8.	Submediant _____

2. Draw the F major scale. Then identify the letter name of each scale degree for F major.

1.	Supertonic _____	5.	Dominant _____
2.	Submediant _____	6.	Mediant _____
3.	Leading tone _____	7.	Submediant _____
4.	Tonic _____	8.	Subdominant _____

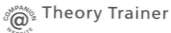 **Theory Trainer**

Exercise 6b Identify tonic or dominant by ear after hearing a major scale.

188

NAME: _____

Exercise 6.7

Match the word with the definition.

  1. Chromatic scale   _____   Scales that sound the same pitches, but are notated differently, using different letter names and accidentals

  2. Dominant   _____   Changing a piece or section of music from one key to another

  3. Enharmonic scale   _____   A scale consisting only of half steps

  4. Fixed "Do"   _____   Fourth note of a scale

  5. Leading tone   _____   When "Do" is equated with "C," "Re" is "D" and so forth

  6. Major scale   _____   First note of a scale; names the key of a piece

  7. Movable "Do"   _____   Singing with syllables

  8. Pentatonic scale   _____   Four diatonic notes consisting of two whole steps followed by a half step (WS WS HS)

  9. Solfège   _____   Fifth note of a scale; the second note of importance

10. Subdominant   _____   Seventh note of a scale; sometimes called a tendency tone

11. Tetrachord   _____   When "Do" is equated with the tonic note of a scale

12. Tonic   _____   Pattern of five notes within the octave

13. Transpose   _____   Pattern of seven notes made of whole and half steps with the half step occurring between 3 and 4, and between 7 and 8

Exercise 6.8

1. Transpose "Bohemian Melody" from D major to F major.

- Draw the D major and F major scales.
- Write the solfège and/or numbers below each scale note and in the music below.
- Then transpose the given melody to F major. The first pitches in F major are given.
- Sing the original and transposed song using solfège or numbers.

D major scale   F major scale

"Bohemian Melody" in D major

"Bohemian Melody" transposed to F major

2. Transpose "Kleine Fuge" by R. Schumann from A major to D major.

•   Draw the A major and D major scales.
•   Write the solfège and/or numbers below each scale note and in the music below.
•   Then transpose the given melody to D major. The first pitch in D major is given.
•   Sing the original and transposed song using solfège or numbers.

D major scale   F major scale

___ ___ ___ ___ ___ ___ ___ ___   ___ ___ ___ ___ ___ ___ ___ ___

"Kleine Fuge" in A major

"Kleine Fuge" transposed to D major

Exercise 6.9

Your instructor will play a major scale followed by either the tonic or dominant note of the scale. Place a check on the appropriate blank below, indicating the note. Each exercise will be played twice.

     Tonic   Dominant

1. _____   _____

2. _____   _____

3. _____   _____

4. _____   _____

MODULE 7

MAJOR SCALE KEY SIGNATURES

Major Scale Key Signatures

The song below, "You Are the Sunshine of My Life" (Stevie Wonder), may appear to be easy to sing or play because it is written in C major and does not have any sharps or flats in the music. However, it may be difficult for many to sing because the composer requires the performer to sing relatively high pitches.

"You Are the Sunshine of My Life" (Stevie Wonder) in C major

A soprano, who has the woman's highest voice range, could sing this piece as written in C major where C is the tonic note. An alto, who has a lower voice range, would probably prefer singing the piece starting on a lower note and perhaps use the E major scale. When E is the tonic note, the highest pitch in the piece is a "B" which would be more comfortable for the alto to sing.

"You Are the Sunshine of My Life" (Stevie Wonder) in E major using accidentals

In the second example, there are many sharps drawn in the music because E major has four sharps in the scale. In order to avoid having to draw these sharps in front of every F, C, G, and D, a composer uses a **key signature**. Notice:

- The key signature is placed after the clef sign at the beginning of each line of music and lists all of the sharps or flats that occur in the scale of a piece. The sharps or flats are always placed in a specific order.
- The sharps or flats in a **key signature** apply to all notes, regardless of the octave; in contrast, an **accidental** written outside of the key signature applies only to the note in that octave.
- The sharps and flats in a key signature apply to the entire line of music; accidentals apply only to the measure in which they are placed.

"You Are the Sunshine of My Life" (Stevie Wonder) in E major using a key signature

The circled notes above are pitches that will be sharped because of the key signature. Compare this version with the previous example using accidentals.

Composers decide to write in different keys for a variety of reasons: (1) to accommodate the range of the singer or instrument; (2) the key of a particular instrument may lend itself to certain scales (for example, a performer on an alto sax in E flat, or a trumpet in B flat may be more accustomed to playing in a key with flats); (3) a particular key may have a "brighter" sound, another may be "darker"; or (4) because the composer is able to and wants to use a particular key, as when J.S. Bach composed 48 Preludes and Fugues for the keyboard because a new tuning system enabled him to do so.

Major Scales with Sharps

In Module 6, scales were drawn with adjoining tetrachords beginning with C major. When the dominant (fifth note) of C major becomes the tonic note of the G major scale, one sharp is added to the scale and likewise to the subsequent key signature. An additional sharp is added with each succeeding scale.

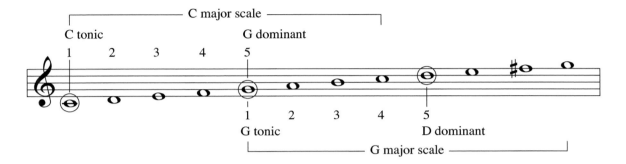

Number of sharps	1	2	3	4	5	6	7
Tonic note	G	D	A	E	B	F♯	C♯
Dominant note	D	A	E	B	F♯	C♯	

On p. 196 is a chart showing the key signatures for C major and the seven scales with sharps. Notice:

* The order of the sharps in the key signature is always the same (F♯ C♯ G♯ D♯ A♯ E♯ B♯) even if the sharps do not appear in the same order or octave in the scale. For example:

Key signature

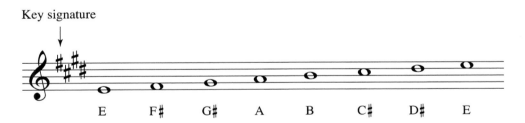

      E   F♯   G♯   A   B   C♯   D♯   E

In E major, the order of the four sharps in the key signature is F♯ C♯ G♯ D♯; in the scale, the order of the notes with sharps from the lowest to the highest pitches is F♯ G♯ C♯ D♯. The F sharp and G sharp in the key signature will affect the F and G in the lower octave of the scale because a sharp in the key signature applies to all octaves of that pitch.

Memorize
THE ORDER OF THE SHARPS IN A KEY SIGNATURE

F♯	C♯	G♯	D♯	A♯	E♯	B♯

- The placement of the sharps from left to right on the staff begins with a down-up-down-pattern. However, the placement of the fifth sharp (A♯) changes direction and does not move up from the previous D sharp. This is to avoid the use of a ledger line above the treble clef for the A sharp.

Incorrect   Correct

Likewise, the last sharp, the B sharp, is not placed above the ledger line in the treble clef. In order to maintain visual symmetry for the clefs, the placement of sharps in bass clef key signatures will parallel those in the treble clef.

Key signatures for C major and seven scales with sharps

Exercise 1

Draw the key signature of C major and the seven scales with sharps.

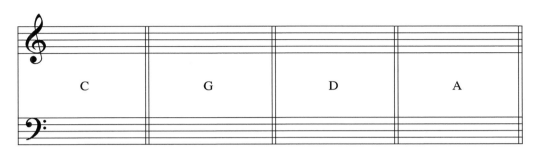

C   G   D   A

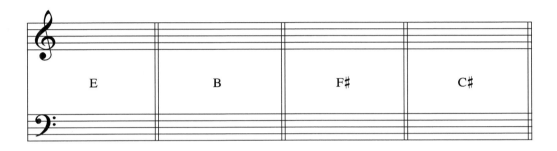

E   B   F♯   C♯

Finding the Tonic Note in a Major Scale with Sharps

The tonic note of a scale with sharps (also called the **key** or the **key tone**) is easy to determine using the key signature: locate the **half step above the last** sharp. This note is the tonic, or key. (The tonic may be drawn in any octave.) Be sure to notice if a sharp in the key signature will affect the pitch of the tonic note.

Last sharp is G♯
Key: A major

Last sharp is A♯
Key: B major

Last sharp is E♯
Key: F sharp major

Exercise 2 | Class Exercise

Name the key and draw the tonic note for the following key signatures. (The letter name of the key and the tonic note should be the same.)

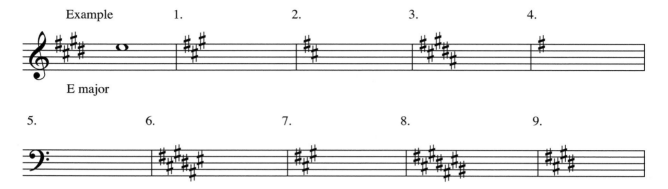

E major

 Theory Trainer

Exercise 7a Key signature identification: sharps.
Exercise 7b Sharps, flats in a key signature: sharps.

Exercise 3

Identify the key and the meter for the following pieces. Circle the notes that are affected by the key signature. Write the consecutive counts below the melodies, then clap.

1. Dutch Folk Song

2. "Good Night, Ladies," American traditional melody

Key _____   Meter _____

Count:

Count:

3. Sonata, K. 209 (D. Scarlatti)

Key _____   Meter _____

Count:

7

Count:

4. "This Land Is Your Land" (W. Guthrie)

Key _____   Meter _____

Count:

7

Count:

13

Count:

199

Major Scales with Flats

Just as there are seven scales with one to seven sharps in their key signatures, there are seven scales with one to seven flats in their key signatures. When we draw adjoining tetrachords for scales with flats we begin with C flat major with seven flats.

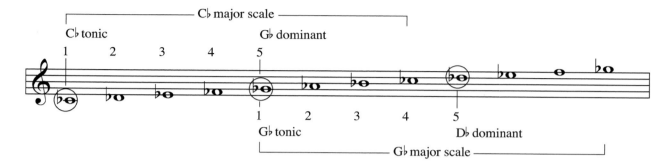

When the dominant note in C flat major (G flat) becomes the tonic note of G flat major, one flat is subtracted from the scale and its subsequent key signature. Similarly, one flat is subtracted from each succeeding scale.

Number of flats	7	6	5	4	3	2	1
Tonic note	C♭	G♭	D♭	A♭	E♭	B♭	F
Dominant note	G♭	D♭	A♭	E♭	B♭	F	

The key signatures for C major and the seven scales with flats are given on the following page. Notice:

- The order of the flats is always the same in the key signature (B♭ E♭ A♭ D♭ G♭ C♭ F♭) even if the flats do not appear in the same order or octave in the scale. For example:

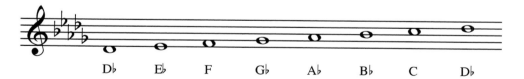

In D flat major, the order of the flats in the key signature is B♭ E♭ A♭ D♭ G♭; in the scale, the order of the flatted notes from the lowest to the highest pitches is D♭ E♭ G♭ A♭ B♭. The D flat and E flat in the key signature will affect the D and E in the lower octave of the scale because a flat in the key signature applies to all octaves of that pitch.

Memorize
THE ORDER OF THE FLATS IN A KEY SIGNATURE
B♭   E♭   A♭   D♭   G♭   C♭   F♭

- The placement of the flats in both clefs moves from left to right in an up-down-up-down pattern until the last flat.

Key signatures of C major and seven scales with flats

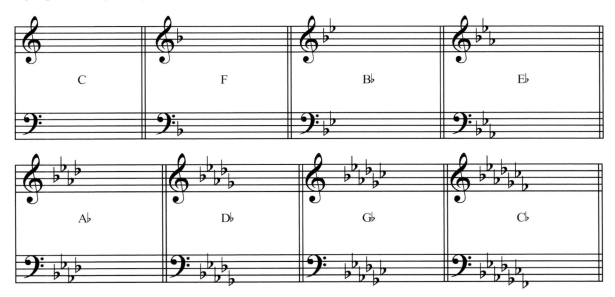

Exercise 4

Draw the key signature of C major and the seven scales with flats.

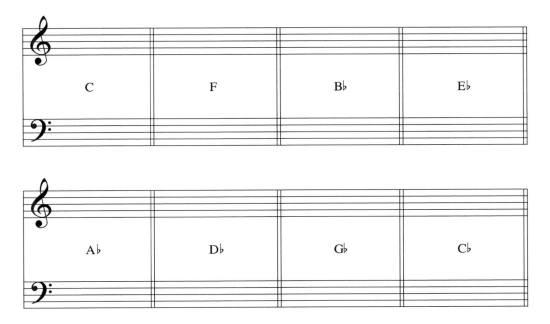

Finding the Tonic Note in a Major Scale with Flats

The tonic note of a scales with flats (the **key**, or the **tonic note**) is easy to determine using the key signature: the **second-to-the-last flat names the tonic or key**. (The tonic note may be drawn in any octave.) In the exceptional case of the scale with only B flat, it is necessary to memorize that as the key of F major. Be sure to notice if a flat in the key signature will alter the pitch of the tonic note. For example:

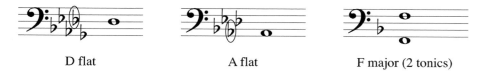

D flat   A flat   F major (2 tonics)

Exercise 5 Class Exercise

Label the key and draw the tonic note for the following key signatures. (The letter name of the key and the tonic note should be the same.)

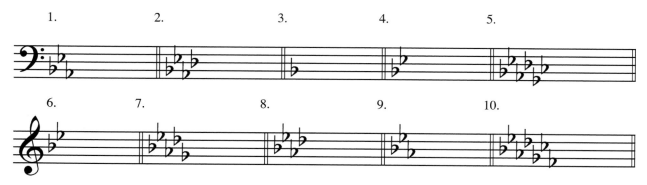

Theory Trainer

Exercise 7a Key signature identification: sharps and flats.
Exercise 7b Sharps, flats in a key signature.

Exercise 6

Identify the key and the meter for the following pieces. Circle the notes that are affected by the key signature. Write the consecutive counts below the melodies, then clap.

1. Theme from *Lohengrin* (R. Wagner)

Key _____   Meter _____

2. "Liza Jane," American folk song

Key _____   Meter _____

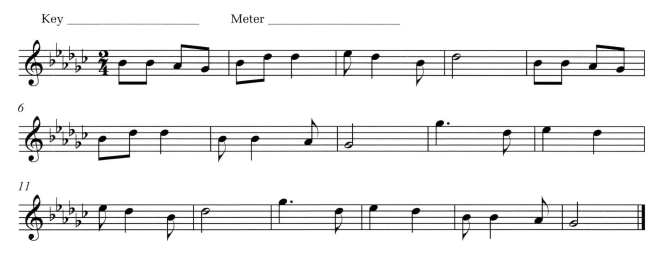

3. "Bridge Over Troubled Water" (P. Simon)

Key _____   Meter _____

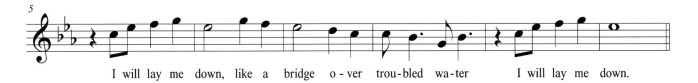

And friends just can't be found. ___ Like a bridge o - ver trou-bled wa - ter

I will lay me down, like a bridge o - ver trou-bled wa - ter   I will lay me down.

4. Waltz (F. Schubert)

Key _____   Meter _____

Vocabulary note

ANOTHER WAY TO USE 𝄇

The sign 𝄇 directs the performer to repeat back to the beginning of the section.

In the preceding piece, there are two repeat signs. Begin with the anacrusis measure and play until the first repeat sign in measure 8. Repeat back to the beginning and play to the end of the piece where there is a second repeat sign. Repeat back to the double bar in measure 8 and play until the end of the piece. (Play A (anacrusis), 1–8 two times, then (A), 9–16 two times.)

Workbook Exercises 7.1–7.3

Circle of Fifths—Major Keys

The Circle of Fifths shows the 15 major scales with their increasing number of sharps or flats. The scales with sharps begin clockwise to the right of C major and the scales with flats begin counterclockwise to the left of C major.

Vocabulary note

CIRCLE OF FIFTHS

The Circle of Fifths was first discussed by the German Baroque composer Johann David Heinichen in a theory treatise written in the early 1700s when it first became possible to compose and perform pieces in all 15 major keys.

When moving **clockwise** around the circle from C major the number of sharps increases from G major with one sharp to C♯ major with seven sharps. When moving **counterclockwise** from C major, the number of flats increases from F major with one flat to C flat with seven flats. Notice that the three pairs of **enharmonic** scales consist of five, six, or seven sharps or flats (C♭/B, G♭/F♯, D♭/C♯). Although other tonics around the Circle also have enharmonic equivalents, major keys do not exist for them—for example, D♯ or F♭.

When moving five notes up from C (the major scale without any accidentals) to the G major scale, we add one sharp, F sharp. This is called moving by a "perfect fifth":

C	D	E	F	G
1 ⟶	2 ⟶	3 ⟶	4 ⟶	5

When we move up a perfect fifth from G to the D major scale, we will add a second sharp for a total of two sharps (F sharp and C sharp), and so forth. Hence the term "Circle of **Fifths**."

Notice (on the next page) that:

- The sharps move up by fifths: F C G D A E B. Look for these letters on the circle overleaf.
- The flats move down by fifths: B E A D G C F. This is the reverse order of the sharps.

Circle of Fifths - Major Keys

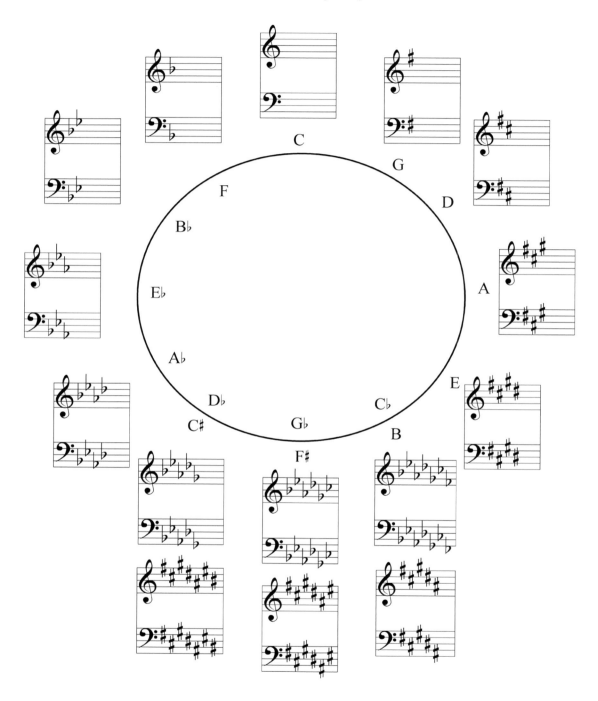

Exercise 7 Class Exercise

Identify the key (the tonic) of the following key signatures. Use any of the following methods to determine the key:

- Use the Circle of Fifths: move clockwise to the right from C major for scales with sharps, move counterclockwise to the left from C major for scales with flats.
- Use the key signature: for a scale with sharps, go up a half step from the last sharp in the key signature to name the key. For a scale with flats, name the second-to-the-last flat.
- Or have you already memorized the key signatures for all 15 major keys?

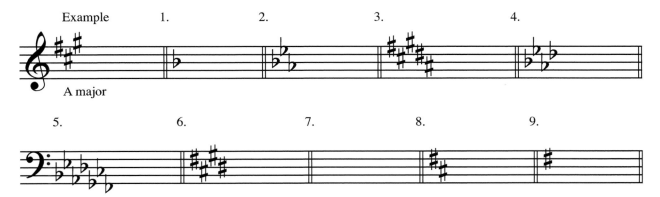

 Theory Trainer

Exercise 7a Key signature identification.
Exercise 7b Sharps, flats in a key signature.

Exercise 8 Class Exercise

Draw the following key signatures in both clefs.

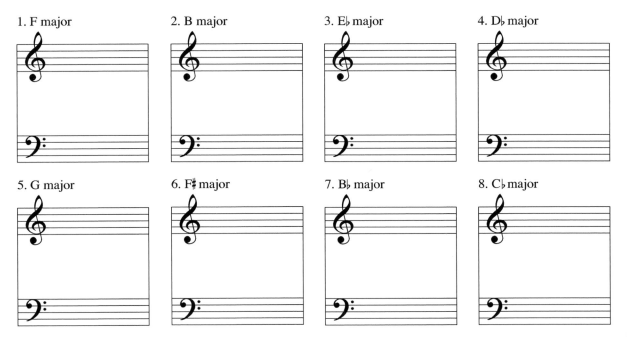

1. F major
2. B major
3. E♭ major
4. D♭ major

5. G major
6. F♯ major
7. B♭ major
8. C♭ major

"Courtesy" Accidentals

Earlier, we discussed that an accidental placed within a measure applies to the appropriate pitch or pitches within that measure or until another accidental cancels it. When a sharp or flat in a *key signature* needs to be cancelled, an accidental is added just in front of the note to be altered. For example, in the song "Blue Hawaii" a natural sign appears in the first complete measure to cancel the B flat in the key signature.

"Blue Hawaii" (L. Robin, R. Rainger)

The flat shown in the third complete measure is added as a "courtesy" accidental reminding the performer that the previous natural sign applies only to the B in the first measure, and returns to Bb in m. 3 again. Courtesy accidentals are placed in the music to remind performers of the correct pitches.

Exercise 9

Circle the courtesy accidentals.

1. Sonatina in F (Third Movement) (F.J. Haydn)

2. Waltz from "Adventures of Ivan" (A. Khachaturian)
    Reminder: Notes with accidentals that are tied across a bar line continue to be altered by the accidental.

3. "Call Me Irresponsible" (S. Cahn, J. Van Heusen)

Transposition: Using a Key Signature

In Module 6, we transposed a melody by shifting all pitches the same distance higher or lower using the corresponding scale number or solfège symbol of the original scale and the transposed scale. We may also transpose a melody by shifting all pitches the same distance higher or lower and applying the key signature of the new scale.

Exercise 10 Class Exercise

The melody "What a Wonderful World" was originally composed in F major. It begins on the dominant (fifth note of the scale) and ends on the tonic (first note of the scale). Below the original written in F major, notate the transposed melody in A major and then B♭ major.

*   Begin by drawing the A major and B♭ major scales using a key signature.
*   Circle the tonic and dominant notes of each scale. (The F major scale is done for you.)
*   Transpose "What a Wonderful World" from F major to both A major and B♭ major. First, draw the key signature and time signature after the treble clef. Begin on the dominant pitches of each respective scale; end on the tonic notes. The first three notes in A major are done for you.
*   Sing the original and transposed melodies. Do they sound "the same"?

F major scale

A major scale

B♭ major scale

"What a Wonderful World" (G. Weiss, B Thiele) in the original key of F major

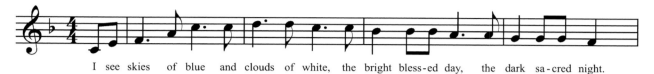

I see skies   of blue and clouds of white, the bright bless-ed day,   the dark sa-cred night.

Transpose to A major

Transpose to B♭ major

Theory Trainer

Exercise 7c Find scale degrees.

Workbook Exercises 7.4–7.9

Name _____

Exercise 7.1

Identify the key (the tonic) of the following key signatures. Use the following methods to determine the key:

- Use the key signature: for a key with sharps, name the key a half step up from the last sharp in the key signature. For a key with flats, name the second-to-the-last flat.
- Memorize the key signatures for all 15 major keys.

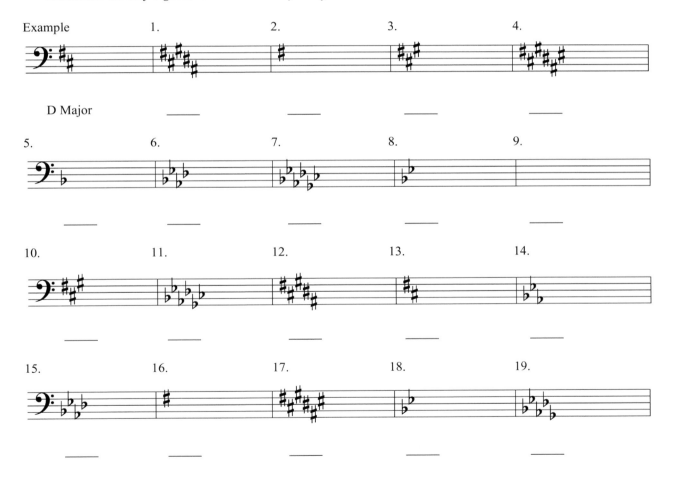

Example   1.   2.   3.   4.

D Major   _____   _____   _____   _____

5.   6.   7.   8.   9.

_____   _____   _____   _____

10.   11.   12.   13.   14.

_____   _____   _____   _____   _____

15.   16.   17.   18.   19.

_____   _____   _____   _____   _____

Exercise 7.2

Draw the following major key signatures in both clefs using sharps or flats as needed. Remember the order of sharps (F C G D A E B) is the opposite order of the flats (B E A D G C F).

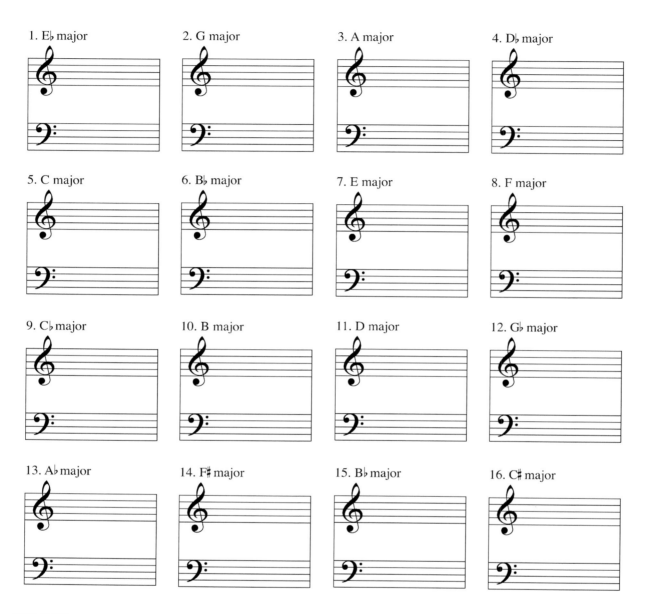

1. E♭ major
2. G major
3. A major
4. D♭ major

5. C major
6. B♭ major
7. E major
8. F major

9. C♭ major
10. B major
11. D major
12. G♭ major

13. A♭ major
14. F♯ major
15. B♭ major
16. C♯ major

Exercise 7.3

Give the number of sharps or flats that are found in the following key signatures.

Example: B major   5 sharps

1. E♭ major _____
2. G major _____
3. A major _____
4. G♭ major _____
5. E major _____
6. C major _____
7. A♭ major _____
8. F major _____
9. F♯ major _____
10. B♭ major _____
11. D♭ major _____
12. D major _____
13. C♯ major _____
14. B major _____
15. F major _____
16. E major _____
17. C♭ major _____

NAME: _____

 Theory Trainer

Exercise 7c Find scale degrees.

Exercise 7.4

Complete the Circle of Fifths. Draw the key signatures for each key. Remember that there are three pairs of enharmonic keys.

Circle of Fifths - Major Keys

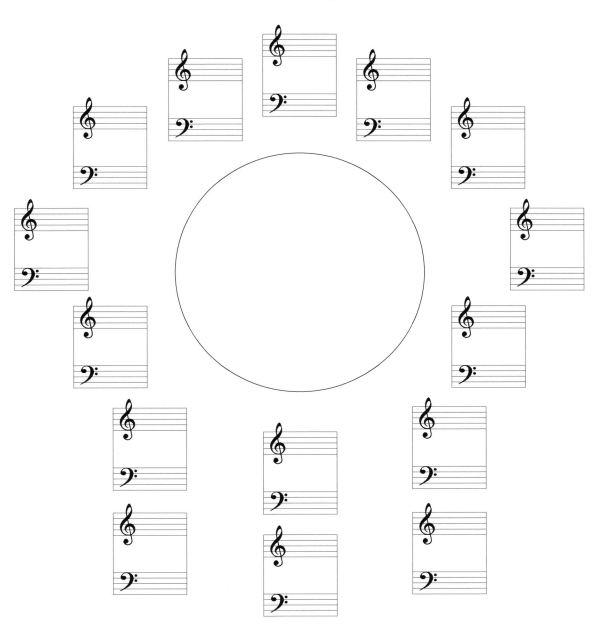

Exercise 7.5

Name the key with the following number of sharps or flats in the key signature.

Example: 2 sharps   <u>D major</u>

1. 5 flats _____
2. 2 flats _____
3. 5 sharps _____
4. 3 sharps _____
5. 0 _____
6. 1 flat _____
7. 7 sharps _____
8. 4 sharps _____
9. 4 flats _____
10. 3 flats _____
11. 1 sharp _____
12. 3 sharps _____
13. 7 flats _____
14. 4 sharps _____
15. 6 flats _____
16. 2 sharps _____
17. 6 sharps _____

Exercise 7.6

Identify the key for the following pieces. Circle the pitches that are altered by the key signature. Identify the meter and write in the counts below the melodies. Count, clap and sing each melody.

1. "Pupu O Ewa" ("Pearly Shells") (W. Edwards, L. Pober)
   This Hawaiian melody divides into two sections called **phrases**. Can you locate the second phrase, which begins the same as the opening measure? How is the beginning of the second phrase the same as the first phrase, and how is it different?

Vocabulary note

PHRASE

A **phrase** is a musical sentence, usually between four and eight measures in length. Frequently, a melody will divide into two phrases, the first ending with the dominant (the antecedent phrase) and the second ending with the tonic (the consequent phrase). Phrase endings are often signaled by a rest or a longer note value.

Key _____   Meter _____

2. "Day-O" (The Banana Boat Song), Jamaican folk song
   When singing "Day-O" you may shout at the "X" in measures 10 and 12.

Vocabulary note

REPEAT SIGN

D.S. al Fine or *Dal Segno al Fine* ("to the sign") directs the performer to return to the sign 𝄋 and end at **Fine** ("the end"). Here, play measures 1–12 then measures 3–4.

Key _____   Meter _____

Day   O!   Day   O!   Day - light   come   an' me   wan - na   go   home.

Come   Mis - ter   Tal - ly   Man,   Come   tal - ly   me   ba - na - na.   Day - light   come   an' me   wan - na   go   home.

Six   hand,   sev - en   hand,   eight   hand   bunch!   Six   hand,   sev - en   hand,   eight   hand   bunch!

D.S. al Fine

3.   "Arirang," Korean folk melody

Key _____   Meter _____

On the staff below, draw the key signature and the major scale that has one flat. Then circle the notes of the scale that are used in "Arirang."

NAME: _____

4. "Georgia on My Mind" (H. Carmichael)

Key _____   Meter _____

Geor - gia _____   Geor - gia, _____   no peace I find.   Just an

old   sweet   song   keeps   Geor - gia   on   my   mind. _____

On the staff below, draw the key signature and the major scale that has one flat. Then circle the notes of the scale that are used in "Georgia on My Mind." Compare the circled notes with those of "Arirang" above. Which of these two pieces sounds "major"? _____ Which piece sounds "pentatonic"? _____

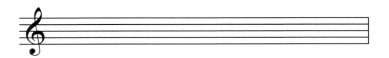

5. "Summer Wind" (H. Mayer, English words J. Mercer)

In this song, the first four notes form a **motive**. Are the next four notes an **exact** repetition or **varied** repetition of the opening motive? _____ Bracket another motive in the second line of music. Is it immediately repeated exactly or it is varied? _____ In what way is the second motive similar to or different from the first motive? _____

Key _____   Meter _____

The   sum-mer wind   came   blow-ing in   from a - cross   the sea.   -

-    -   -   It   lin-gered there   to   touch your hair   and   walk with me.

Exercise 7.7

Match the word with the definition.

1. Circle of Fifths _____ Fifth note of the scale; the second note of importance

2. "Courtesy" accidental _____ When "Do" is equated with "C," "Re" is "D," and so forth

3. D.C. al Fine _____ Sharps or flats placed in a specific order after the clef at the beginning of a line of music indicating the key of a piece

4. Dominant _____ Musical sentence

5. Enharmonic scale _____ Short rhythmic and melodic idea used in a phrase

6. "Fixed Do" _____ Changing a piece of music from one key to another; all pitches retain the same intervallic relationship throughout

7. Key signature _____ When "Do" is equated with the tonic note of a scale, "Re" is the supertonic, and so forth

8. Major scale _____ First note of the scale; names the key of a piece

9. Motive _____ Return to this sign and repeat, ending at the word "Fine"

10. "Movable Do" _____ The 15 major scales with their increasing number of sharps or flats; scales with sharps move clockwise to the right of C major, and the scales with flats move counterclockwise to the left of C major

11. Phrase _____ Directs the musician to return to the beginning and repeat, ending at the word "Fine"

12. Tonic _____ Accidental placed in music as a reminder to alter a note

13. Transposition _____ Scales that sound the same but are notated differently, using different letter names and accidentals

14. 𝄋 _____ Pattern of eight notes made of whole and half steps, with half steps occurring between 3 and 4, and between 7 and 8

NAME:

Exercise 7.8

1. Transpose the second phrase of Beethoven's "Ode to Joy" from the original key of D major to B♭ major and then to G major. Draw the key signature and time signature for the new keys.

"Ode to Joy" (L.v. Beethoven) in D major

Transpose to B♭ major

Transpose to G major

2. Transpose Schubert's Ecossaise from the original key of C major to A major and then to F major. Draw the key signature and time signature for the new keys.

Transpose to A major

Transpose to F major

Exercise 7.9

On your own staff paper or on the staff lines below, notate an original melody. (Determine the clef, time signature and key.) Then transpose it to a different key; share this with the class.

Title _____   Original key _____

MODULE 8

RHYTHM: COMPOUND METER

Melodies in Compound Meter

Let's look at the piece, "A Little Hunting Song" by Robert Schumann, a short descriptive piece written for piano.

Notice:

- The **new time signature**
- The beaming of eighth notes into **groups of three** in the last two measures

---

Vocabulary note: Articulation marks

> **ACCENT MARKS**

tell the performer to play the note or notes louder than surrounding ones.

STACCATO

dots above or below note heads tell the performer to play the notes disconnected or detached.

🔊 **TRACK 70—CLASS EXERCISE**

Listen to "A Little Hunting Song" by Schumann or another piece in 6/8. Discuss accents, staccatos, and the grouping of the three eighth notes in the last two measures of "A Little Hunting Song." Listen to the piece again; clap the two main beats along with the music while emphasizing the first beat slightly louder than the second.

Meter is the regular grouping of strong and weak beats or pulses. Earlier, we studied **simple meter** where the upper number of the time signature is **2**, **3**, or **4**; the division of the main pulse is into **groupings of two** or multiples of two and the lower number of the time signature represents the pulse note. (For example, the lower number four is used to represent the quarter note.)

In **compound meter**, the pulse note is a dotted note which divides equally into **groups of three** or multiples of three. Therefore the **upper number** of a compound time signature is divisible by three: 6, 9, 12.

• 6 signifies compound duple.
• 9 signifies compound triple.
• 12 signifies compound quadruple.

In compound meter, the lower number in a time signature cannot represent the pulse note since the pulse note is a dotted note. Therefore, the **lower number** represents the *subdivision* of the dotted note.

Vocabulary note

COMPOUND METER

In compound meter, the upper number of the time signature is 6, 9, or 12 (all multiples of three). To determine the meter of a compound rhythm, divide the upper number of the time signature by 3. Therefore, when the upper number is a 6, this is **compound duple**; when the upper number is a 9 this is **compound triple**, and when the upper number is 12 this is **compound quadruple**.

Note: Although the number 3 in the time signature 3/4 is a multiple of three, 3/4 is a simple meter because the main pulse, the quarter note, is divided into groups of two, NOT groups of three. This will be discussed later in this module.

We will begin our study of compound meters by comparing the most common compound meter time signatures, 6/8, 9/8, and 12/8, with comparable time signatures in simple meter, 2/4, 3/4, 4/4.

The chart opposite compares simple and compound meters and their corresponding time signatures.

In the left column showing simple meters, the main pulse is a quarter note, which can be divided into groups of **two eighth notes**. In the right column showing compound meters, the main pulse is a dotted quarter note, which can be divided into groups of **three eighth notes**.

In a 6/8 compound time signature, we may count six eighth notes in one measure. These six eighth notes are beamed into groups of three; we therefore count (and feel) two groups of three eighth notes (♫♪ ♫♪), or two dotted quarter notes (♩. ♩.).

Consequently, there are two simultaneous rhythms in compound music: one is the main dotted note pulse, and the other is the division of the dotted note into three equal parts.

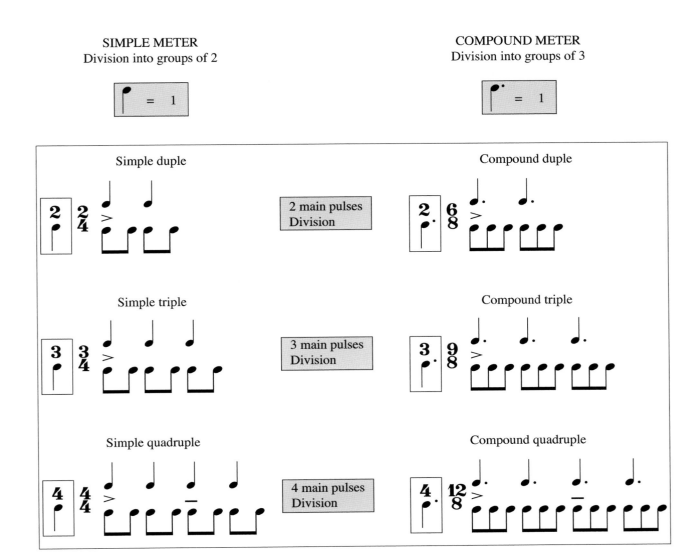

As a result of these two concurrent rhythmic patterns, there are two ways of counting compound time signatures.

- The first method of counting utilizes the main beats in each measure.
- The second method utilizes the divided beat.

Your instructor will determine which method of counting to use for compound meters. Some musicians use both methods: the first method for melodies with larger note values that are played at faster tempos, and the second method for melodies with smaller note values that are played at slower tempos. Both methods should emphasize the main beats in each measure—and both should "sound the same."

First Method of Counting Compound Meter

We can look at the grouping of three eighth notes in the treble clef of Ross Lee Finney's "Mirrors" to demonstrate the first method of counting compound meter.

Notice:

- There are **two** main beats (pulses) in each measure (the top number, 6, when divided by 3 will equal 2).
- The main pulse is the dotted quarter note (♪♪♪ = ♩. = 1).

"Mirrors" (R.L. Finney)
Meter: Compound duple

🔊 **TRACK 71**

> *Listen to "Mirrors" by Ross Lee Finney. To establish the tempo, two measures will be given before the piece begins: count "1—2—1—2". Continue to count out loud as you listen to the piece. Can you feel the underlying division of the main beats into three smaller units?*

In 6/8 there are six eighth notes in a measure, with the grouping of the eighths into two groups of three, resulting in two dotted quarter notes. Therefore, the meter of 6/8 is compound duple. Likewise, 9/8 is **compound triple** meter (9 divided by 3). It consists of three main beats, each a dotted quarter note which can be divided into three eighth notes. The same applies to **compound quadruple** meter, with four beats.

Exercise 1 Class Exercise

Utilizing the main beat, count and clap the rhythms below.
Method 1: Counting compound meter—utilizing the main beat

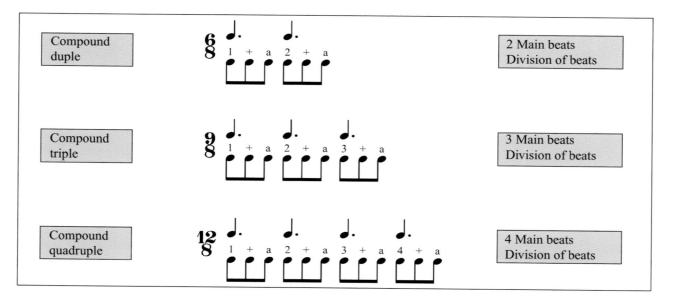

Second Method of Counting Compound Meter

In the **second method** of counting rhythms in compound meter, the lower number of the time signature indicates the type of note serving as each beat. In a 6/8 time signature where the main beat is an eighth note, there are six eighth notes. Beginning with the first eighth note, every fourth eighth note is accented:

1 2 3 4 5 6

Let's look again at "Mirrors" by Ross Lee Finney to count using the eighth note beat. Notice that each of the eighth notes forming the two main beats is given one count, and the first and fourth counts are accented.

🔊)) **TRACK 72**

> *Listen to "Mirrors" by Ross Lee Finney. To establish the tempo, two measures will be given before the piece begins: count "**1**—2—3—**4**—5—6." Continue to count out loud as you listen to the piece. Feel the two stronger main beats in each measure. Notice that counting "Mirrors" using the second method will result in a performance identical to that using the first method of counting the main beats.*

In **compound duple** meter there are six eighth notes in a measure with the first and fourth eighth notes accented, creating two main beats. In **compound triple** meter, beats 1, 4, and 7 are accented; in **compound quadruple** meter, beats 1, 4, 7, and 10 are accented.

Exercise 2 Class Exercise

Utilizing the eighth note beat, count and clap the rhythms below. Count one measure before beginning to clap. At first, do this at a slow tempo. Then count at a faster tempo.

Method 2: Counting compound meter—utilizing the divided beat as a pulse note

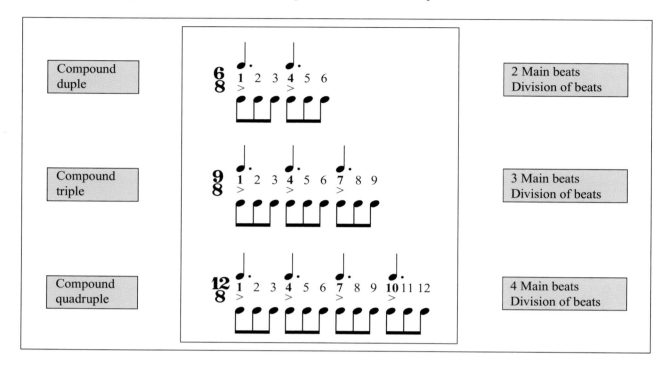

Rests

Rests in compound meter are given the same counts as their comparable notes. For example:

As we learned in Module 3, rests may be dotted, but they may not be tied. Composers frequently use two rests to represent a dotted rest in order to maintain the grouping of three eighth notes. For example:

Beams

To show the pulse note in compound meter, notes are beamed into groups in the following ways:

- Beam notes of similar value together to equal one main pulse.

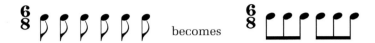

- Beam different note values together into groups to equal one main pulse.

- Do *not* beam notes together from different main beats; only beam notes together that occur in the same main pulse.

Exercise 3

In the following exercises, write the time signature on the empty staff below and rewrite the melody, changing the flags of single eighth notes to beams when appropriate. Group eighth notes so that they equal the dotted quarter note, or a total of three eighth notes.

Example: Violin Concerto (Third Movement) (L.v. Beethoven)

1. "For He's a Jolly Good Fellow," American traditional melody

2. "The Old Hag in the Kiln" (D. Delaney), Celtic session song

3. Piano Sonata in G Major, Op. 79 (Second Movement) (L.v. Beethoven)

Dividing the Dotted Quarter

Use one of the two methods below to count and clap the following patterns in 6/8. Your instructor may prefer one method over the other—use the method that is assigned.

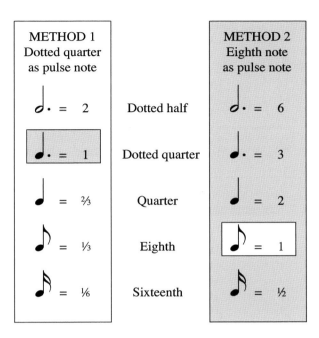

METHOD 1 Dotted quarter as pulse note		METHOD 2 Eighth note as pulse note
𝅗𝅥. = 2	Dotted half	𝅗𝅥. = 6
♩. = 1	Dotted quarter	♩. = 3
♩ = ⅔	Quarter	♩ = 2
♪ = ⅓	Eighth	♪ = 1
𝅘𝅥𝅯 = ⅙	Sixteenth	𝅘𝅥𝅯 = ½

Exercise 4

Practice each pattern separately. Count out loud, always emphasizing the two main beats.

To the instructor: You may wish to use percussion instruments to give students a more varied aural experience.

Method 1: Count the dotted quarter as the pulse note. (Use the left column.) This method works better for pieces in faster tempos.

Method 2: Count the eighth note as the pulse note. (Use the right column with the shaded box.) This method of counting works better for slower tempos and for smaller note values.

Exercise 5

The following rhythms use the six patterns of Exercise 4. Identify the meter of each and notate the counts below each example; clap and count out loud. Identify the pieces that begin with incomplete measures.

_____

1. Meter _____

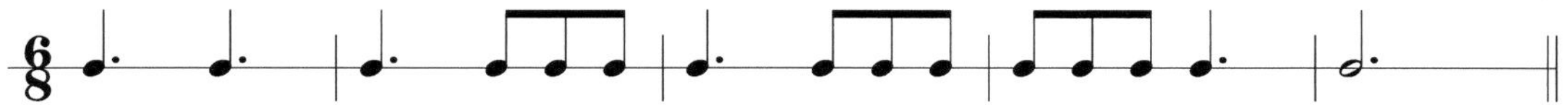

Count: 1 (+a)   2 (+ a)
OR: **1** (2 3)   **4** (5 6)

2. Meter _____

Count: 1   +   a   2(+a)
OR: 1   2   3   4(56)

3. Meter _____

Count:
OR:

4. Meter _____

Count:
OR:

The following rhythms use ties and rests.

5. Meter _____

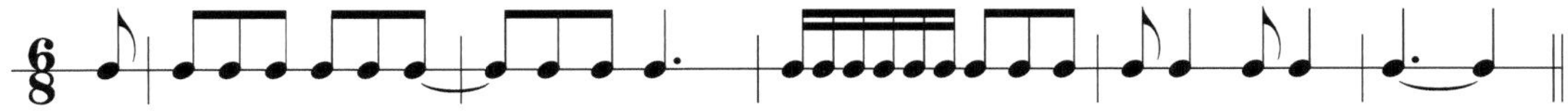

Count:
OR:

231

6. Meter _____

Count:
OR:

7. Meter _____

Count:
OR:

Exercise 6

The musical examples below use the six patterns of Exercise 4. Identify the meter of each piece and notate the counts below each example. Do all of the pieces have complete measures?_____

1. "Aogeba Tô Toshi," Japanese traditional graduation song

Count: a   1 (+) a   2 (+) a

OR   6   **1** (2) 3 **4** (5) 6

Count:

2. Celtic session tune (J. Walsh)
    Using measure numbers, explain how the music repeats. _____

Count: 1 (+ a) 2   +   a   1 (+ a) (2 +)   a
OR   **1** (2 3) **4**   5   6   **1** (2 3) (**4** 5)   6

Count:

Count:

3. Songs Without Words, Op. 53, No. 4 (F. Mendelssohn)

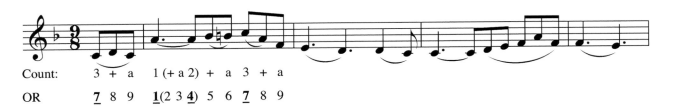

Count: 3   +   a   1 (+ a 2)   +   a   3   +   a
OR   **7**   8   9   **1** (2 3 **4**)   5   6   **7**   8   9

How many slurs does Mendelssohn use?_____
How many ties does Mendelssohn use?_____

4.   Piano Sonata, Op. 28 (Fourth Movement) (L.v. Beethoven)

Write the counts below each clef. First, tap the bass staff rhythm with your left hand, then the treble staff rhythm with your right hand. Finally, tap both parts together. Identify the rhythmic device Beethoven uses that complicates the tapping with two hands. _____

Count:

5.   Etude Tableau, Op. 33, No. 2 (S. Rachmaninoff)

Count: 1 (+ a) 2 (+ a 3 +) a   4   +   a

OR   **1** (2   3) **4** (5   6   **7**   8) 9   **10**   11   12

6.   "Touch the Sky" from Brave (A. Mandel, M. Andrews)

Write the counts below each clef. Notice the bracket above m. 10: this measure has momentarily changed to 3/4 time, before returning to 6/8 the following measure. This rhythmic device, frequently used in the Middle Ages, is called hemiola.

Quickly

Vocabulary note

HEMIOLA

A rhythmic device that utilizes two beats in the time of three, or three beats in the time of two; for example, going from 6/8 to 3/4, or 3/4 to 6/8 without changing the time signature. In "Touch the Sky," although the time signature for the piece is 6/8, the rhythm for m. 10 is in 3/4.

 Theory Trainer

      Exercise 8a Rhythm tapping in compound meter.
      Exercise 8b Compound rhythm tapping with rests

Workbook Exercises 8.1 and 8.2

Comparing 6/8 and 3/4

Measures written in 6/8 and 3/4 time signatures have the same number of eighth notes. However, the metric accents are different.

Exercise 7 Class Exercise

Clap the **subdivided eighth notes** drawn below, keeping the eighth notes in each time signature at the same speed—feel the change in the placement of the accents.

    Before you begin clapping, count one measure out loud, emphasizing the beats that get the accents.

- For **compound duple** count: **1** + a **2** + a   OR   **1** 2 3 **4** 5 6
- For **simple triple** count: **1** + **2** + **3** +

Keep the speed of the eighth notes the same for both the compound and simple meters.

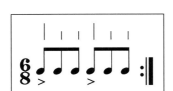

Count: **1** + a **2** + a
OR   **1** 2 3 **4** 5 6

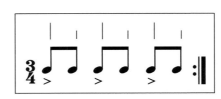

Count: **1** + **2** + **3** +

Exercise 8 Class Exercise

Clap the main pulses (beats) of each time signature drawn below—feel the change in the placement of the accents.

   To establish the tempo, count one measure out loud. Students may take turns counting out loud before beginning the exercise.

- For **compound duple** count: **1** + a **2** + a   OR   **1** 2 3 **4** 5 6
- For **simple triple** count: **1** + **2** + **3** +

Keep the speed of the underlying subdivided eighth notes constant.

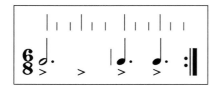   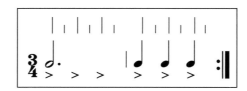

Count: 1 + a 2 + a   1 + a 2 + a   Count: 1 + 2 + 3 +   1 + 2 + 3 +
OR   1 2 3 4 5 6   1 2 3 4 5 6

Notice that the half note may be used in music written in 3/4 but not in 6/8; to use the half note in 6/8 would obscure the main pulse. Following are examples showing the correct and incorrect usage of the half note.

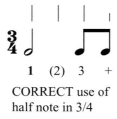   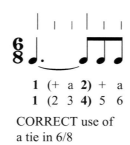   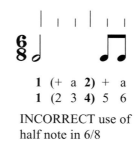

1 (2) 3   +   **1** (+ a **2**) +   a   **1** (+ a **2**) +   a

CORRECT use of   **1** (2   3 **4**) 5   6   **1** (2   3 **4**) 5   6
half note in 3/4
                         CORRECT use of   INCORRECT use of
                         a tie in 6/8   half note in 6/8

236

Exercise 9

Determine the time signature for the following rhythms: 3/4 or 6/8. Write the time signature for each rhythm in the box at the beginning. Add bar lines and a double bar at the end. Each exercise has four complete measures.

Exercise 10

In each exercise, locate three measures that are notated incorrectly according to the given time signature; draw brackets above them. Rewrite the exercise on the staff below, correcting the errors. Identify the meter. The first measure is done for you.

1. Meter _____

2. Meter _____

3. Meter _____

Two-part Rhythm Exercises

Exercise 11 Class Exercise

Write the meter. Tap the notes above the line with your right hand (RH); tap the notes below the line with your left hand (LH). Then tap hands together. Counting out loud, practice slowly at first, then faster.

1. Meter: _____

2. Meter: _____

3. Meter: _____

@ Theory Trainer

Exercise 8c Listening to rhythms in compound meter: reproduce the rhythm.

Workbook Exercise 8.3

Further Exercises in Compound Meter: Dotted Eighth Note Rhythms

The eighth note, like the quarter note, is commonly dotted. For example:

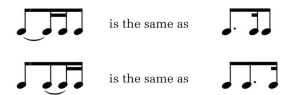

is the same as

Exercise 12 Class Exercise

Practice each pattern separately. Count out loud, always emphasizing the two main beats.

To the instructor: Assign the method to be used by the class. You may wish to use percussion instruments or instruments "found" in students' backpacks.

Method 1: Count the dotted quarter as the pulse note. (Use the first line of counting.) This method works better for pieces in faster tempos.

Method 2: Count the eighth note as the pulse note. (Use the counts in the shaded box.) This method of counting works better for slower tempos and for smaller note values.

Pattern 5

1	+	(a) –	2	+	(a) –	3	+	(a) –
1	2	(3) +	**4**	5	(6) +	**7**	8	(9) +
>			>			>		

Exercise 13

Identify the meter and notate the consecutive counts below each example; clap and count out loud.

1. Meter _____

Counts:
OR:

2. Meter _____

Counts:
OR:

3. Meter _____

Counts:
OR:

4. Meter _____

Counts:
OR:

5. Meter _____

9/8 ♪♪♪♪♪♪♪. ♪♪ | ♪♪♪♪♪♪♪. ♪♪. | ♩ ♪♩. ♪♪ | ♩. ♩. ‖

Counts:
OR:

6. Meter _____ ¬¬¬¬¬ _____

12/8 ♪. ♪♩. ♪. ♪♩. | ♪. ♪♪♩ ♪♪♪♩ | ♪♩ ♪♪♪♩. | ♩. ‖

Counts:
OR:

Exercise 14

Label the key for selections that are in a major key; identify the meter. Below the music, write the consecutive counts; clap and count out loud.

1. "Believe Me If All Those Endearing Young Charms," Irish traditional melody

Key _____   Meter _____

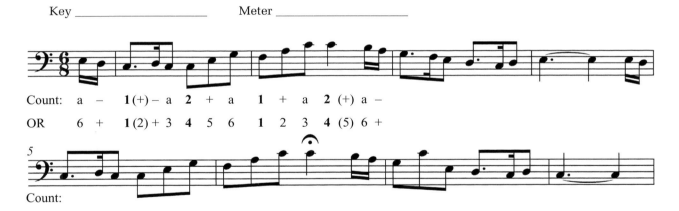

Count: a –   **1**(+)– a **2** + a   **1** + a **2** (+) a –
OR   6 +   **1**(2)+ 3 **4** 5 6   **1** 2 3 **4** (5) 6 +

Count:

- The music divides into two sections. Where does the music repeat? _____
- Find one motive in the music, bracket and label each time it is used.
- What is ⌢ called? What does it tell you to do? _____
- How many counts do the pairs of tied notes receive? _____

241

2.   Moment Musical, Op. 94, No. 2 (F. Schubert)

Key _____   Meter _____

Count: **3**(+) – a   **1(2)**   **3**(+) – a
OR: **7**(8) + 9   **1**(23 **4**56) **7**(8) + 9

Schubert wrote this piece for piano. The treble clef notes are played entirely by the right hand.

3.   Trumpet Concerto (Second Movement) (F.J. Haydn)

Key _____   Meter _____

Count:

4.   "Veulay" ("Perhaps") (J. Sharet), Israeli folk song

Meter _____

Count:

Count:

Vocabulary notes

SIGNS TO REPEAT A SECTION

| 1. | | 2. | | **First ending** and **Second ending** are signs that instruct the performer to repeat the beginning of a section but to play the endings differently.

In "Veulay" play measures A, 1, 2, 3, 4, 1, 2, 3, 5, 6, 7.

CHANGING METER, POLYMETER, COMPLEX METER

When the time signature in a piece changes, the meter is called **changing meter, polymeter**, or **complex meter**.

In Veulay, the time signature changes from 6/8 to 9/8. When performing this, be sure to keep the pulse constant.

5.   "Shan ge," Chinese folk song

Meter _____

Count:

Count:

Rhythm Review—1-, 2-, 3-part Exercises

Exercise 13

Rhythm Review—Compound Meter

Write the consecutive counts below each of the following rhythms. Tap or clap.

1.

2.

3.

4.

5.

6.

7.

8.

Rhythm Review—Simple Meter

Write the consecutive counts below each of the following rhythms. Tap or clap.

9.

10.

11.

Tap the two-part rhythm. Begin by tapping or clapping each line separately. Then divide the class into two, each section performing a different line. For greater interest, each line may be produced in a different manner; for example, tapping on a tabletop, clapping, snapping fingers. For a greater challenge, tap both parts simultaneously: play the upper line with your right hand, and the lower line with your left hand.

3.

4.

5.

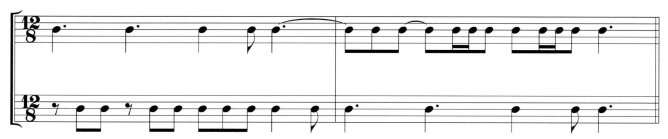

Theory Trainer

Exercise 8a Rhythm tapping in compound meter: dotted quarter subdivision.

Exercise 8b Compound rhythm tapping with rests.

Exercise 8c Listening to rhythms in compound meter: reproduce the rhythm.

Workbook Exercises 8.4–8.6

Name _____

Exercise 8.1

Count and clap the following rhythms. Count one complete measure before you begin in order to establish the tempo. For example, count: **1** 2 3 **4** 5 6 *or* **1** + a **2** + a.

Exercise 8.2

Complete the melody using the notes and time signature that are provided. Add bar lines and end with a double bar line.

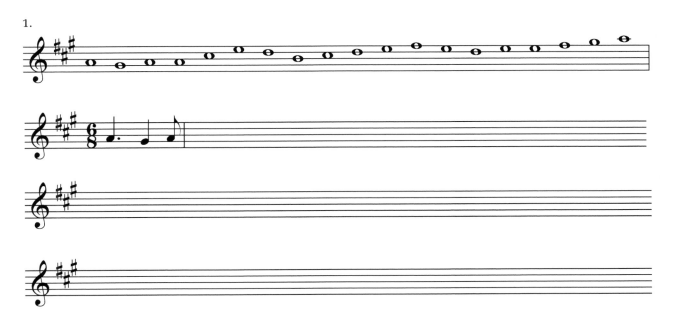

2.

3.

4. Compose your own melody. Decide on the clef, key, and compound time signature. Utilize a motive; think about phrase structure. Take it a step further: add lyrics and a title. If possible, play it on a keyboard, sing it, or ask your instructor to play it for the class.

Title_____

NAME: _____

Exercise 8.3

Write in the missing time signature for the exercises below. Each of the following seven time signatures will be used once. Then write in the counts, clap and sing.

1. "The Dingle Regatta," Celtic sessions song

Where does the music repeat? _____ Is the repetition exact or varied? _____

2. "Du und Du," *Die Fledermaus*, Op. 367 (J. Strauss)

3. "Soushunbu" ("Song for Early Spring") (N. Shou), Japanese melody

4. Song Without Words, Op. 53, No. 4 (F. Mendelssohn)

How many slurs and how many ties are found in this piece? Slurs _____ Ties _____ How many beats do the tied notes receive? _____ Identify the ornament in the anacrusis measure. _____

5. "Time in a Bottle" (J. Croce)

How many counts do the three sets of tied notes receive?_____ _____ _____

6. Sonata in A Major, Op. 120 (Third Movement) (F. Schubert)

In the music above, a motive is marked by a bracket. Locate and bracket three other times this motive occurs. Are the repetitions the same? If not, explain how they differ.

_____

_____

7. "What Kind of Fool Am I?" (L. Bricusse, A. Newley)

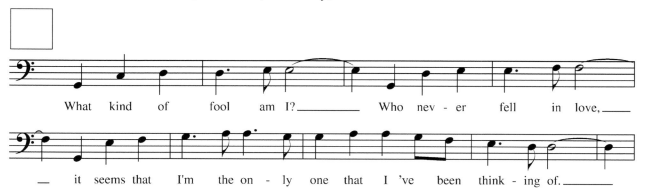

Exercise 8.4

Match the word with the definition.

1. Accent

   _____ Note that represents the beat; note that receives one count

2. Articulation mark

   _____ When the top number of a time signature is 2, 3, or 4; the main pulse note divides into groups of 2 or 4

3. Changing meter, polymeter

   _____ A dot placed above or below a note head indicating to play that note detached; an articulation mark

4. Compound meter

   _____ A sign (>) placed above or below a note head indicating to play that note louder than surrounding notes; an articulation mark

5. Meter

   _____ When the top number of a time signature is 6, 9, or 12; the main pulse note is a dotted note that divides into groups of 3 or 6

6. Pulse note

   _____ Symbol or word used to indicate how a note or notes are to be played; for example, smoothly (legato), detached (staccato), stressed (accent or tenuto)

7. Simple meter

   _____ First ending and second endings are signs that instruct the performer to repeat the beginning of a section but to play the endings differently; also called multiple endings

8. Staccato

   _____ Recurring division of the pulse into a pattern of strong and weak beats

9. | 1. | 2. |

   _____ Meters that change within a piece of music; for example, when the time signature changes from 3/4 to 3/8

Exercise 8.5 | Class Exercise

Various combinations of the following four rhythms will be played. Each example will be three measures long. One measure will be counted out loud to establish the tempo.

- Count to yourself—and keep counting
- At first, notate the number of notes that you hear in each measure. Use a short diagonal line to represent each note. (How many notes do you have in each measure?)
- **If you cannot complete a measure, go on to the next.**
- Change the diagonal line into a note head. Add a stem to each note head.
- Fill in note heads, add beams, flags, or dots as needed.

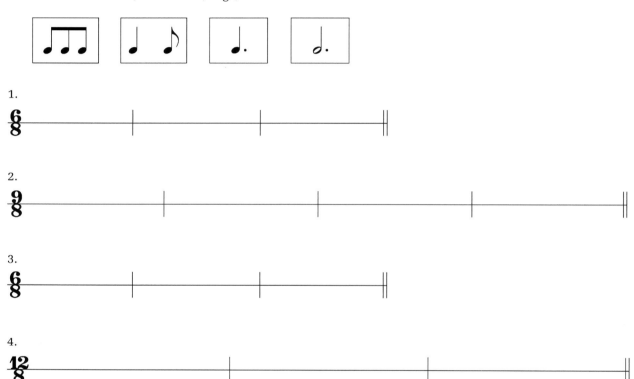

Exercise 8.6

Compose rhythms to fill measures that are left blank.

- Use a combination of notes or rests that are similar to those in surrounding measures.
- It is usually most satisfying if rhythms begin slowly and progressively speed up. Ending with a longer note value gives a sense of finality.
- Write in the counts; clap.

1.

2.

3.

4.

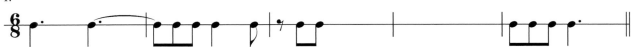

5. Compose your own two-hand rhythm in compound meter. Write the time signature at the beginning of the first line. Notate the right-hand rhythms above the line and stem them up; notate the left-hand rhythms below the line and stem them down. If hands alternate, indicate rests as required. See page 238 for examples.

_____

_____

_____

MODULE 9

MINOR SCALE

Minor Key Signatures

Looking at the "James Bond Theme," it might appear that the piece is in the key of C major because there are no sharps or flats in the key signature.

"James Bond Theme" (M. Norman)

Key signature

However, the melody centers on A and the downbeat, the strongest beat of every measure, is an A. This piece is not in C major but in the key of **A minor**. Every key signature can signify either a major or a minor key. In this module we will explore pieces written in minor keys and how they compare with those written in major keys. (Note: The key of a piece written in major may be labelled "C major" or simply "C." The key of a piece in minor should always state "minor" as in "A minor.")

🔊 **TRACKS 73–78—CLASS EXERCISE**

Discuss the "quality" of major versus minor keys: does a piece written in major sound brighter and happier, and a piece written in minor sound sadder or more mysterious? Can a piece written in a minor key sound happy—and why or why not?

73. "James Bond Theme" in A minor (M. Norman)

74. Symphony No. 40 in G minor, K. 550 (First Movement) (W.A. Mozart)

75. "The Entertainer" in C major (S. Joplin)

76. *"Moonlight" Sonata in C♯ minor (L.v. Beethoven)*
77. *"Die Forelle" ("The Trout") in D♭ major (F. Schubert)*
78. *"El Choclo" (Tango Criolla) in D minor (A. Villoldo)*

Relative Major and Minor Key Signatures

Major and minor keys that share the same key signature are called **relative keys**. Neither C major nor A minor has any sharps or flats in the key signature; they are relative keys. Because the notes of each scale are the same but the scales begin with different tonic notes, the half step and whole step arrangement for each scale will not be the same.

C major

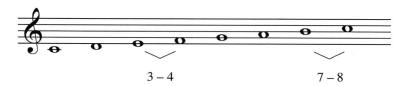

A minor

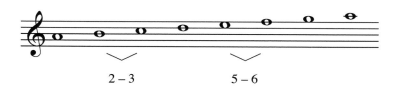

The distance between the tonic notes of relative minor and major keys is three half steps. For example:

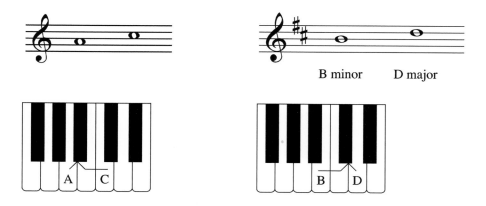

256

Finding the Tonic Note in a Minor Key with Sharps

To find the tonic note (also called the key or key tone) for a minor scale **key signature with sharps**, count three half steps below the major tonic note, or name the note a whole step below the last sharp.

F♯ sharp minor   A major   C♯ sharp minor   E major
Tonic relatives drawn on LINES   Tonic relatives drawn on SPACES

Notice:

* The tonic note may be affected by the key signature. In the first example with three sharps, the F is sharped owing to the F sharp in the key signature. In the second example with four sharps, the C is sharped owing to the C sharp in the key signature.
* On the staff, if the major tonic note is written on a line, the minor tonic note is also written on a line (F sharp minor and A major). Or both major and minor tonic notes may be written on spaces (C sharp minor and E major). However, the tonic note may be drawn in any octave as shown below.

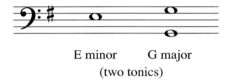

E minor   G major
(two tonics)

Below is a chart showing the key signatures for A minor and the seven minor scales with sharps. Notice:

* The order of the sharps is the same as for the major scales with sharps (F♯ C♯ G♯ D♯ A♯ E♯ B♯).

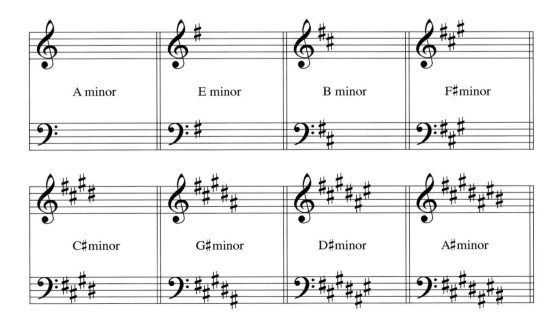

Exercise 1 Class Exercise

Draw the major (M) and minor (m) tonic notes for the following key signatures and label the keys below. (The letter names of the key and the corresponding tonics should be the same.)

CM   Am

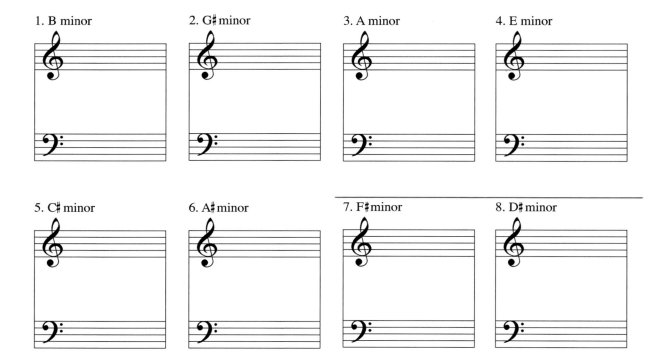

Exercise 2

Draw the minor key signature for the following keys.

1. B minor

2. G♯ minor

3. A minor

4. E minor

5. C♯ minor

6. A♯ minor

7. F♯ minor

8. D♯ minor

 Theory Trainer

Exercise 9b Key signature identification: sharps.

Finding the Tonic Note in a Minor Key with Flats

To find the tonic note in a minor scale using a **key signature with flats**, locate the major tonic note and count down three half steps. On the staff, notice that the major and minor tonic notes may be drawn from a line to a line or a space to a space.

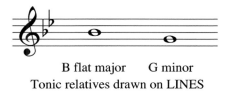

B flat major   G minor
Tonic relatives drawn on LINES

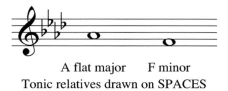

A flat major   F minor
Tonic relatives drawn on SPACES

However, the tonic note may be drawn in any octave as shown below.

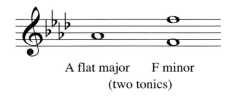

A flat major   F minor
(two tonics)

Following is a chart showing the key signatures for A minor and the seven minor scales with flats. Notice:

- The order of the flats is the same as for flatted major scales: B♭ E♭ A♭ D♭ G♭ C♭ F♭.

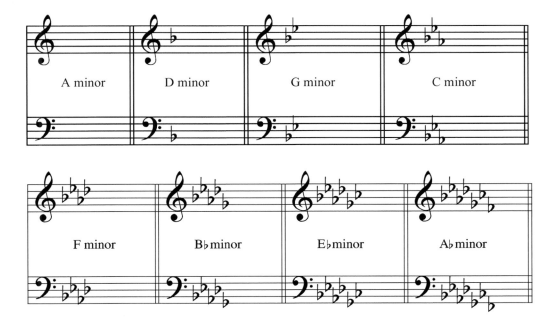

Exercise 3 Class Exercise

Draw the major (M) and minor (m) tonic notes for the following key signatures and label the keys below. (The letter names of the key and the corresponding tonics should be the same.)

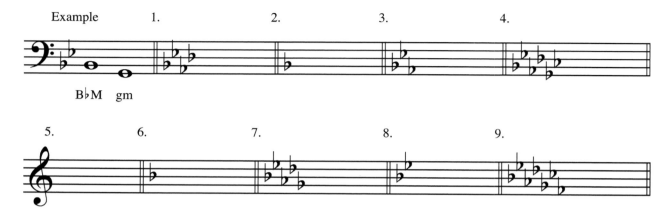

B♭M   gm

Exercise 4

Draw the key signatures for the following minor scales.

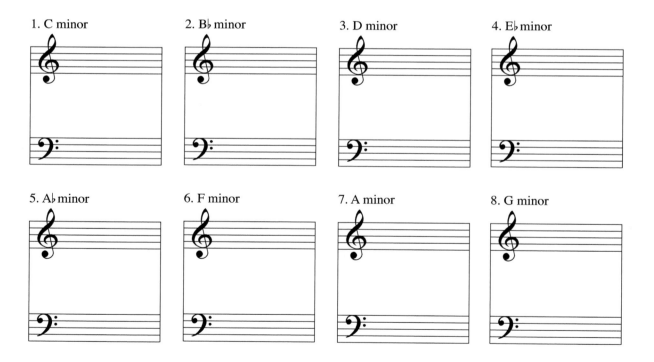

1. C minor
2. B♭ minor
3. D minor
4. E♭ minor

5. A♭ minor
6. F minor
7. A minor
8. G minor

Theory Trainer

Exercise 9b Key signature identification.
Exercise 9c Sharps, flats in a key signature.

Parallel Major and Minor Key Signatures

Major and minor keys that share the same tonic notes are called **parallel keys**. Notice:

- Parallel keys do not have the same key signature. For example:

F major
Key signature: 1 flat

F minor
Key signature: 4 flats

- Not every major and minor key has a parallel key. For example, D sharp minor does not have a parallel D sharp major key, and G flat major does not have a parallel G flat minor key.

Circle of Fifths—Minor Keys

The minor Circle of Fifths shows the 15 minor scales with their increasing number of sharps or flats. As in the major Circle of Fifths, the sharped minor scales begin clockwise around the circle (this time from A minor) and the flatted scales begin counterclockwise. Moving clockwise from A minor, the number of sharps increases from E minor with one sharp to A sharp minor with seven sharps. When moving counterclockwise from A minor, the number of flats increases from D minor with one flat to A flat minor with seven flats. Notice:

- The sharps in a key signature move by fifths: F♯ C♯ G♯ D♯ A♯ E♯ B♯.
- The flats in a key signature move by fifths: B♭ E♭ A♭ D♭ G♭ C♭ F♭.
- The three pairs of enharmonic scales consist of 5, 6, or 7 sharps or flats (A♯/B♭, D♯/E♭, G♯/A♭).
- Every key on the minor Circle of Fifths has a **relative** major; however, not every key will have a **parallel** major. For example, G♯ minor and B major are relative keys. However, G♯ minor does not have a parallel G♯ major key.
- Letter names for minor keys are sometimes written with lower case letters, especially when the word "minor" is omitted. This style is used here as an example (overleaf).

Exercise 5

Identify the minor key for the following key signatures. Use any of the following methods to determine the key:

- Use the minor Circle of Fifths: move clockwise to the right from A minor for scales with sharps, move counterclockwise to the left from A minor for scales with flats.
- Use the key signature: move three half steps down from the major key (tonics will both be notes on lines or notes on spaces).
- Memorize the key signatures for all 15 minor keys.

Circle of Fifths - Major and Minor Keys

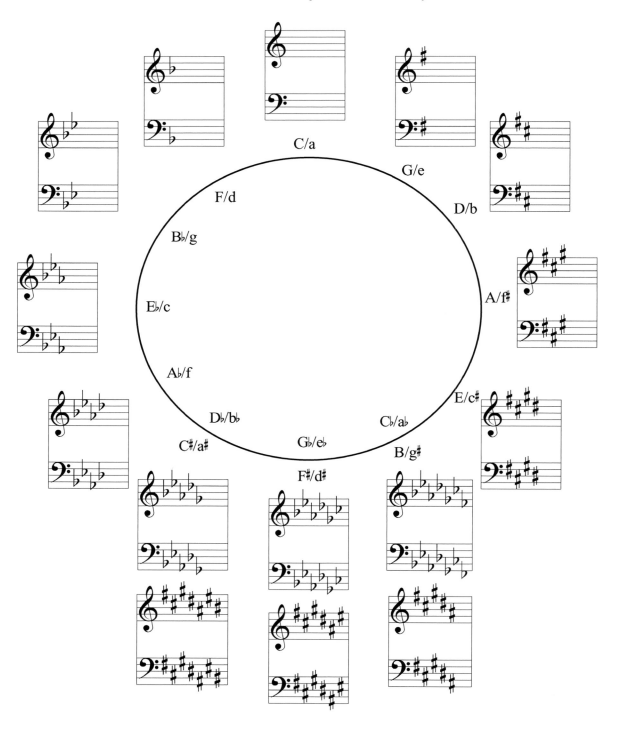

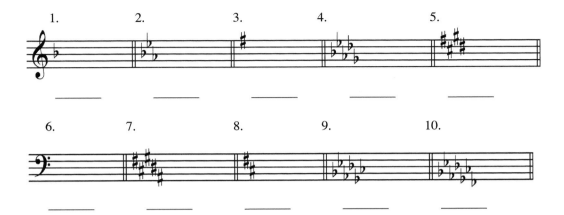

1.   2.   3.   4.   5.

_____ _____ _____ _____ _____

6.   7.   8.   9.   10.

_____ _____ _____ _____ _____

 **Theory Trainer**

Exercise 9b Key signature identification.

Three Forms of Minor Scales

Every minor scale has three forms:

• Natural (or pure)
• Harmonic
• Melodic

Each form has the same tonic note and key signature but its specific arrangement of whole steps and half steps is different. Each form begins with the same five notes ascending from the tonic.

The **natural** (or **pure**) form of the minor scale, like the major scale, will utilize the sharps or flats (never both) of the key signature. The natural minor scale may be drawn using three methods.

Method 1: The arrangement of whole and half steps is **W H W W H W W**. Notice that the half steps are between notes 2 and 3, and 5 and 6. For example:

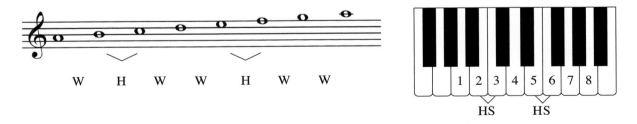

Method 2: Using the minor Circle of Fifths, locate the letter name of the tonic and apply the accidentals of the key signature, if any, according to the scale's placement clockwise or counterclockwise around the circle.

Key signature (no sharps or flats)

Method 3: Memorize the number of sharps or flats, if any, in the minor key signatures. As we saw earlier, A minor is the only minor scale that has no accidentals.

Elements of the NATURAL MINOR:

- Consists of 8 diatonic notes.
- Arrangement of whole and half steps: W H W W H W W.

The **harmonic** form of the minor has the same key signature as the natural minor. However, in the harmonic form, the seventh note is raised a half step, which emphasizes **harmonic** tendencies by creating the leading tone—hence the name of this form.

In the harmonic form, there are three half steps between 2–3, 5–6, and 7–8.

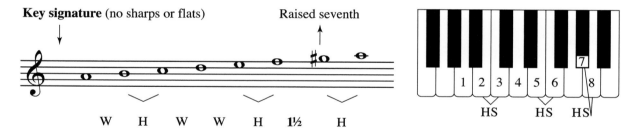

- Note that the *key signature* does not reflect the raised G sharp.
- By raising the seventh note, there will be 1½ steps between notes 6 and 7 from F to G sharp. This is what makes this form of the minor difficult to sing or play; this also gives the scale its distinctive sound.

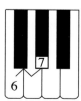

Elements of the HARMONIC MINOR

- Consists of 8 diatonic notes.
- From the natural minor scale (using the key signature) **raise the seventh note a half step** keeping the letter name the same. *Do not* change the key signature.
- Arrangement of whole and half steps: W H W W H 1½ H.

The **melodic** form also has the same key signature as the natural and harmonic forms; unlike the other two forms, the *ascending* melodic scale is different from the *descending* scale. In the harmonic form, the raised seventh note makes it difficult to sing or perform the larger 1½ steps between the sixth and seventh notes. To facilitate singing or playing a **melody**, the melodic form was developed—hence the name of this form. When **ascending**, both the sixth and seventh notes are raised a half step, so half steps are now between 2 and 3, and 7 and 8.

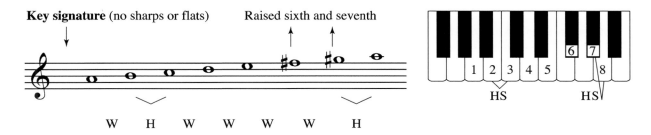

Note that the *key signature* does not reflect the raised sixth and seventh notes.

In the **descending** form of the melodic minor, the sixth and seventh notes that had been raised are now lowered a half step, which returns the scale to the natural form.

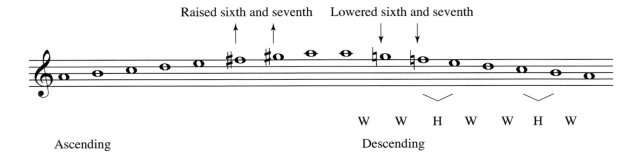

Ascending   Descending

Elements of the MELODIC MINOR

- Consists of eight diatonic notes.
- The ascending and descending forms of the melodic minor have different arrangements of whole and half steps.
- To ascend: from the natural minor scale (using the key signature), *raise* the sixth and seventh notes a half step keeping the letter names the same. Arrangement of whole and half steps: W H W W W W H. To descend: *lower* the sixth and seventh notes a half step, returning the scale to the natural form. *Do not* change the key signature when ascending or descending.

Workbook Exercises 9.1–9.6

Musical Examples in the Three Forms of Minor Scales

Following are musical examples in the three forms of the E minor scale.
    To study pieces in minor scales:

1. Locate the minor scale on the Circle of Fifths. Is the scale a sharped or a flatted scale? What is its relative major?
2. Draw the three forms of the scale using either accidentals or a key signature.
3. Determine the form of the minor scale that is used in the musical example:

- Are accidentals used in the example?
- If so, are they the sixth or seventh notes of the scale?

E natural (pure) minor (relative is G major)

"O Come, O Come, Immanuel," Gregorian chant, eighth century

Only the notes in the E natural minor are used in "O Come, O Come, Immanuel"—the F sharp is shown in the key signature.

E harmonic minor: Raise the seventh note

D sharp

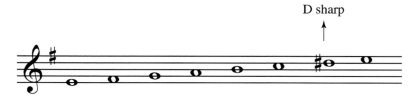

"Charade" (H. Mancini)

In the second line, notice the D sharp in the bass clef in measures 10, 12, 14, signaling the harmonic form of E minor.

E melodic minor—Ascending: Raise the sixth and seventh notes. Descending: Lower the sixth and seventh notes.

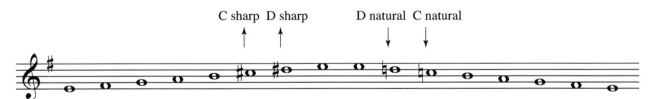

Toccata in E minor, BWV 914 (J.S. Bach)

Notice the D's and C's in the first measure (and elsewhere) and the C sharp and D sharp in the second measure, signaling the melodic form of E minor.

 Theory Trainer

Exercise 9a Input minor scales.

Exercise 6

Using a **key signature just after the clef**, draw the three forms of the following minor scales. Indicate half steps. Notice:

- When drawing the **natural** minor scale using a key signature, accidentals do not need to be placed in the scale. (If you do, you will be adding *courtesy* accidentals.)
- When drawing the **harmonic** minor using a key signature, the raised seventh note *must* have an accidental.
- When drawing the **melodic** minor using a key signature, the sixth and seventh notes ascending and descending *must* have accidentals.

1. E minor (**use a key signature just after the clef** and accidentals as needed)

Natural   *Harmonic*

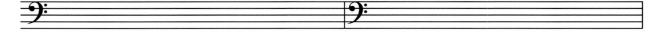

Melodic (*ascend and descend*)

2. D minor (**use a key signature just after the clef** and accidentals as needed)

Natural   *Harmonic*

Melodic (ascend and descend)

3. F minor (**use a key signature just after the clef** and accidentals as needed)

Natural   *Harmonic*

Melodic (ascend and descend)

4.   B minor (**use a key signature just after the clef** and accidentals as needed)

   Natural   *Harmonic*

Melodic (ascend and descend)

 Theory Trainer

   Exercise 9d Identify scale type by ear.

Workbook Exercise 9.7

Comparing Pieces in Major and Minor Keys

It is important to distinguish whether a piece is written in a major or a minor key because every key signature has two tonics, one major and one minor. In addition, the minor scale also has three different forms. Therefore: (1) how do we determine the key; and (2) if the piece is in a minor key, what is the form of minor?

1.   Begin by identifying the relative major and minor keys. Draw the two scales.
2.   Locate the tonic (first) and dominant (fifth) notes of each scale.
3.   Identify the first and last pitches of the piece. Almost always the last pitch in a melody will be the tonic. Frequently, the first pitch will be tonic or the dominant note of the scale.
4.   Accidentals in the piece may indicate the harmonic or melodic forms of the minor. (Look for sharps, flats, naturals, double sharps on the sixth or seventh notes of the scale.) (Double flats are not used in minor scales.)

REVIEW: ACCIDENTALS

  The **sharp** *raises* a note a half step.
   On the keyboard, move to the nearest note to the right.

   The **natural** *cancels* a previous accidental. All naturals are white keys.

> ♭ The **flat** *lowers* a note a half step.
>
> On the keyboard, move to the nearest note to the left.
>
> 𝄪 The **double sharp** *raises* a note a **whole step**.

Exercise 7

Using the four steps outlined above, draw the relative major and minor scales for each piece. Circle the tonic and dominant pitches. Identify the key of the piece; if in minor, determine the form. Finally, notate the counts for each piece, sing and clap. The four scale options are: major, natural minor, harmonic minor, and melodic minor.

Example: "Go Down, Moses," Spiritual

Altered pitch: F sharp

Count: 4   1   2   3 4   1   2   3(4)   1   2   3   4   1(2 3)4   1   2   3   4   1   2   3(4)   1   2   3   4   1   (2   3)

B♭ major   G minor   (F sharp is raised seventh)

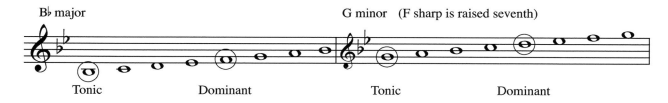

Tonic   Dominant   Tonic   Dominant

- Relatives are B♭ major and G minor.
- First pitch of the piece is D and the last pitch is G; these are the tonic and dominant notes in G minor.
- The altered F sharp is the seventh note in G harmonic minor.
- **Answer: G harmonic minor**

1. Bourrée (J.S. Bach)

    Key: _____ (If in minor, state the form of minor.)

2.   Allegro (from *Magic Flute*) (W.A. Mozart)

   Key: _____ (If in minor, state the form of minor.)

3.   "Ro Kilong Bao" (Aklanon dialect), Filipino ballad
     "Poor old turtle . . . with his house on top . . ."

   Key: _____ (If in minor, state the form of minor.)

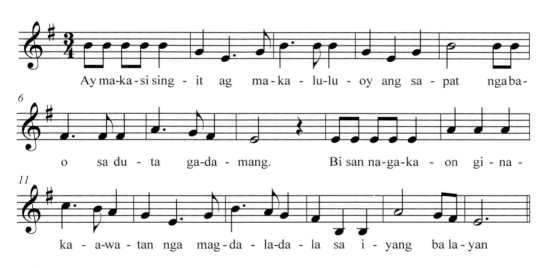

Ay ma-ka-si sing - it ag   ma-ka-lu-lu-oy ang sa - pat   nga ba-

o   sa du - ta   ga-da-mang.   Bi san na-ga-ka - on   gi - na -

ka - a-wa-tan nga mag-da - la-da - la sa i - yang   ba la - yan

4. "My Heart Will Go On" (Love Theme from *Titanic*) (J. Horner, W. Jennings)

Key: _____ (If in minor, state the form of minor.)

We'll stay for ev - er this way. ___ You are safe in my

heart, and my heart will go on and on. ___

5. Toccata, K. 141 (D. Scarlatti)

Key: _____ (If in minor, state the form of minor.)

6. Nocturne, Op. 15, No. 3 (F. Chopin)

Key: _____ (If in minor, state the form of minor.)

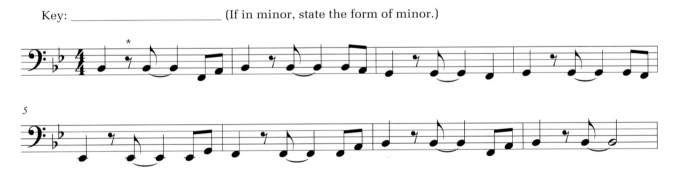

7. "Stand By Me" (J. Leiber, M. Stoller, B. King)

Key: _____ (If in minor, state the form of minor.)

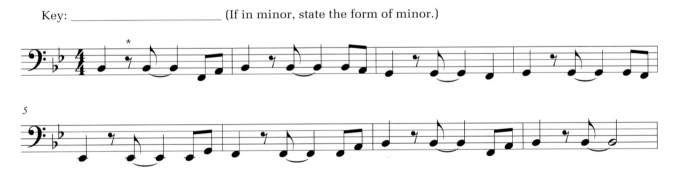

*At every rest, snap your finger.

8. Fugue (*Well Tempered Clavier*, Book II, BWV 877) (J.S. Bach)

Key: _____ (If in minor, state the form of minor.)

Workbook Exercises 9.8 and 9.9

Scale Degree Names in Minor

Each of the seven notes of a minor scale is given a scale degree name. In the harmonic and melodic minor forms, the scale degree names are the same as for the major scale. For the natural minor, the seventh note is a whole step below the tonic and therefore is called the **subtonic**.

Following are the scale degree names for the A natural minor. Notice: only the seventh scale degree is changed from those in a major scale. (Review Module 6.)

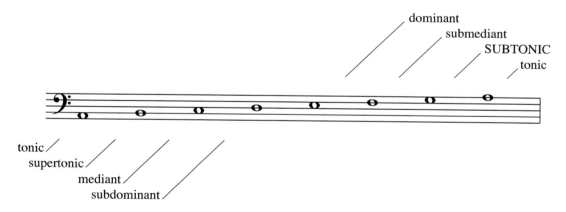

The scale degree names for the harmonic and melodic minors remain unchanged from the major scale.

Theory Trainer

Exercise 9e Find the scale degree in a minor key.

Exercise 8 Class Exercise—Singing Minor Scales

You may use any of the following methods of singing.

- The scale degree number
- "Movable Do" where the tonic is "Do" (only in this system will the syllables change with each form of the minor)
- "Fixed Do" where "Do" is C
- Sing any syllable such as "La."

1. Track 79—Natural minor (pure)

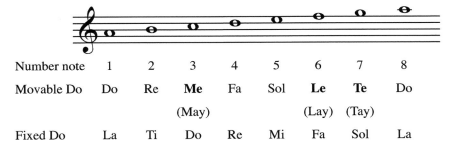

Number note	1	2	3	4	5	6	7	8
Movable Do	Do	Re	**Me**	Fa	Sol	**Le**	**Te**	Do
			(May)			(Lay)	(Tay)	
Fixed Do	La	Ti	Do	Re	Mi	Fa	Sol	La

2. Track 80—Harmonic minor

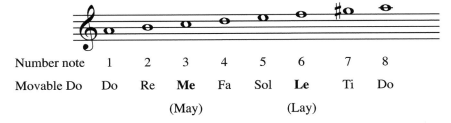

Number note	1	2	3	4	5	6	7	8
Movable Do	Do	Re	**Me**	Fa	Sol	**Le**	Ti	Do
			(May)			(Lay)		

3. Track 81—Melodic minor

Number note	1	2	3	4	5	6	7	8	8	7	6	5	4	3	2	1
Movable Do	Do	Re	**Me**	Fa	Sol	La	Ti	Do	Do	**Te**	**Le**	Sol	Fa	**Me**	Re	Do
			(May)							(Tay)	(Lay)			(May)		

🔊 **TRACKS 79–81**

Listen, then sing: each of the above scales will be played twice at a slow tempo. Listen the first time, then sing the second time, matching each pitch.

Workbook Exercises 9.10–9.12

Name _____

Exercise 9.1

Identify the minor key for the following key signatures.

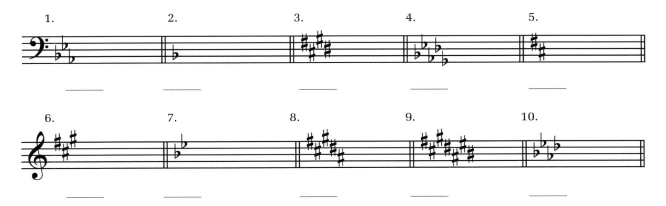

1.   2.   3.   4.   5.

____   ____   ____   ____   ____

6.   7.   8.   9.   10.

____   ____   ____   ____   ____

Exercise 9.2

Draw the following minor key signatures in both clefs using sharps or flats as required.

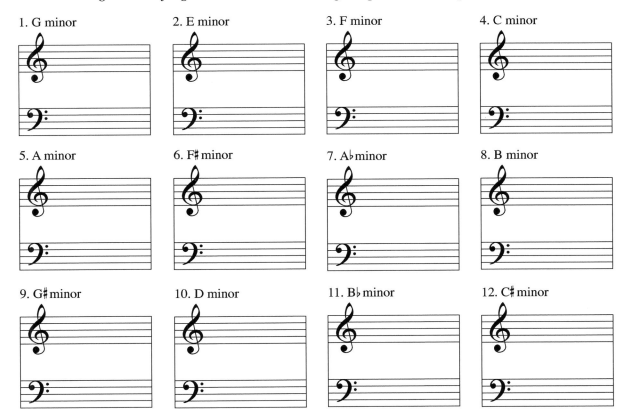

1. G minor   2. E minor   3. F minor   4. C minor

5. A minor   6. F♯ minor   7. A♭ minor   8. B minor

9. G♯ minor   10. D minor   11. B♭ minor   12. C♯ minor

Circle of Fifths - Minor Keys

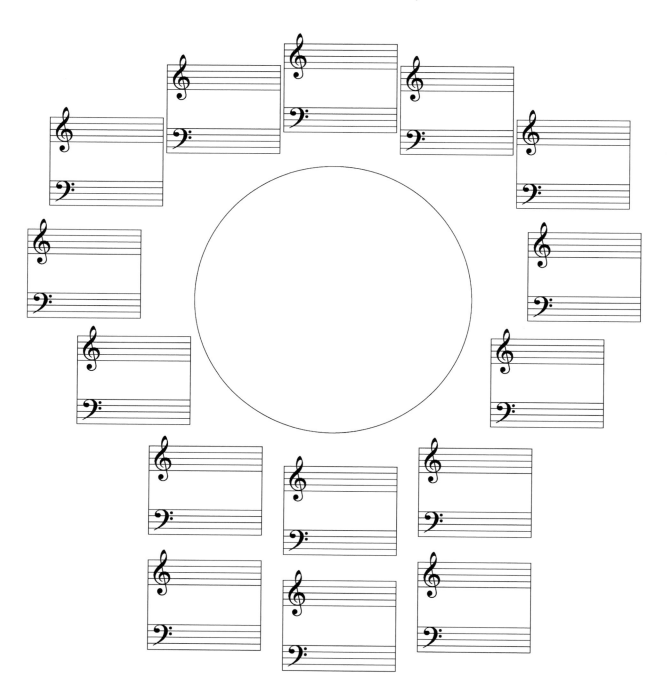

Exercise 9.3

Identify the relative major key for the following minor scales.

1. F minor _____
2. D♯ minor _____
3. G minor _____
4. B♭ minor _____
5. A minor _____

6. F♯ minor _____
7. E♭ minor _____
8. B minor _____
9. G♯ minor _____
10. C minor _____

11. A♭ minor _____
12. E minor _____
13. A♯ minor _____
14. D minor _____
15. C♯ minor _____

Exercise 9.4

Identify the relative minor key for the following major keys.

1. G major _____
2. E♭ major _____
3. F♯ major _____
4. A♭ major _____
5. B♭ major _____

6. E major _____
7. A major _____
8. F major _____
9. C♭ major _____
10. D major _____

11. D♭ major _____
12. C major _____
13. G♭ major _____
14. C♯ major _____
15. B major _____

Exercise 9.5

Complete the minor Circle of Fifths (opposite). Draw the key signature for each key. Remember that there are three pairs of enharmonic keys.

Exercise 9.6

Using accidentals draw the three forms of the following minor scales. Indicate half steps. After the bar line, draw the key signature. Example:

C natural (pure) minor (relative is E flat major)   *C harmonic minor—Raise the seventh note of the scale.*

C melodic minor—Ascending: Raise the sixth and seventh notes. Descending: Lower the sixth and seventh notes.

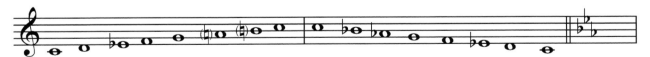

1. D minor (Use accidentals. At the end of each line, draw the key signature.) Notice that sharps and flats may be used together in the harmonic and melodic forms of the scale, but not in the key signature.

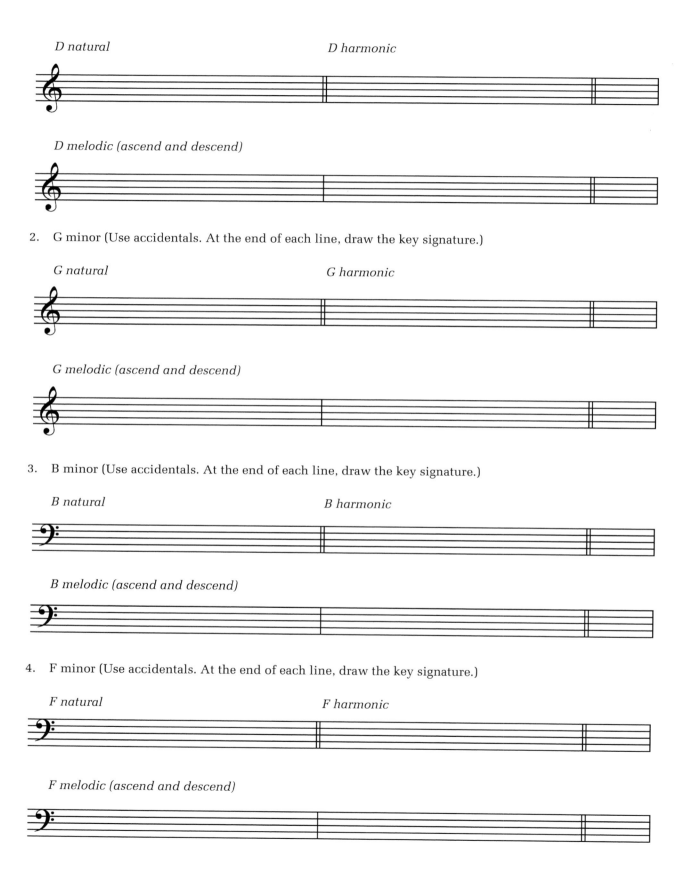

D natural   D harmonic

D melodic (ascend and descend)

2. G minor (Use accidentals. At the end of each line, draw the key signature.)

G natural   G harmonic

G melodic (ascend and descend)

3. B minor (Use accidentals. At the end of each line, draw the key signature.)

B natural   B harmonic

B melodic (ascend and descend)

4. F minor (Use accidentals. At the end of each line, draw the key signature.)

F natural   F harmonic

F melodic (ascend and descend)

NAME: _____

Exercise 9.7

Using a key signature, draw the following scales: major, natural, harmonic, or melodic minors. Note whether to draw the scales ascending or descending.

1. E natural minor, ascending

2. C harmonic minor, ascending

3. F♯ major, descending

4. D harmonic minor, ascending

5. G natural minor, descending

6. F melodic minor, ascending

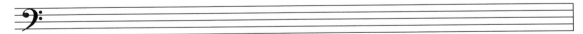

7. B melodic minor, descending

8. E♭ major, ascending

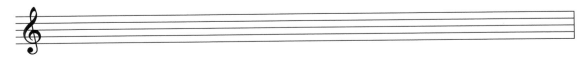

9. G♯ harmonic minor, ascending

10. A♭ major, ascending

11. E♭ melodic minor, ascending

12. C♯ natural minor, descending

13. D♯ harmonic minor, ascending

14. A♭ melodic minor, ascending

NAME: _____

Exercise 9.8

Identify the scale used in the following excerpts; if in minor, determine the form of the minor scale. Each of the following seven scale options will be used once.

1. Major
2. Natural minor
3. Harmonic minor
4. Melodic minor

5. Chromatic
6. Pentatonic—major
7. Pentatonic—minor

Vocabulary note

PENTATONIC SCALES

Pentatonic scales consist of five notes, either utilizing half steps ("hemitonic") or without half steps ("anhemitonic"). Those without half steps are called either **major** pentatonic scales or **minor** pentatonic scales. For example:

- **Major pentatonic scale:** consists of notes 1, 2, 3, 5, 6 of a major scale.

- **Minor pentatonic scale:** consists of notes 1, 3, 4, 5, 7 of a natural minor scale.

---

1. Grand Galop (F. Liszt)

   Key: _____ (If in minor, identify the form.)

2. "Layla, Layla" (M. Zeira, N. Alterman), Israeli folk melody

Key: _____ (If in minor, identify the form.)

3. "Ame, Ame" ("Rain Song"), Japanese folk melody

A - me, a - me, fur - e, fur - e, ka - a-san - ga, Jya - no me de o mu kae, -

u - re shi - na. Pi chi, pi chi, cha pu, cha pu, ran, ran, ran.

The words "Pichi, pichi, chapu, chapu" are onomatopoeic, and meant to sound like rain.

This melody is pentatonic. Notate the five notes used in this piece. Are they derived from a major scale or a minor scale? _____

4.   "Land of the Silver Birch," Canadian folk song

This melody is pentatonic. Notate the five notes used in this piece. Are they derived from a major scale or a minor scale? _____

5.   Etude No. 3, *La Campanella* (F. Liszt)

Key: _____ (If in minor, identify the form.)

6. Piano Sonata No. 2, Op. 35, Third Movement (*Marche funèbre*) (F. Chopin)

Key: _____ (If in minor, identify the form.)

7. Symphony No. 5, Op. 67 (L.v. Beethoven)

Key: _____ (If in minor, identify the form.)

This is a reduction of Beethoven's Symphony No. 5 from an orchestral piece to a few voices in the treble clef. To help separate the voices (also called "parts"), the notes are stemmed upward or downward. For example in the first line, the notes of the first voice representing the first violins are stemmed upward. Later in measure 7, a second voice representing the second violins enters; here the notes are stemmed down.

What is the main motive of this piece? Bracket and label the motive the first time it appears.

8. "María Elena" (L. Barcelata)
   "*. . . as falling rain is to a flower . . . so you are to me.*"

   Key: _____ (If in minor, identify the form.)

Exercise 9.9 | Class Exercise—Listening

Identify the scale: major, natural, harmonic, or melodic. Place a check below. Your instructor will play each scale twice.

	Major	Natural minor	Harmonic minor	Melodic minor
1.	_____	_____	_____	_____
2.	_____	_____	_____	_____
3.	_____	_____	_____	_____
4.	_____	_____	_____	_____
5.	_____	_____	_____	_____
6.	_____	_____	_____	_____

Exercise 9.10

1. Using a key signature, draw the F♯ natural minor scale. Then identify the letter name of the scale degree according to the natural, harmonic, or melodic form of minor.

Natural (pure) minor

1. Subdominant __B__
2. Subtonic _____
3. Mediant _____
4. Supertonic _____

Harmonic minor

5. Leading tone _____
6. Dominant _____
7. Supertonic _____
8. Tonic _____

Melodic minor

9. Mediant _____
10. Submediant _____
11. Subdominant _____
12. Leading tone _____

2. Using a key signature, draw the C natural minor scale. Then identify the letter name of the scale degree according to the natural, harmonic, or melodic form of minor.

Natural (pure) minor

1. Dominant _____
2. Submediant _____
3. Subtonic _____
4. Tonic _____

Harmonic minor

5. Supertonic _____
6. Subdominant _____
7. Leading tone _____
8. Mediant _____

Melodic minor

9. Dominant _____
10. Tonic _____
11. Subdominant _____
12. Submediant _____

Exercise 9.11

Match the word with the definition.

1. Circle of fifths _____ Fifth note of the scale; the second note of importance

2. Dominant _____ Pattern of 8 notes made of whole and half steps, with half steps occurring between 2 and 3, and 5 and 6, and having the same notes (letter names) and key signature as its relative major

3. Harmonic minor scale _____ Sixth note of the scale

4. Melodic minor scale _____ Major and minor keys that share the same key signature, but have different tonic notes

5. Natural (pure) minor scale _____ Fourth note of the scale

6. Parallel keys _____ Ascending: raise the 6th and 7th notes from the minor key signature; descending: lower the 6th and 7th notes, returning to the natural minor

7. Relative keys _____ First (and last) note of the scale; identifies the scale

8. Scale degree names _____ From the minor key signature, raise the 7th note; half steps occur between 2–3, 5–6, and 7–8

9. Subdominant   _____   The 15 minor scales with their increasing number of sharps or flats; scales with sharps move clockwise to the right of A minor, and the scales with flats move counterclockwise to the left of A minor

10. Submediant   _____   Seventh note of the natural minor scale

11. Subtonic   _____   Major and minor keys that share the same tonic, but have different key signatures

12. Tonic   _____   Names given to each note of the scale

Exercise 9.12

Compose melodies using the motives provided below. Continue using rhythms that are similar to those in the motive, and incorporate repetition and variation in your melody. In the final exercise, select the time signature and a minor key, and compose your own motive.

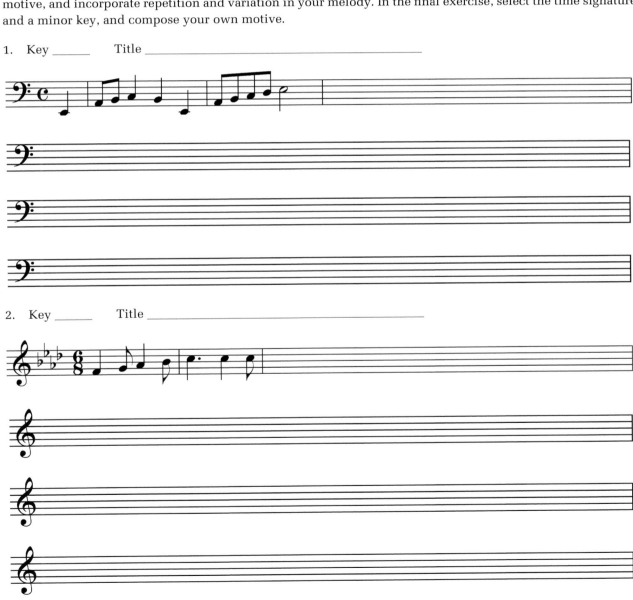

1. Key _____   Title _____

2. Key _____   Title _____

3. Key _____   Title _____

4. Compose a motive in a minor key; use it to complete a melody. Select the clef, key signature, and time signature.

   Key _____   Title _____

MODULE 10

INTERVALS

Identifying Intervals

Intervals are the distance between two pitches and are the building blocks of melody and harmony. While intervals may be expressed as acoustic ratios of frequencies (see Appendix 2), we will study intervals expressed as the distance between pitches on the staff and the keyboard. Remember to also sing and listen to them. We have already discussed three intervals in Modules 1 and 4: the octave, whole step, and half step.

Intervals may be drawn and performed in two ways:

- **Harmonically**, or blocked—notes sounding simultaneously, forming **harmony**.

- **Melodically**, or broken—notes sounding consecutively, forming **melody**.

An interval consists of two parts: an interval **quantity** and an interval **quality**.

- The interval **quantity** (expressed as a number) is determined by counting the inclusive adjacent letter names between two pitches. For example, the interval from C ascending to E is a third.

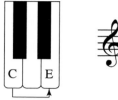

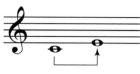

Count:

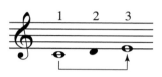

- Interval **quality** specifies the exact size of the interval number, which is determined by the number of half steps between the two pitches. Quality determines the "color" of the interval. There are five qualities: perfect, major, minor, augmented, and diminished. Quality will be discussed in more depth later in this module.

We will begin our discussion with interval **number** or quantity. Following are the ascending intervals from C, counting the first note "C" as "1". This interval "1" is also called the **unison** ("one sound"). The interval of a second (written as "2") is determined by counting from C (as 1) to D (which is 2). The interval from C to E, as shown earlier, is called a "third" and written as "3". All other intervals follow similarly, up to the octave from C to C which is written as "8."

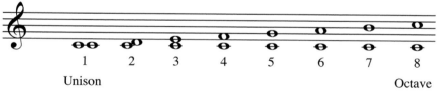

Exercise 1 Class Exercise

Sing the following exercises using solfège or numbers. In the second exercise, relate the distance separating each pair of pitches (the interval) with the sound of the corresponding pitches.

1. Track 82

Do	Re	Mi	Fa	Sol	La	Ti	Do	Do	Ti	La	Sol	Fa	Mi	Re	Do
1	2	3	4	5	6	7	8	8	7	6	5	4	3	2	1

2. Track 83

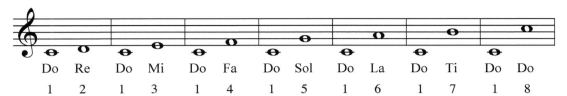

Do Re Do Mi Do Fa Do Sol Do La Do Ti Do Do
1 2 1 3 1 4 1 5 1 6 1 7 1 8

🔊 **TRACKS 82–83**

Listen, then sing; the exercises above will be played at a slow tempo. Listen the first time, then sing the second time, matching each pitch. Repeat.

Exercise 2 Class Exercise "Even" Numbered Intervals: 2, 4, 6, 8

Listen to each interval as it is played both harmonically and melodically.

When written, notice that "even" numbered intervals (2, 4, 6, 8) encompass a pitch written on a space and one written on a line, or a pitch written on a line and another written on a space.

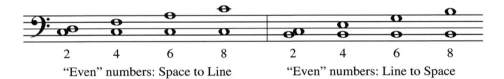

2 4 6 8   2 4 6 8
"Even" numbers: Space to Line   "Even" numbers: Line to Space

Let's relate intervals written on the staff to the keyboard. Count interval numbers beginning with the first pitch (key); count all ascending consecutive **letter names** up the staff (keyboard). (Notice we are counting adjacent letter names of the alphabet, *not* all adjacent white and black keys.)

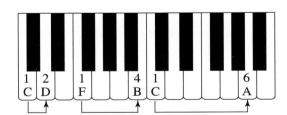

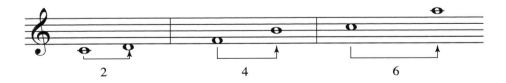

2   4   6

Exercise 3 Class Exercise "Odd" Numbered Intervals: 1, 3, 5, 7

Listen to each interval as it is played both harmonically and melodically. When written, notice that "odd" numbered intervals (1, 3, 5, 7) encompass pitches written on a space and another on a space, or a line and a line.

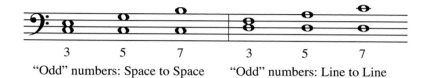

| 3 | 5 | 7 | 3 | 5 | 7 |

"Odd" numbers: Space to Space   "Odd" numbers: Line to Line

Again, count all consecutive letter names beginning with the first pitch (key).

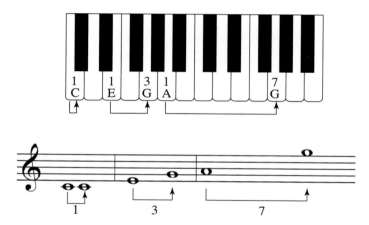

Exercise 4

Label the interval number of the pitches drawn below. Write the letter name on the keyboard below the staff and bracket them as shown in the example.

Note: The interval number is not affected by whether notes ascend or descend; always count from the lowest note to the highest.

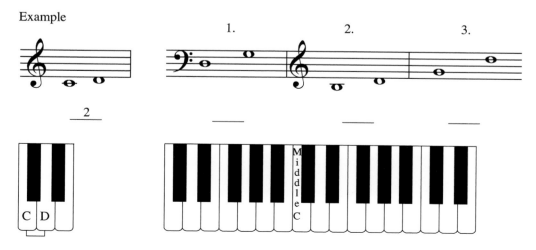

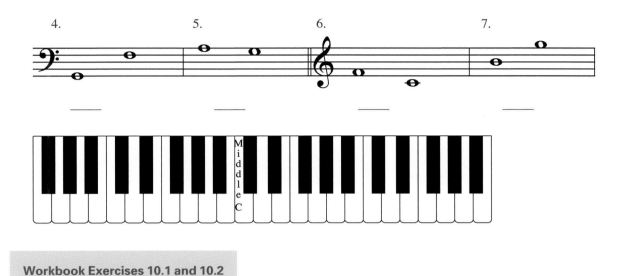

Workbook Exercises 10.1 and 10.2

Consonance and Dissonance

Cultural and historical perspectives help to define the concepts of **consonance** and **dissonance**. What is considered to be consonant (sounds that are pleasing to the ear) and what is considered to be dissonant (sounds displeasing to the ear) are usually learned responses, dependent on the sounds to which an individual has been exposed. There are two intervals, the unison and the octave, that all cultures consider to be a consonance; when men and women sing together they will most often sing an octave apart.

Principles of acoustics may also assist in defining consonance and dissonance. The simpler ratios of sound frequencies of notes are usually labeled "consonant" (for example, octave pitches C to the next C vibrate at a ratio of 2:1). However, more complex ratios are usually labeled "dissonant" (for example, the seventh C to B vibrates at a ratio of 17:9). For further study, see Appendix 2 on Acoustics.

TRACKS 84–90—CLASS DISCUSSION

Listen to the following selections. Discuss what sounds consonant and dissonant to you—and why.

84. *"Ting Song," Chinese erhu (a two-stringed bowed instrument, popular in China)*
85. *Water Music, Suite No. 2 in D (G.F. Handel), suite for winds*
86. *"True Life Blues" (B. Monroe), American blues*
87. *"Pizza's Not for Breakfast" (Skeleton Closet), punk rock*
88. *"Heartsong Aria" (F. Ho, R. Margraff), opera*
89. *"Sabá Medley," Arab folk improvisation*
90. *"Benedicamus Domino," Gregorian Chant, performed by Schola Cantorum of Amsterdam*

As we proceed through this module, we will continue this discussion on consonance and dissonance—as you listen to music, compare your responses with the definitions given in this book.

Defining Quality

In music of the West where the octave is divided into twelve equal semitones, the interval numbers of the unison (1) to the octave (8) may be further defined by five **qualities**:

- Perfect
- Major
- Minor
- Diminished
- Augmented

The quality of an interval may be determined in two ways: (1) by relating the interval to a major scale; or (2) by counting the number of half steps between the two pitches forming the interval. Your instructor may have a preference; use the method that is assigned to determine the interval number and quality.

Intervals of the Major Scale: Perfect and Major

Method 1: Using the major scale to determine perfect and major intervals
    Intervals formed from the tonic pitch up to each note of a major scale are either perfect or major.

- **Perfect intervals** are 1, 4, 5, 8.
- **Major intervals** are 2, 3, 6, 7.
- Use the diagram to help you visualize this. (Note: the overlapping section of the circles will be discussed later in this module.)

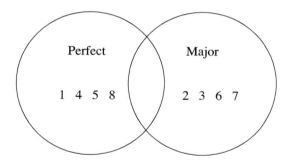

For example, let's look at the A major scale with three sharps in its key signature.

The quality for intervals 1, 4, 5, 8 is **perfect** (abbreviated to "P"). These intervals may also be expressed as a ratio of sound frequencies of 1:1, 4:3, 3:2, and 2:1, respectively. (See Appendix 2 for a further discussion on acoustics and sound frequencies.)

Perfect intervals for the key of A major are shown below, first melodically, then harmonically.

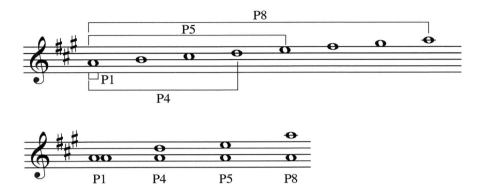

The quality for intervals 2, 3, 6, 7 is **major** (abbreviated to "M").

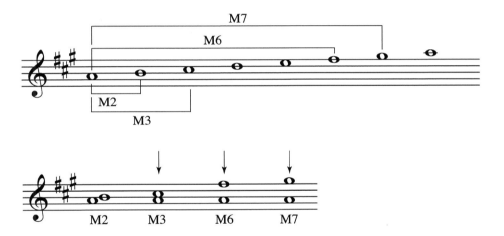

Notice:

- The A major key signature affects the C, F, and G by raising the note half step, resulting in the M3, M6, and M7 as shown by the arrows above.
- If the appropriate major key signature is applied to a scale, the resulting interval qualities are either perfect or major. **Always apply the key signature of the lower pitch of an interval.**

Exercise 5

Using accidentals, draw each note of a major scale above its tonic note, forming all major and perfect intervals. In this exercise, do not use a key signature. Write the interval quantity and quality below the notes. If you have access to a keyboard, play the intervals drawn below. In music of the West, the M2 and M7 are considered to be dissonant. Do you agree?

Example—Key: D major

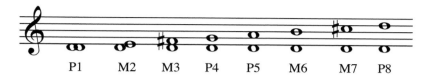

P1   M2   M3   P4   P5   M6   M7   P8

1. Key: B flat major

2. Key: E major

Method 2: Counting half steps to determine perfect and major intervals
Memorize the chart below for perfect and major intervals—count half steps above the lower note.

P1 = 0 half steps (the same note)
M2 = 2 half steps
M3 = 4 half steps
P4 = 5 half steps
P5 = 7 half steps
M6 = 9 half steps (or 3 half steps below the octave)
M7 = 11 half steps (or 1 half step below the octave)
P8 = 12 half steps (octave higher)

Perfect intervals

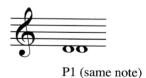

P1 (same note)

P4

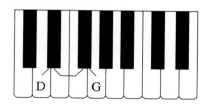

Count 5 half steps

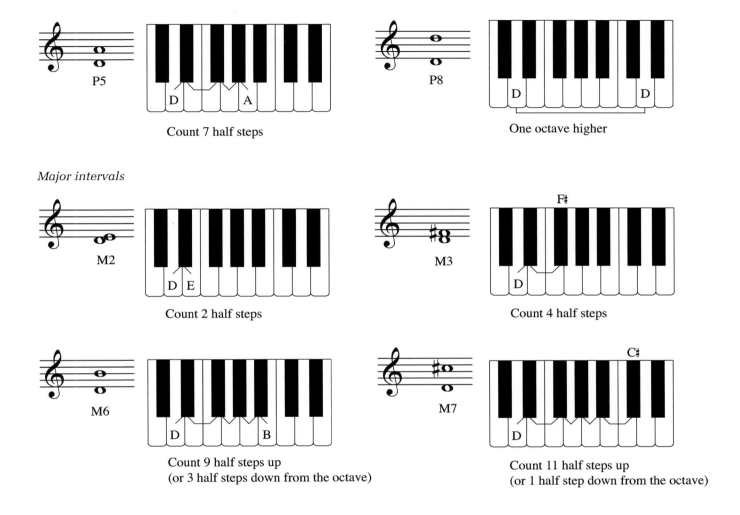

Interval Shortcuts

- When writing **perfect fourths** (P4) on the staff, both notes will be naturals, flats, or sharps. (*Exception: F to Bb and F# to B.*)

- When writing **perfect fifths** (P5) on the staff, both notes will be naturals, flats or sharps. (*Exception: B to F# and Bb to F.*)

Theory Trainer

Exercise 10b Identify intervals when written on staff: Perfect, major.

Exercise 6

Identify the following interval and quality (for example: M3).

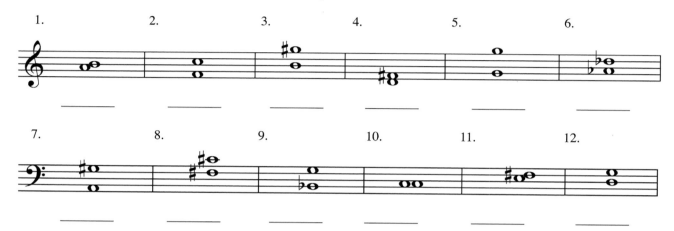

Exercise 7

Using accidentals, draw the following intervals above the given pitch. Use either method discussed above to determine the interval. If working for speed, the first method may be a quicker method.

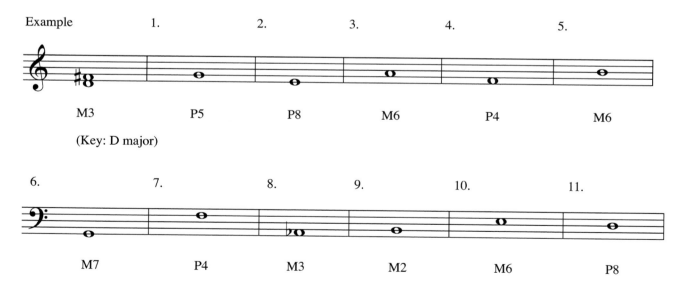

 Theory Trainer

Exercise 10c Draw intervals when given the bottom note: Perfect, major.

Exercise 8 Class Exercise

Circle the **perfect** intervals in the song below. The first one is circled for you. Play or sing the melody, listening to the sound of the perfect intervals.

"Take Me Out to the Ball Game" (A. von Tilzer)

Take me out to the ball game, take me out with the crowd. Buy me some pea-nuts and

Crack-er Jacks, I don't care if I nev-er get back. Let me root, root, root for the home team. If

they don't win it's a shame. For it's one, two, three strikes you're out at the old ball game.

Exercise 9 Class Exercise—Singing Perfect and Major Intervals

Sing the exercise below using any of the following methods: solfège, numbers, or qualities. Identify songs that begin with the following intervals. For example, "Happy Birthday" begins with a M2.

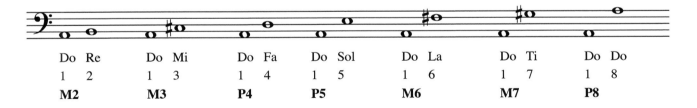

Do Re	Do Mi	Do Fa	Do Sol	Do La	Do Ti	Do Do
1 2	1 3	1 4	1 5	1 6	1 7	1 8
M2	**M3**	**P4**	**P5**	**M6**	**M7**	**P8**

List songs that begin with the following intervals:

M2   "Happy Birthday," "Chopsticks" (M2 played harmonically)

M3

_____

P4

_____

P5

_____

M6

_____

M7

_____

P8

_____

 Theory Trainer

Exercise 10a Identify intervals by ear: Perfect, major.

Workbook Exercises 10.3–10.5

Changing Major Intervals: Minor

To change a major (M) interval to minor (m), lower the upper note by a half step without changing the letter name of the notes. For example:

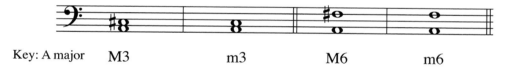

Key: A major   M3   m3   M6   m6

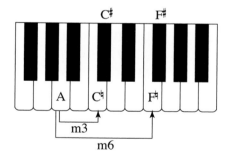

- In the first example, the M3 is decreased in size by moving the C sharp down a half step to C natural.
- In the second example, the M6 is decreased in size by moving the F sharp down a half step to F natural.

Method 1: Determining a minor interval using a key signature: 2, 3, 6, 7

- Determine the interval number: 2, 3, 6, or 7.
- Use the key signature of the lower pitch to determine the **major** interval.
- The **minor** interval is a half step smaller than the major interval. *Do not use the key signature of the minor scale to determine the minor interval.* (To do so would result in an incorrect interval of the minor second.)

For example, let's determine the interval and quality of the following two pitches:

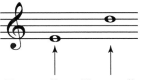

Note on line   Note on line

- Determine the interval number: is the interval an "even" numbered interval (line to space) or "odd" numbered interval (line to line *or* space to space)?

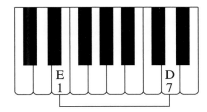

- Determine the major key signature of the lower note: the lower note E has four sharps in its key signature: F♯ C♯ G♯ D♯.

Key: E major Major 7   **Correct answer:** minor 7

- The D sharp belongs to the E major scale, so E to D sharp is a M7. However, our second pitch is a D natural. Because this is a half step lower, the interval is smaller. The answer is: m7.

Method 2: Determining a minor interval by counting half steps: 2, 3, 6, 7

- Determine the interval number: 2, 3, 6, 7.
- Memorize the number of half steps in the major interval. The minor interval is one half step smaller than the major interval.

- P1 = 0 half steps
- m2 = 1 half step
- M2 = 2 half steps
- m3 = 3 half steps
- M3 = 4 half steps
- P4 = 5 half steps

- P5 = 7 half steps
- m6 = 8 half steps (or 4 half steps below the octave)
- M6 = 9 half steps (or 3 half steps below the octave)
- m7 = 10 half steps (or 2 half steps below the octave)
- M7 = 11 half steps (or 1 half step below the octave)
- P8 = 12 half steps (one octave higher)

   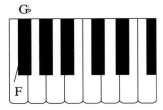

Key: F major M2 = 2 half steps   m2 = 1 half step

Key: F major   M3 = 4 half steps   m3 = 3 half steps

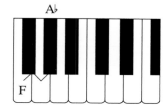

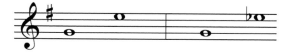

Key: G major   M6 = 9 half steps   m6 = 8 half steps
                                         (or 4 half steps below the octave)

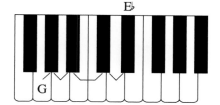

Key: G major   M7 = 11 half steps   m7 = 10 half steps
                                         (or 2 half steps below the octave)

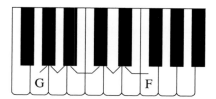

 Theory Trainer

> **Exercise 10b** Identify intervals when written on staff: Perfect, major, minor.

Exercise 10

Label the interval number (2, 3, 6, 7) and quality (M or m) of the following intervals. Use either of the two methods outlined above. You may use a combination of the two methods—count half steps for smaller intervals and use the key signature for larger intervals.

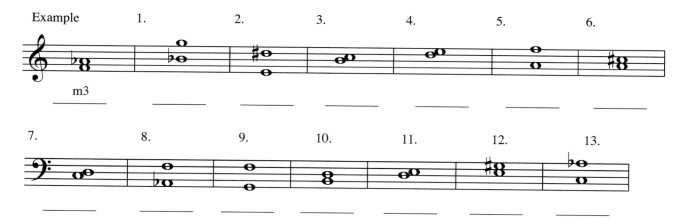

Theory Trainer

Exercise 10c Draw intervals when given the bottom note: perfect, major, minor.

Exercise 11

Draw intervals above the given pitch. Add accidentals as needed.

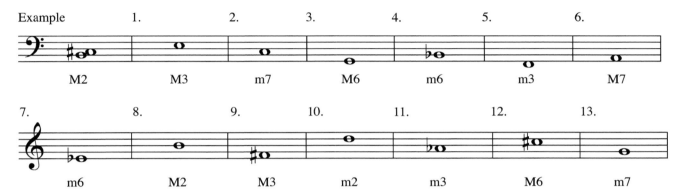

Example   1.   2.   3.   4.   5.   6.

M2   M3   m7   M6   m6   m3   M7

7.   8.   9.   10.   11.   12.   13.

m6   M2   M3   m2   m3   M6   m7

 Theory Trainer

Exercise 10a Identify intervals by ear: Perfect, major, minor.

Exercise 12

Identify the interval (1 to 8) and quality (P, M, m) of the underscored pitches in the following melody.

"La Cumparsita" (Tango) (G.H.M. Rodriguez)

Vocabulary note

TANGO

The **tango** originated in Argentina and Uruguay in the late nineteenth century, first as a style of music and later as a distinctive dance. Spanish, African, and Cuban musical styles and rhythms mixed together. Eventually, the dance was characterized by a sudden stop followed by various gestures, and also by gyrations of the hips.

Class Exercise. Accompany "La Cumparsita" with the following pattern.

Exercise 13 Class Exercise—Singing

Sing, listening to the quality of the intervals.

1. Key: F major

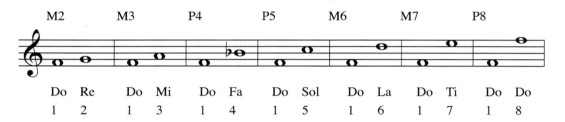

M2   M3   P4   P5   M6   M7   P8

Do Re Do Mi Do Fa Do Sol Do La Do Ti Do Do
1 2   1 3   1 4   1 5   1 6   1 7   1 8

2. Key: F major

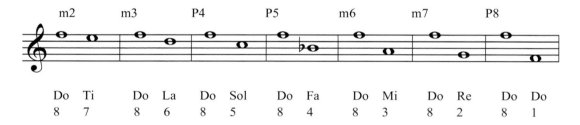

m2   m3   P4   P5   m6   m7   P8

Do Ti Do La Do Sol Do Fa Do Mi Do Re Do Do
8 7   8 6   8 5   8 4   8 3   8 2   8 1

3. Key: G major

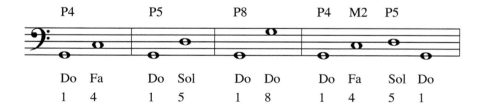

P4   P5   P8   P4 M2 P5

Do Fa Do Sol Do Do Do Fa Sol Do
1 4   1 5   1 8   1 4   5 1

Workbook Exercises 10.6 and 10.7

Changing Major and Minor Intervals: Augmented, Diminished

A major interval (2, 3, 6, 7) may be increased in size to form an **augmented** interval (written "Aug" or "A"). A minor interval (2, 3, 6, 7) may be decreased in size to form a **diminished** interval (written "dim" or "d"). For example:

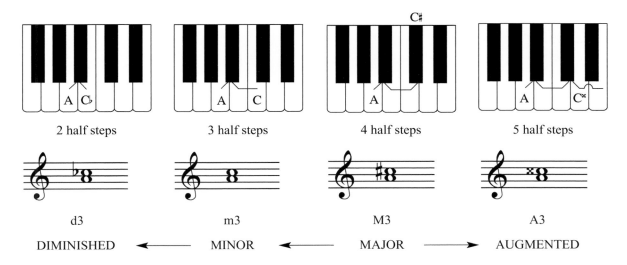

2 half steps	3 half steps	4 half steps	5 half steps
d3	m3	M3	A3

DIMINISHED ← MINOR ← MAJOR → AUGMENTED

Exercise 14

Identify the interval (2, 3, 6, 7) and quality (M, m, Aug, dim) of the following pitches.

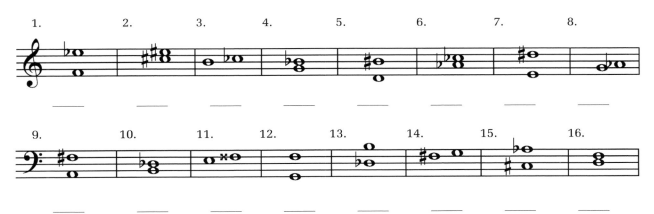

Exercise 15

Draw intervals harmonically above the given note. Reminder:

- Begin by drawing the pitch above the given note by counting lines and spaces without regard to accidentals.
- Apply the key signature of the given note and, if necessary, alter the second pitch to make the interval bigger or smaller.
- *Or* count half steps to determine the second pitch.

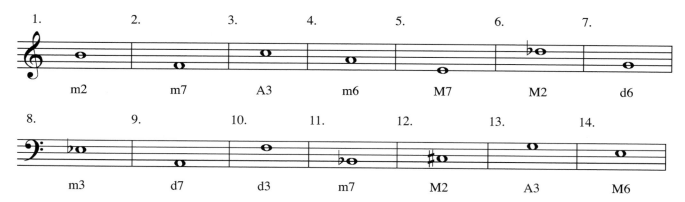

Exercise 16

Label the melodic intervals in the music below. Notice:

- The key signature may alter pitches; be sure to find all altered pitches through the entire piece.
- Continue to use the major key signature of the lower note to determine the major interval—and raise or lower the upper note for the augmented or diminished qualities. *Or* count the half steps between the pitches.

1. "Tiny Bubbles" (L. Pober)

2. Menuet (J.S. Bach)

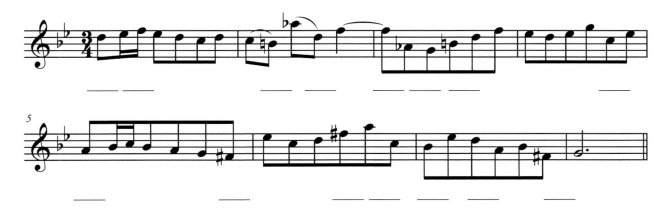

Changing Perfect Intervals: Augmented, Diminished

A **perfect** interval may be either increased in size by a half step to form an **augmented** interval (written "Aug" or "A"), or decreased by a half step to form a **diminished** interval (written "dim" or "d"). For example:

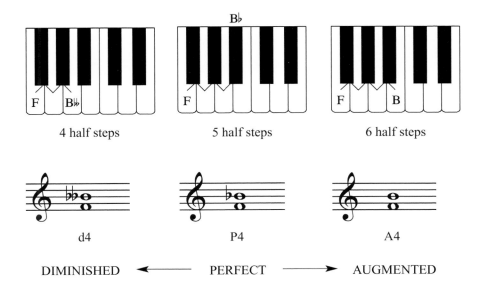

Exercise 17 | Class Exercise

Play the intervals below, listening for the changes in **quality**. All augmented and diminished intervals are considered to be dissonances. However they may not all *sound* dissonant; listen particularly to the augmented fifth and the diminished fourth. Discuss why they sound consonant.

- All perfect intervals may be **enlarged** to form an augmented interval.

P1   Aug1   P4   Aug4   P5   Aug5   P8   Aug8

- All perfect intervals except the unison may be **decreased** in size to form a diminished interval.

P4   dim 4   P5   dim 5   P8   dim 8

- Intervals 1, 4, 5, 8 may not be major or minor. All intervals may be augmented or diminished (exception: no diminished unison).

Use this diagram to reinforce memory of interval qualities.

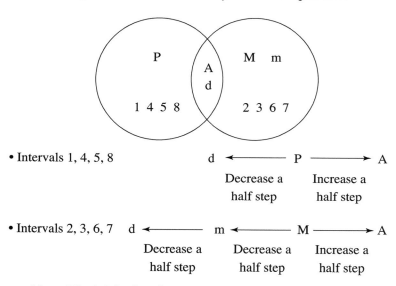

- Intervals 1, 4, 5, 8   d ⟵ ——— P ——— ⟶ A
                                      Decrease a   Increase a
                                      half step   half step

- Intervals 2, 3, 6, 7   d ⟵ ——— m ⟵ ——— M ——— ⟶ A
                    Decrease a   Decrease a   Increase a
                    half step   half step   half step

- Note: Diminished and augmented intervals may be respelled enharmonically: the interval number and quality will change. For example, A to C𝄪 is an Aug 3. Respelled as A to D, the interval is a P4. If you count half steps to determine the interval quality, it is especially important to first determine the interval number.

Key: AM   Aug 3   P4
     OR: 6 HS 6 HS

For discussion of the enharmonic "tritone," the Aug 4 and dim 5, see page 313.

 **Theory Trainer**

Exercise 10b Identify intervals when written on staff: All qualities.

Exercise 18 Class Exercise

Identify the following intervals.

* Determine the interval number.
* Determine the major key signature of the **lower** note. When notes descend, the second note will be the lower note.
* Ask: does the upper note belong to the scale, or has it been altered?
* *Or* you may count half steps to determine the interval quality. (*Note*: This requires memorization of the number of half steps in every interval and quality. The prior method tends to be faster and more accurate.)

Example:

Interval number: 5

Key: G major   P5 ——→ Answer: Aug 5
OR: 7 HS   (The D is raised a half step to D sharp)

Harmonic intervals

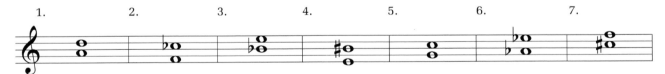

Melodic intervals

Exercise 19

Draw intervals harmonically above the given note.

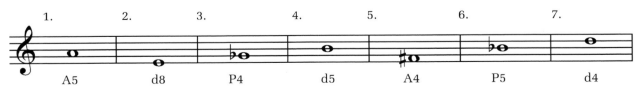

A5   d8   P4   d5   A4   P5   d4

Exercise 20 Class Exercise

Identify the melodic intervals and qualities of the underscored pitches in the following selections. Listen to your instructor play these excerpts, paying particular attention to the quality of the intervals.

1. Prelude in D minor (J.S. Bach)

P5   M3

2. "Ma Omrot Enayich" ("What Are Your Eyes Saying?"), Israeli Love Song (M. Zeira)

The above melody utilizes two different forms of a minor key. The two forms are given below. Write the name of each form; sing the scales and the piece. (Review pages 263–266.)

Form of minor: _____

Form of minor: _____

Theory Trainer

Exercise 10c Draw intervals when given the bottom note: All qualities.

The Tritone

Tritone (or "three tones") is the term used to describe both the augmented fourth (A4) and the diminished fifth (d5). The tritone, because of its dissonance, will be discussed in Module 15 along with the dominant seventh chord. The tritone consists of three whole steps, hence the term "tritone." For example:

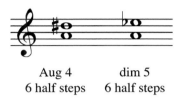

Aug 4   dim 5
6 half steps   6 half steps

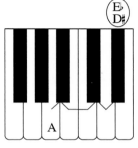

6 half steps = 3 whole steps

Cultural note: The tritone

The **tritone** is considered to be one of the most dissonant intervals. Before 1600 it was originally termed the "devil in music" (*Diabolus in musica*) and was forbidden to be used melodically.

Sing the opening notes to "Maria" from *West Side Story*, or the beginning of "The Simpsons." Both songs begin with the tritone. Notice also how the tritone resolves up in both songs.

 Theory Trainer

Exercise 10a Identify intervals by ear: All qualities.

Workbook Exercises 10.8–10.11

Simple and Compound Intervals

We have been studying **simple** intervals, or those that are an octave or smaller. **Compound** intervals are larger than an octave. For example:

9   10   11   12

313

To identify the quality of a compound interval, bring the upper note down an octave while retaining the lower note. Doing so does not change the quality of the interval.

Notice:

- The compound interval and its corresponding simple interval share the same quality.
- Although we are moving the upper note down an octave (eight notes) we will subtract seven from the compound interval to get the comparable simple interval.
- You may also move the lower note *up* an octave while retaining the upper note.

Exercise 21

Draw the simple interval by moving the upper note of the compound interval down an octave (or moving the lower note up an octave). Identify the compound interval and its comparable simple interval.

Example: In the first answer, the upper G is moved down an octave; in the second answer, the lower E is moved up an octave. Notice that the resulting notes in both answers are the same (E to G); they are only written in different octaves. Example:

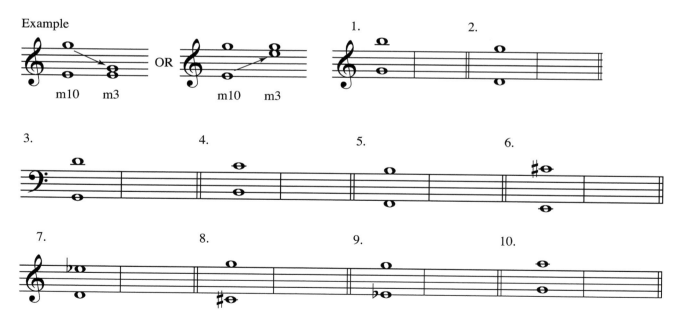

Workbook Exercises 10.12–10.15

Descending Intervals (Interval Inversion)

We have been drawing simple intervals **above** notes. To draw a simple interval **below** a given note, begin by inverting the interval to be drawn (one of the notes will move up or down an octave; the other note remains unchanged).

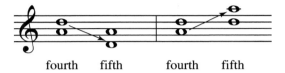

fourth   fifth   fourth   fifth

Lower the D an octave OR Raise the A an octave

Notice:

- The inverted interval consists of the same pitches in a different octave.
- When intervals invert, the two interval numbers will total nine.

Note: use either of the following diagrams to visualize this concept.

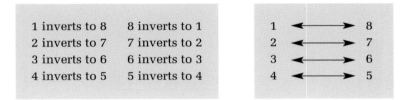

- Qualities of inverted intervals will change in this manner:

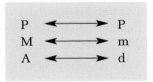

For example:

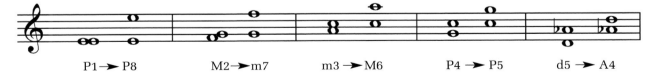

P1 → P8   M2 → m7   m3 → M6   P4 → P5   d5 → A4

Exercise 22 | Class Exercise

Draw the interval **below** the given pitch.

Method 1
Draw the interval below the given pitch by inverting the interval.

Example: Draw a M3
below the given pitch.

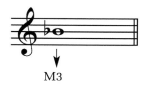

M3

1. Begin by drawing the
   inversion of the M3.
   Use B♭M key signature.

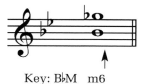

Key: B♭M   m6

2. Invert the interval. Circled
   notes are the answer.

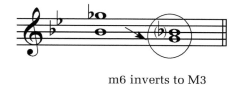

m6 inverts to M3

Method 2
Draw the interval below the given pitch by counting half steps. Review pages 298–299 for the number of half steps in major and perfect intervals, and adjust for minor, augmented, and diminished qualities.

Example: Draw a M3
below the given pitch
(The letter name must be G.)

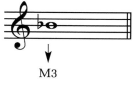

M3

1. M3 = 4 half steps

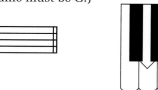

2. Answer: G♭.

Method 3
Draw the interval below the given pitch; do not add accidentals at this time. Determine the quality (P, M, m, A, d) of the interval using the key signature of the lower note. Adjust the lower note if needed. Note: Do not alter the given pitch.

Example: Draw a M3
below the given pitch

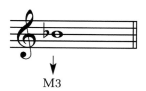

M3

1. Begin by drawing a
   third below. Determine
   the interval (m3).

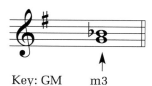

Key: GM   m3

2. Enlarge the m3 (G–B♭)
   by lowering the G one half
   step. Answer: G♭

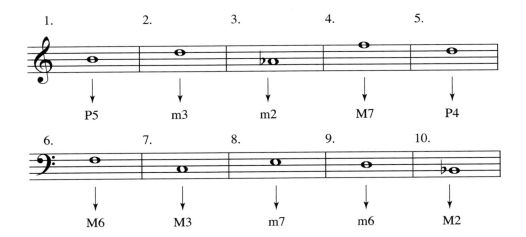

Theory Trainer

Exercise 10d Draw intervals when given to top note.

Workbook Exercise 10.16

Name _____

Exercise 10.1

Identify the interval number for the following pitches.

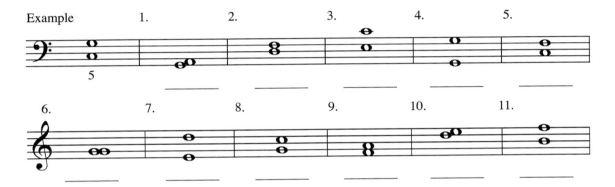

Exercise 10.2

Draw harmonic intervals above the given note.

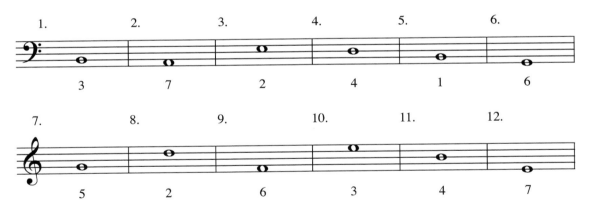

Exercise 10.3

Identify the following interval and quality (for example: M3).

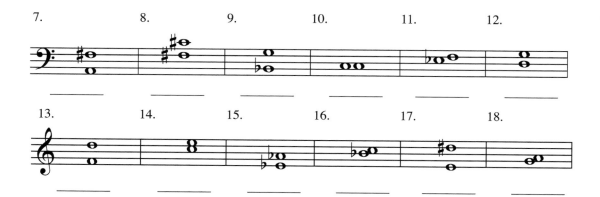

Exercise 10.4

Circle the perfect intervals in the song below.

"Qing Hai Ming Ge," Chinese folk song

Exercise 10.5 Class Exercise—Listening

1. Circle the interval that you hear. Each interval will be played melodically and harmonically twice.

   1. M2   M3   2. P4   M6   3. M3   P5
   4. M6   M7   5. P1   P8   6. M2   M3
   7. P4   P5   8. M2   P4   9. P5   P8

2. Circle the interval that you hear.

   1. M2   M3   M6   2. M3   P5   P8   3. P4   M6   M7
   4. M2   P4   P5   5. M3   M6   M7   6. P4   P5   P8

3. Identify the interval and quality that you hear.

   1. ____   2. ____   3. ____
   4. ____   5. ____   6. ____

Exercise 10.6

Identify the interval (1 through 8) and quality (P, M, m) of the pitches in the following melodies (for example: m2).

1. "Over the Rainbow" (H. Arlen)

P8   m2   M3   ___   ___   ___

2. Trio, K. 1(1e) (W.A. Mozart)

Exercise 10.7

Draw intervals **above** the given pitch. Add accidentals as needed.

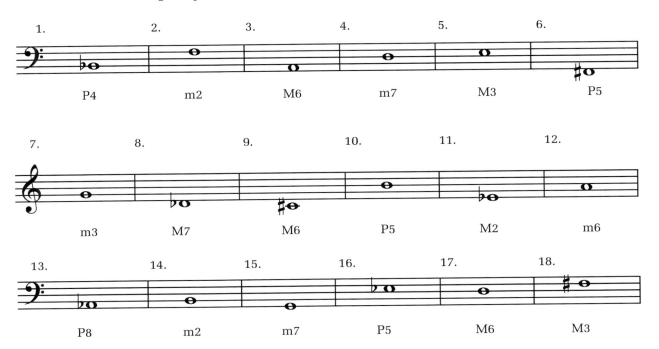

1.	2.	3.	4.	5.	6.
P4	m2	M6	m7	M3	P5

7.	8.	9.	10.	11.	12.
m3	M7	M6	P5	M2	m6

13.	14.	15.	16.	17.	18.
P8	m2	m7	P5	M6	M3

321

Exercise 10.8 | Class Exercise—Listening (Major, minor, Perfect)

1. Circle the interval that you hear. Each interval will be played twice, melodically and harmonically.

1. M3 m3	2. M2 m2	3. M7 m7
4. m2 m3	5. P4 P5	6. m6 m7
7. P5 P8	8. M2 M3	9. m2 m7

2. Circle the interval that you hear. Each interval will be played twice, melodically and harmonically.

1. P5 P8 M6	2. m2 m3 M3	3. M6 m7 M7
4. P4 P5 P8	5. M3 m6 M6	6. M2 M3 P4
7. m6 m7 M7	8. P5 M6 P8	9. M2 m3 M6

3. Identify the interval and quality that you hear (Major, minor, Perfect)

1. _____   2. _____   3. _____   4. _____
5. _____   6. _____   7. _____   8. _____

Exercise 10.9

Identify the interval (1, 4, 5, 8) and quality (P, A, d) of the following notes.

Exercise 10.10

Identify the intervals (2, 3, 6, 7) and quality (M, m, Aug, dm) of the following pitches.

Exercise 10.11

Draw the interval and quality **above** the given pitch—all intervals and qualities.

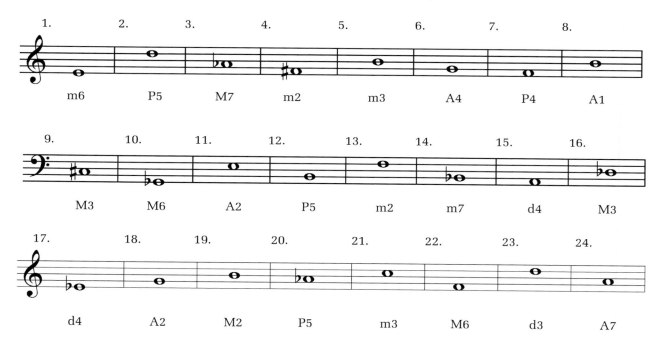

1. m6 2. P5 3. M7 4. m2 5. m3 6. A4 7. P4 8. A1

9. M3 10. M6 11. A2 12. P5 13. m2 14. m7 15. d4 16. M3

17. d4 18. A2 19. M2 20. P5 21. m3 22. M6 23. d3 24. A7

Exercise 10.12

Match the word with the definition.

1. Compound interval   _____   Intervals 1, 4, 5, 8

2. Consonance   _____   Two notes that sound simultaneously

3. Dissonance   _____   Term to describe both A4 and D5; three whole steps ("three tones")

4. Harmonic interval   _____   Number of letter names between two pitches including the first and the last

5. Interval   _____   Interval of two identical pitches ("one sound")

6. Interval inversion   _____   Interval larger than an octave

7. Interval quality   _____   Two notes that sound consecutively

8. Interval quantity   _____   Specifies exact size of an interval number: Perfect, major, minor, augmented, or diminished

9. Melodic interval   _____   Distance between two pitches identified by "quantity" and "quality"

10. Perfect intervals   _____   Sounds considered to be unstable, needing to be resolved; in Western music: 2nds, 7ths, augmented, and diminished intervals

11. Simple intervals   _____   Interval an octave or smaller

12. Tritone   _____   Interval "turned upside down"

13. Unison   _____   Sounds considered to be stable; in Western music: 3rds, 6ths, and perfect intervals

Exercise 10.13

Identify the compound interval and quality for the following pitches.

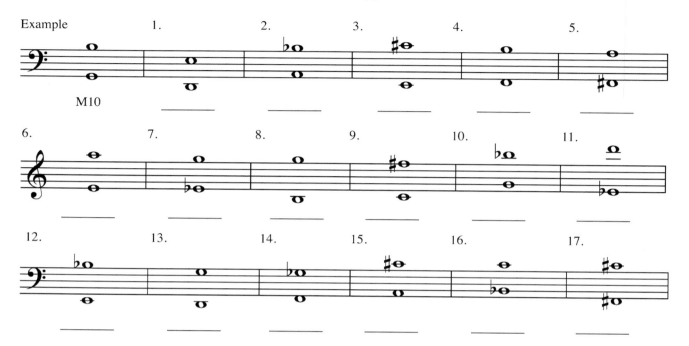

Exercise 10.14

Identify the harmonic intervals between two notes in each clef in the example below.
"Du Friedensfürst, Herr Jesu Christ," Chorales, No. 42 (J.S. Bach)

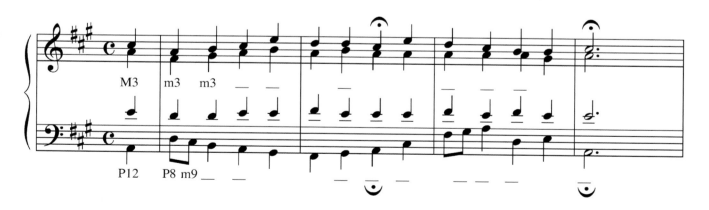

Exercise 10.15

Identify the harmonic intervals between the two notes of the treble and bass clefs.
"Jyugoya Otsukisan" ("Full Moon Night"), Japanese folk melody

P8 All ___ ___ ___ ___ ___ ___ ___

Exercise 10.16

Draw the interval **below** the given pitch.

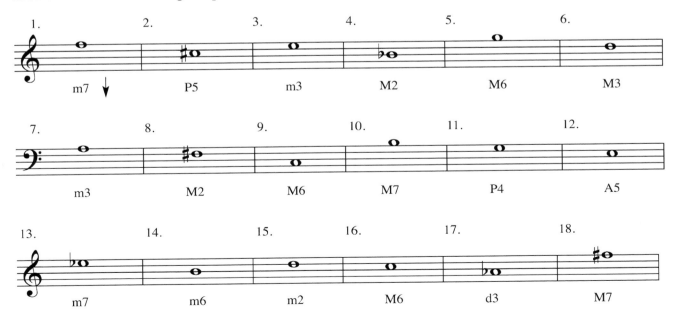

MODULE 11

TRIADS

Defining and Drawing Triads

In the first 10 modules we discussed two basic musical elements: **melody** (pitch and intervals) and **rhythm** (simple and compound meter). In this module we will discuss a third musical component, **harmony**, which is the defining element in Western music. Let's listen to "Love Me Tender" while reading the music given on the next page.

Vocabulary note

HARMONY

From the Greek word "*harmonia*" or "agreement." Harmony is the relationship between consecutive groupings of simultaneous (vertical) sounding pitches. In Western music beginning around 1600, the vertical sounding of notes a third apart (called "tertian" harmony) became the foundation of chords.

CHORD

Three or more notes that sound simultaneously. (When only two notes sound, they form an "interval.")

- Blocked chord: Three or more different pitches sounding simultaneously (harmonically); notes may be drawn in one or more clefs.
- Broken chord: Notes of a chord played successively (melodically).
- Implied chord: An incomplete chord where the third or the fifth of the chord is missing; the chord may be blocked or broken.

TRIAD

In its simplest form, a triad has three notes, each a third apart.

🔊 **TRACK 91—CLASS EXERCISE**

Listen to "Love Me Tender."
Discuss the different way chords are written and performed in this song: blocked, broken and implied.

"Love Me Tender" (E. Presley and V. Matson)

"Blocked" chords

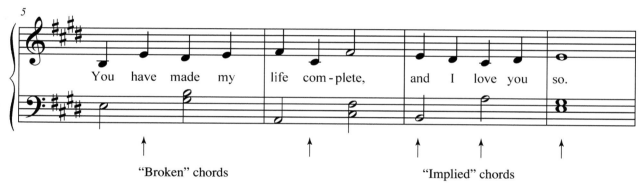

"Broken" chords   "Implied" chords

Notice that the bass clef notes below the melody provide the **harmony**, which may be "blocked" chords as in the first three measures, "broken" chords as in mm. 5 and 6, or "implied" chords as in mm. 7 and 8.

🔊 **TRACKS 92–94**

Listen to three musical examples which represent the following: a melody accompanied by a variation of the same melody, a melody accompanied by a harmony, or a melody alone.

92. *Karnatak "Budham aśrayami," Southeast Asian music*
93. *"Black Girl (in the Pines)" (Lead Belly), American blues music*
94. *Vai Call to Prayer, Liberian music*

Exercise 1 Class Exercise

Listen to your instructor play each of the chords written below. Discuss whether or not the chords sound consonant or dissonant.

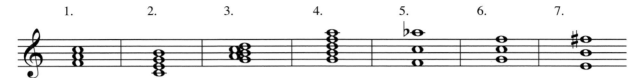

In this module, the chord we will be discussing is the **triad**. In the Module 1 exercises, we practiced skipping every other letter of the alphabet. A triad is formed when we combine three pitches, each a third apart ("skips").

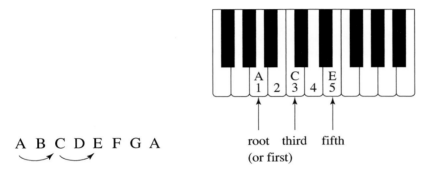

These three notes (A C E) form the "A" triad. Notice:

- On the staff, triads may be written in either staff and in any octave; the three notes of the triad will be written all on lines or all on spaces.

- The lowest note gives the triad its name. This note (the first) is also called the "root." The middle note is the "third" and the top note is the "fifth."

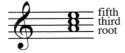

A is the root of the triad

- A triad may be written harmonically (all of the notes sound simultaneously) or melodically (notes are played in succession, as in a melody).

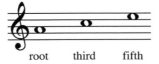

Triad played **harmonically**

Triad played **melodically**

Exercise 2 Class Exercise

Complete the triad harmonically by drawing two consecutive thirds above the given pitch. Identify the root. Play the triads.

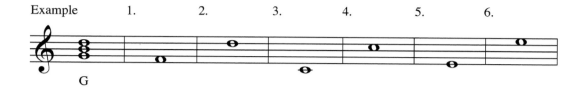

Qualities of Diatonic Triads

Triads may be classified by **quality**, which is determined by measuring the interval size of each of the thirds of the triad. There are four qualities of triads: major, minor, diminished, and augmented. We will begin our study with the major triad.

Major Triad

A **major** triad consists of the first, third, and fifth pitches of a major scale. For example:

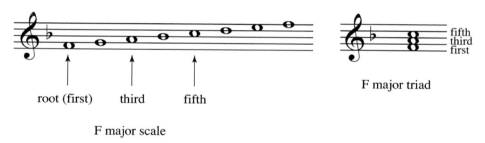

Constructing Major Triads

There are three methods for constructing a major triad. Your instructor will tell you which method(s) to use.

Method 1: Use the intervals of a major triad

- A triad may be defined as a combination of intervals. A major triad consists of notes a major third (M3) and a perfect fifth (P5) above the root. A minor third (m3) occurs between the upper two notes.

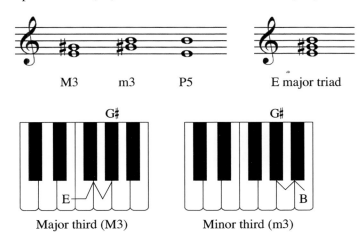

Method 2: Use tetrachords

- Determine the accidentals used in a major scale by joining tetrachords (see Module 6).

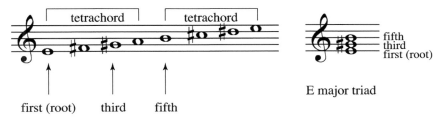

- The first, third, and fifth notes of the scale form a major triad.

Method 3: Use the major key signature

- Determine the key signature of a major scale by using the Circle of Fifths (see Module 7). E major has four sharps: F♯, C♯, G♯, and D♯.

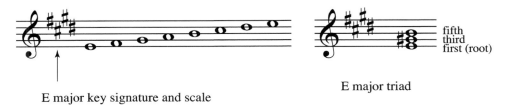

- G becomes G sharp because of the E major key signature.

Exercise 3 Class Exercise

On the keyboards below, label the keys that form major triads. Draw the triads on the staff in any octave. Use any of the three methods to construct the triads (DM = D major triad).

Example

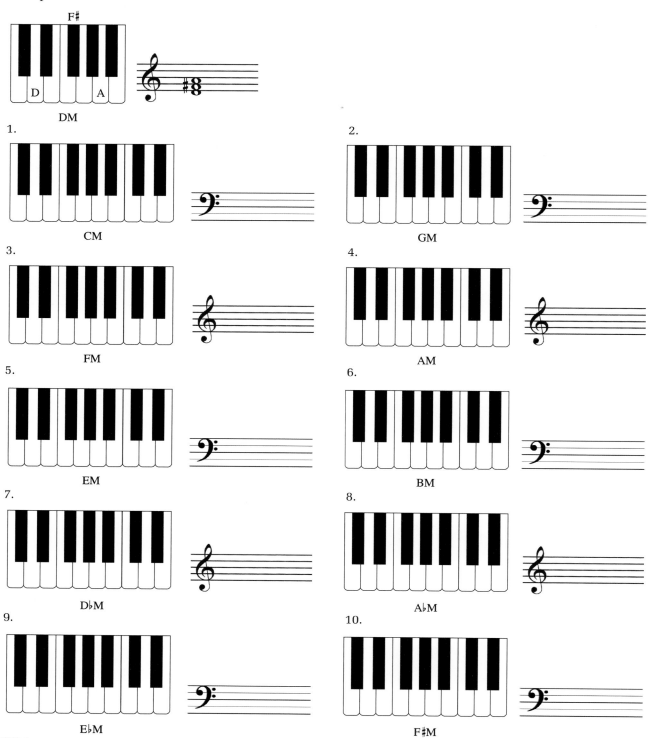

334

Exercise 4 Class Exercise

Draw major triads using any of the three methods given above. Triads may be drawn in any octave (AM = A major triad).

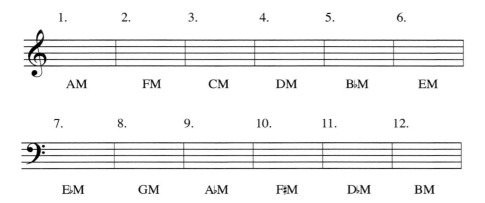

 Theory Trainer

Exercise 11b Triad drawing: major triad

Harmonizing Music Using Major Triads

Triad letter names (called "chord symbols") may be written above a melody line; the letter names are the root of the triads used to accompany the melody.

Vocabulary note

CHORD SYMBOL

Letter name of the root of a chord frequently placed above a melody line, used to accompany the melody.

HARMONIZATION

The use of chords (harmony) to accompany a melody.

NON-HARMONIC TONE

A note that is not a member of a chord; for example, "D," which does not belong to a C major triad (C E G), is a non-harmonic tone of CM.

Listen to your instructor or another class member play "Ye Banks and Braes O'Bonnie Doon." Listen first to the treble clef melody and then the bass clef triads, and finally both parts together. Notice that:

• Triads may be written in any octave; here, the treble clef range may determine the octave placement of the triads below.

335

- All triads are placed directly below the melodic note that is sounded or played with the triad; all measures have the correct number of counts.
- When the letter name does not change across a bar line as in m. 4, the triad remains the same.
- Some melodic notes do not belong to the given triad; these notes are called "non-harmonic" tones. The first two non-harmonic tones are circled.

"Ye Banks and Braes O'Bonnie Doon" ("The Banks and Hillsides of the Pretty River Doon"), Scottish folk song from the eighteenth century

Cultural note

"Ye Banks and Braes O'Bonnie Doon" ("The Banks and Hillsides of the Pretty River Doon") is one of the most popular Scottish folk songs. It sets to music the poem written by Robert Burns, the famous Scottish poet. According to popular lore, the poem tells the story of Miss Kennedy who was spurned by her lover and thus her heart was broken. "*Ye Banks and braes o' bonnie Doon, how can ye bloom sae fresh and fair? . . . Wi' lightsome heart I stretch'd my hand, and pu'd a rosebud from the tree. But my fause lover stole the rose, and left the thorn wi'me.*"

Notice the "Scotch snap" rhythm in m. 3:

Exercise 5 Class Exercise

Using the chords symbols (triad letter names) given above the melody, harmonize "Las Mañanitas." Refer back to your discussion about "Ye Banks and Braes" to assist with this exercise. The first triad is given.

Las Mañanitas" ("Morning Song"), traditional Mexican song

Cultural note

"LAS MAÑANITAS"

"Las Mañanitas" is a Mexican birthday song, traditionally sung in the early morning to wake up and serenade the birthday celebrant. "Wake up, my dear, wake up, look, it is already dawn." It may also be sung at a party before the cake is cut.

* At "mi bien," the name is sung.

Minor Triad

The **minor** triad, like the minor scale, may elicit a different mood or response in the listener depending on one's cultural background. Listen to the four pairs of triads drawn below; the first one is major and the second one is minor. Listen for their different **quality**.

Exercise 6 Class Listening Exercise

You will hear two triads, one major and one minor. Each exercise will be played twice. Place a check to indicate the triad that you hear first.

	Major	Minor
1.	_____	_____
2.	_____	_____
3.	_____	_____
4.	_____	_____
5.	_____	_____

Theory Trainer

Exercise 11a Identify triad quality by ear: major and minor triads.

Constructing Minor Triads

There are three methods for constructing a minor triad. Your instructor will tell you which method(s) to use.

Method 1: Use the intervals of a minor triad

- A minor triad consists of a minor third (m3) and a perfect fifth (P5) above the root. A major third (M3) occurs between the upper two notes.

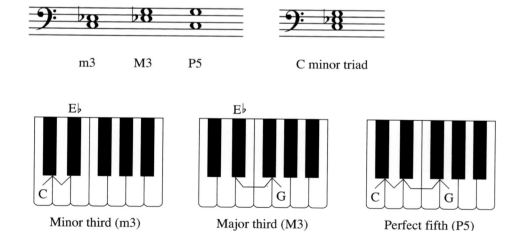

| m3 | M3 | P5 | | C minor triad |

| Minor third (m3) | Major third (M3) | Perfect fifth (P5) |

- Compare the intervals in major and minor triads.

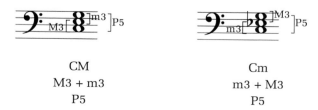

CM
M3 + m3
P5

Cm
m3 + M3
P5

Method 2: Change a major triad to minor

- To construct a minor triad, lower the third (the middle) note of a major triad a half step, keeping the original letter names. For example:

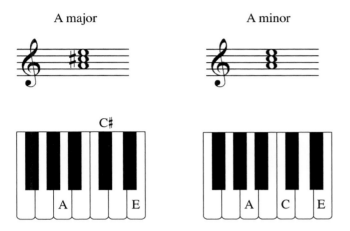

Method 3: Use the minor key signature

- Determine the key signature of a minor scale by using the minor Circle of Fifths (see Module 9). E minor has one sharp: F♯.

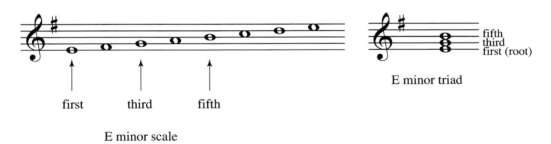

- Although there is an F♯ in the key signature, it does not affect the triad (E G B).

Exercise 7 Class Exercise

- On the keyboards below, label the keys that form the major and minor triads.
- Draw the corresponding major and minor triads on the staff below each keyboard. Triads may be drawn in any octave.
- Note: To change a major triad to minor, lower the middle key (the third above the root) a half step; keep all letter names the same.

Example

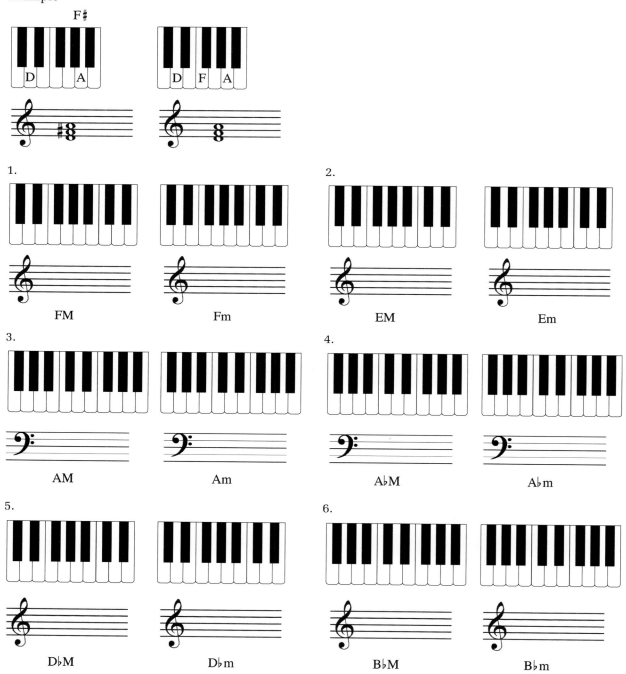

Exercise 8 | Class Exercise

Draw minor triads using any method shown above. Triads may be drawn in any octave.

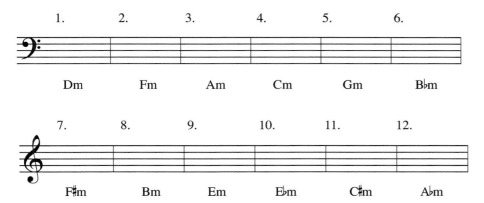

1. Dm 2. Fm 3. Am 4. Cm 5. Gm 6. B♭m

7. F♯m 8. Bm 9. Em 10. E♭m 11. C♯m 12. A♭m

 ## Theory Trainer

Exercise 11b Triad drawing: major and minor triads.

Exercise 9 | Class Exercise

Below each triad, label the triad root and quality (M or m).

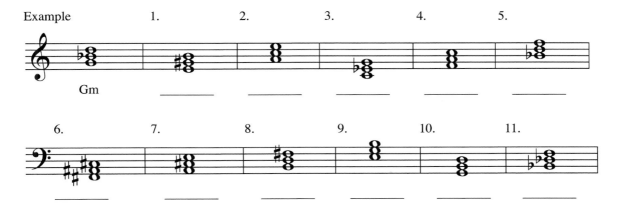

Example — Gm

1. ____ 2. ____ 3. ____ 4. ____ 5. ____

6. ____ 7. ____ 8. ____ 9. ____ 10. ____ 11. ____

 ## Theory Trainer

Exercise 11a Identify triad quality by ear: major and minor triads.
Exercise 11c Identify triads when written on staff: major and minor triads.

Exercise 10 Class Exercise

Using the **chord symbols** (triad letter names) given above the melody, harmonize the following song. Write the triads in the bass clef below using the appropriate rhythms. The first two triads are given.

- Notice the key signature given at the beginning of every line. Will you need to add any additional accidentals when you notate the triads? _____
- Be sure to draw the triads in the bass clef directly below the melody note that corresponds to the harmony changes. Triads may be repeated or tied and drawn in any octave. Does each measure have the correct number of beats? _____
- In "Tōryanse" only minor triads are used; in what ways does this piece sound "Western" or "Asian"? _____

Reminder: When a chord symbol is not written at the beginning of a measure, continue the harmony of the previous measure.

"Tōryanse" ("Let Me Pass"), Japanese traditional folk song

Cultural note

In this traditional Japanese song, "Tōryanse" ("Let Me Pass"), pilgrims ask permission to pass through the narrow gate to the castle housing the Tenjin Shrine. Long ago, children's third, fifth, and seventh birthdays were celebrated. *"Please allow me to pass through . . . to celebrate this child's seventh birthday. I've come to dedicate my offering . . ."* Today, this song is heard at many street crossings to tell blind people when to cross.

Workbook Exercises 11.1–11.4

Diminished Triad

The **diminished** triad consists of two ascending consecutive minor thirds from the root. This creates a diminished fifth between the root and the fifth, hence the name "diminished" which means to "make smaller."

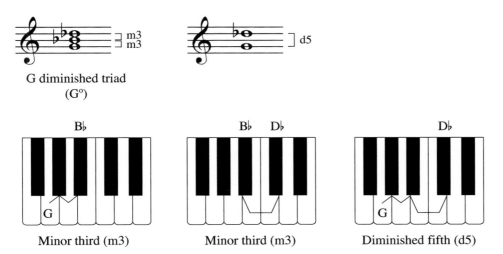

When labeling the quality of a diminished triad, frequently the "degree" sign ° is used. It is preferable either to label a diminished triad using the "°" or to write "dim" to avoid any confusion with the letter "D."

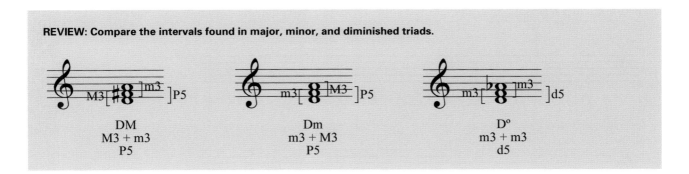

REVIEW: Compare the intervals found in major, minor, and diminished triads.

Constructing Diminished Triads

There are two methods for constructing a diminished triad.

Method 1: Use the intervals of a diminished triad

- A diminished triad consists of a minor third (m3) and a diminished fifth (d5) above the root. A minor third (m3) occurs between the upper two notes.

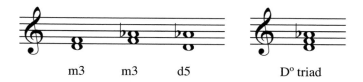

m3   m3   d5   D° triad

Method 2: Change a major triad to a diminished triad

- To construct a diminished triad, lower the third (the middle) and the fifth (the top) notes of a major triad each a half step without changing the letter names. For example:

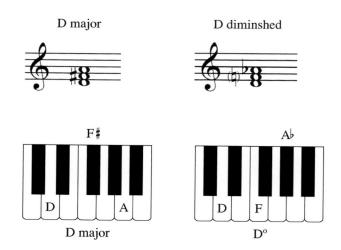

D major   D diminshed

F♯   A♭

D major   D°

Exercise 11 Class Exercise

Draw diminished triads using either method shown above. Triads may be drawn in any octave.

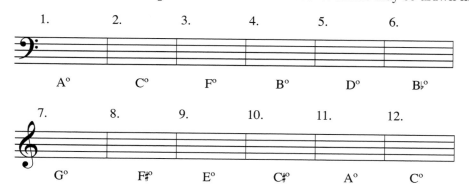

1.	2.	3.	4.	5.	6.
A°	C°	F°	B°	D°	B♭°

7.	8.	9.	10.	11.	12.
G°	F♯°	E°	C♯°	A°	C°

Theory Trainer

Exercise 11b Triad drawing: major, minor, diminished triads.

Exercise 11a Identify triad quality by ear: major, minor, diminished triads.

Exercise 12 Class Exercise

Indicate with a check the triad that you hear: major, minor, or diminished. You will hear the triad played twice, once harmonically and once melodically.

	Major	Minor	Diminished
1.	___	___	___
2.	___	___	___
3.	___	___	___
4.	___	___	___
5.	___	___	___
6.	___	___	___

Theory Trainer

Exercise 11c Identify triads when written on the staff: major, minor, diminished triads.

Augmented Triad

The **augmented** triad consists of two ascending consecutive major thirds from the root. This creates an augmented fifth between the root and the fifth, hence the name "augmented" which means "made bigger."

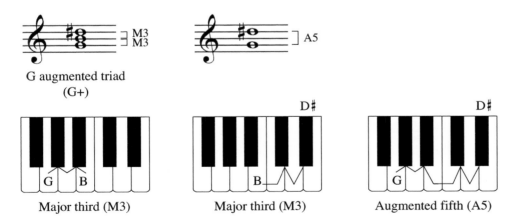

When labeling the quality of an augmented triad, frequently the "plus" sign + is used. It is preferable to either label an augmented triad using the "+" or to write "Aug" to avoid any confusion with the letter "A".

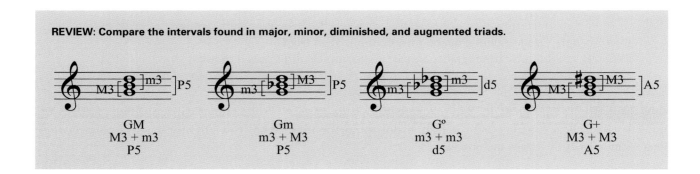

REVIEW: Compare the intervals found in major, minor, diminished, and augmented triads.

GM
M3 + m3
P5

Gm
m3 + M3
P5

G°
m3 + m3
d5

G+
M3 + M3
A5

Constructing Augmented Triads

Use either method to draw an augmented triad.

Method 1: Use the intervals of an augmented triad

- An augmented triad consists of a major third (M3) and an augmented fifth (A5) above the root. A major third (M3) occurs between the upper two notes.

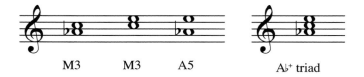

M3   M3   A5   A♭⁺ triad

Method 2: Change a major triad to an augmented triad

- Raise the fifth (top) note of a major triad a half step to construct an augmented triad. For example:

A♭ major   A♭ augmented

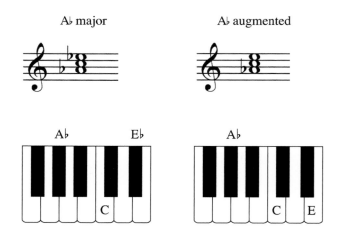

Exercise 13 Class Exercise

Draw augmented triads using either method shown above. Triads may be drawn in any octave.

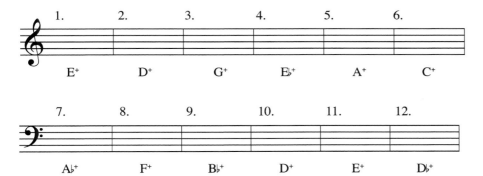

Theory Trainer

Exercise 11b Triad drawing: major, minor, diminished, augmented triads.

Exercise 14 Class Exercise

Identify the following triads, naming the root and the quality (major, minor, augmented, or diminished).

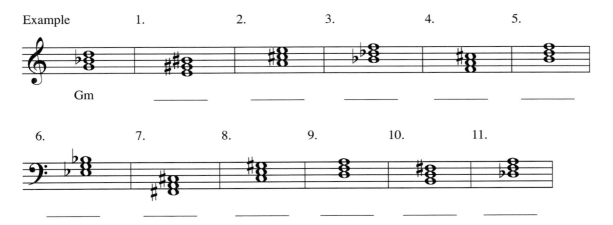

Theory Trainer

Exercise 11c Identify triads when written on staff: major, minor, diminished, augmented triads.
Exercise 11a Identify triad quality by ear: major, minor, diminished, augmented triads.

Augmented and Diminished Triads Using Double Sharps and Double Flats

In order to draw some augmented and diminished triads, it may be necessary to use double sharps or double flats. For example:

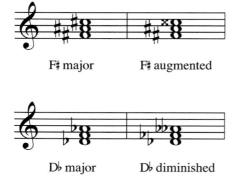

F♯ major   F♯ augmented

D♭ major   D♭ diminished

Exercise 15

Draw the following augmented and diminished triads. Some triads may need double sharps or double flats.

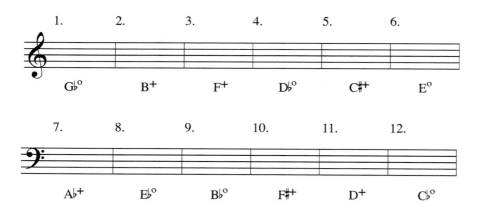

1. G♭° 2. B+ 3. F+ 4. D♭° 5. C♯+ 6. E°

7. A♭+ 8. E♭° 9. B♭° 10. F♯+ 11. D+ 12. C♭°

Workbook Exercises 11.5–11.10

Name _____

Exercise 11.1

Draw parallel major and minor triads using accidentals as needed. Note the similarities between each group of triads.

Reminder: parallel keys share the same tonic, for example, GM and Gm.

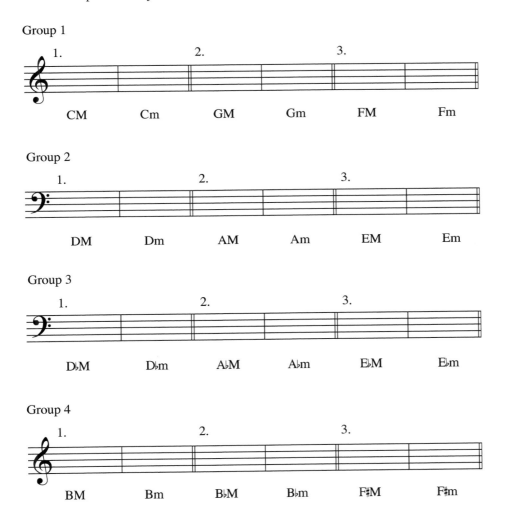

Group 1

1.   2.   3.

CM   Cm   GM   Gm   FM   Fm

Group 2

1.   2.   3.

DM   Dm   AM   Am   EM   Em

Group 3

1.   2.   3.

D♭M   D♭m   A♭M   A♭m   E♭M   E♭m

Group 4

1.   2.   3.

BM   Bm   B♭M   B♭m   F♯M   F♯m

Exercise 11.2

Below each triad, label the triad root and quality (M or m).

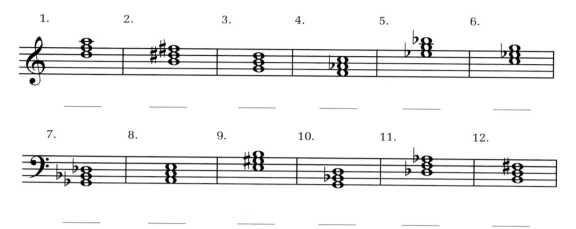

Exercise 11.3

Using the chord symbols (triad letter names) given above the melody, harmonize the following song. Write the triads on the bass staff below using the appropriate rhythms. The first triad is given.

Note: It is common convention that chord names are assumed to be major unless minor is indicated.

"Danny Boy," Irish folk melody *Londonderry Air* (words by F. Weatherly)

NAME: _____

Exercise 11.4

Using the chord symbols (triad letter names) given above the melody, harmonize the following song. Write the triads on the bass staff below using the appropriate rhythms. The first two triads are given.

　　Note: As shown in this example, it is common convention that chord names are assumed to be major unless minor is indicated.

"Water Come a Me Eye," Jamaican folk song

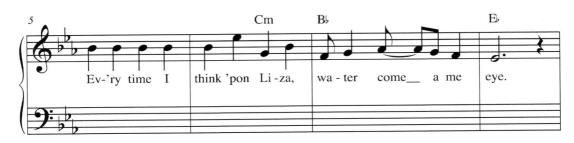

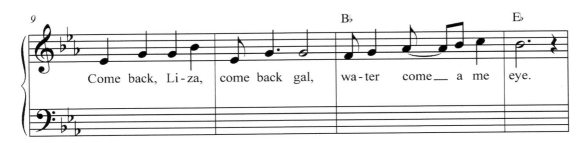

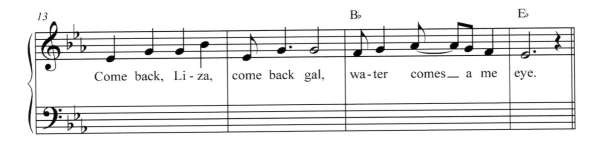

Exercise 11.5

Identify the following triads by naming the letter name of the root and the quality of the triad (major, minor, or diminished).

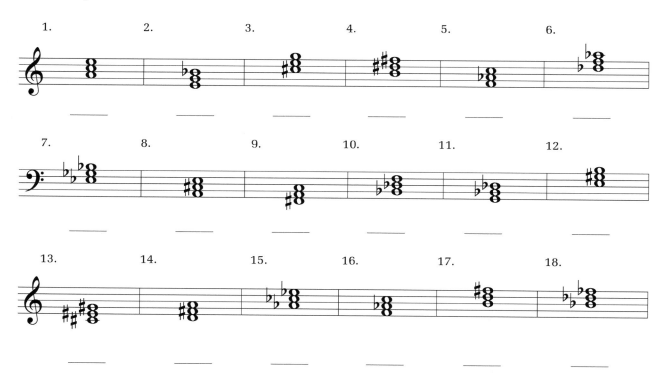

Exercise 11.6

Draw major, minor, augmented, and diminished triads for the following roots.

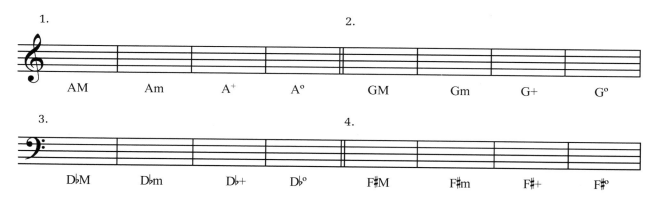

Exercise 11.7

Identify the following triads by naming the letter name of the root and the quality of the triad (major, minor, augmented, or diminished).

1.   2.   3.   4.   5.   6.

7.   8.   9.   10.   11.   12.

13.   14.   15.   16.   17.   18.

Exercise 11.8

Draw the following triads using accidentals as needed.

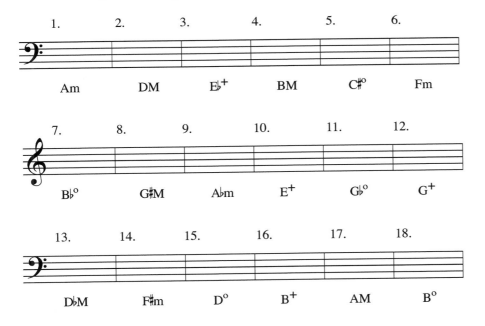

1.   2.   3.   4.   5.   6.

Am   DM   E♭+   BM   C#o   Fm

7.   8.   9.   10.   11.   12.

B♭o   G♯M   A♭m   E+   G♭o   G+

13.   14.   15.   16.   17.   18.

D♭M   F♯m   Do   B+   AM   Bo

Exercise 11.9

Harmonize the following excerpt using the letter names and triad qualities written above the melody. Add triads on the bass staff directly below the melody note that corresponds to the triad, and apply accidentals as needed. Be sure each measure has the correct number of beats.

"That's All" (A. Brandt, B. Haymes)

Exercise 11.10

Match the word with the definition.

1. Augmented triad _____ Consists of three notes: a major third and a perfect fifth above the root; the first, third, and fifth notes of a major scale

2. Chord _____ Scotch snap rhythm

3. Chord symbol _____ From the Greek word "*harmonia*" or "agreement"; the relationship between consecutive groupings of simultaneous sounding pitches

4. Diminished triad _____ In its simplest form, three notes each a third apart

5. Harmony _____ Consists of three notes: a minor third and a perfect fifth above the root; the first, third, and fifth notes of a minor scale

6. Harmonization _____ Classification of triads determined by measuring the interval size of each of the thirds of the triad: major, minor, augmented, diminished

7. Major triad _____ (°) Consists of two ascending consecutive minor thirds from the root, creating a diminished fifth between the root and the fifth

8. Minor triad _____ Triad letter names

9. Non-harmonic tone _____ Three or more notes that sound simultaneously

10. Triad _____ (+) Consists of two ascending consecutive major thirds from the root, creating an augmented fifth between the root and the fifth

11. Triad quality _____ Chords or triads accompanying a melody

12. [musical notation] _____ Melodic note that does not belong to a chord or triad

MODULE 12

RHYTHM: COMPOUND METER EXPANDED

Changing the Pulse Note in Compound Meter: The Dotted Half Note and Dotted Eighth Note

The most common pulse note value in compound meter is the dotted quarter note. (Review Module 8 beginning on page 221.) Less frequently, composers use the dotted half note or the dotted eighth note as the main pulse note. The chart compares these different note values: dotted quarter, dotted half, and dotted eighth.

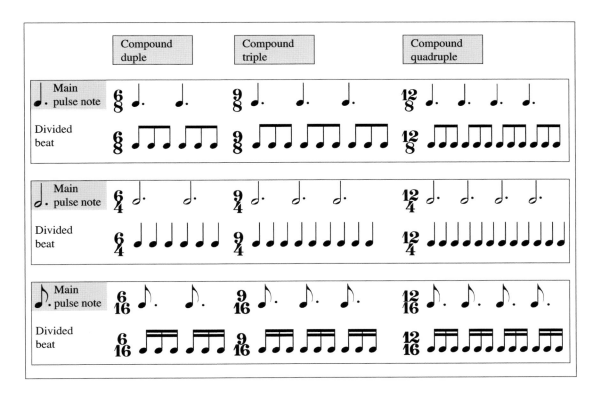

Exercise 1 Class Exercise

Count and clap the rhythms below.

- The first method of counting utilizes the main beats in each measure and may work better with melodies with larger note values and faster tempos.
- The second method of counting utilizes the divided beat and may work better with melodies with smaller note values and slower tempos.

Your instructor will tell you which counting method to use. Both methods should emphasize the main beats in each measure—and both should "sound the same."

Method 1
Main pulse

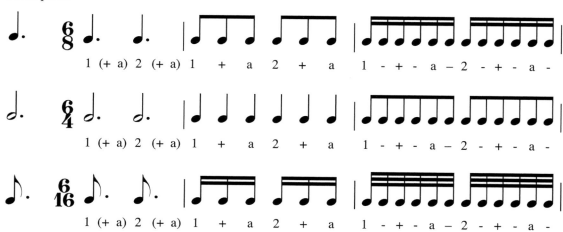

Method 2
Main pulse

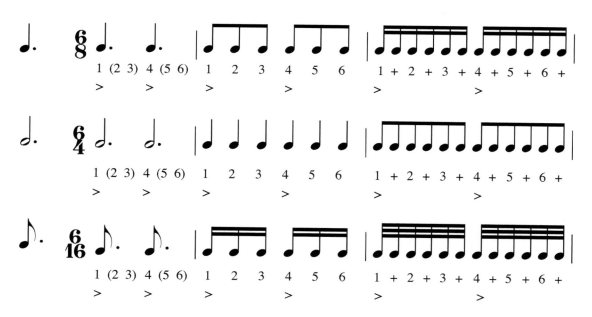

Exercise 2

Using the upper number of the time signature, identify the meter. Using the lower number, determine the pulse note. Write the counts below the melodies and clap each exercise.

1. Liebesträume No. 3 (F. Liszt)
    Meter: Compound duple
    Pulse note: Quarter note

Poco Allegro, con affetto

Musical note: Liebesträume

Franz Liszt composed a set of three solo piano pieces collectively called "Liebesträume" ("Dreams of Love") which were published in 1850. Originally, the pieces were written for soprano and piano and later transcribed for both piano duet and solo piano. Liebesträume No. 3, which is the most popular of the solo piano collection, looks at mature love that mourns death: "Love as long as you can. The hour will come when you will stand at graves and mourn." Note that the tempo marking, "con affetto" translates to "with tenderness."

2. Prelude, from *Le Tombeau de Couperin* (M. Ravel)
    Meter: Compound quadruple
    Pulse note: _____

Vocabulary note

TOMBEAU

Le Tombeau de Couperin (*tombeau* is French for "tomb") is a suite of six pieces written by Maurice Ravel between 1914 and 1917, each piece commemorating a friend who had died in World War I. (Ravel served during the war as a driver.) Rather than paying homage to the famous seventeenth-century French composer Francois Couperin, Ravel was honoring the Baroque keyboard suite which is a collection of dances. This Tombeau opens with a Prelude dedicated to Lieutenant Jacques Charlot who had transcribed one of Ravel's duets for solo piano.

3.   Sonata in E♭, Op. 22, Second Movement (L.v. Beethoven)
     Meter: _____
     Pulse note: _____

Notice the syncopation in mm. 4–5.

 Theory Trainer

Exercise 12a Rhythm tapping with dotted half as pulse note

Workbook Exercises 12.1–12.4

The Triplet

In simple meter, the beat may be divided into three equal parts by use of the **triplet**. Note that:

*   The triplet divides the beat into three equal parts where you normally have two equal parts.
*   Triplets are commonly identified by a "*3*" placed above or below the group of notes, sometimes with the addition of a bracket.

"3" ABOVE the notes   Triplet with BRACKET

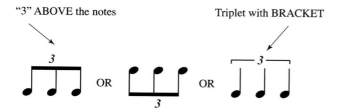

*   In a series of triplets, only the first groups may have the "*3*" and the bracket.

- Any note value may be divided into triplets; the most common is the eighth note triplet. For all triplets, the combined value of the triplets is equal to the next larger note value.

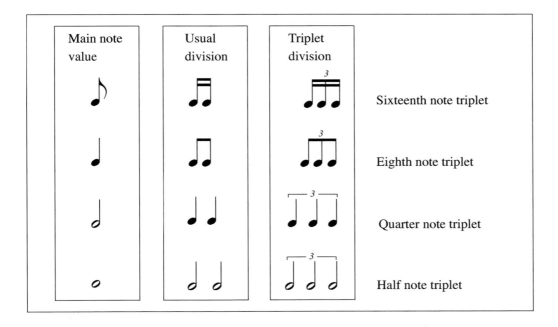

- Triplets are used for short segments of music when the normal division into groups of two is changed momentarily to three. For an extended section using a division into groups of three, the music is usually written in compound meter.

Listen to your instructor play this excerpt from Claude Debussy's "La Puerto del Vino" which uses eighth note and thirty-second note triplets. Note the "courtesy" accidentals.

La Puerto del Vino (C. Debussy)

Notice Debussy's designation "Mouvement de Habanera" at the beginning of the Prelude. Here, Debussy uses the Habanera rhythm to accompany the melody. Ask your instructor to play the excerpt again, this time tapping the following Habanera rhythm:

Musical note

HABANERA

The Habanera is a slow, graceful Cuban dance which developed in the early nineteenth century from the French contradanza, and incorporated African rhythms. It became popular in Spain and throughout the Americas and Europe, and is used in compositions by Georges Bizet (*Carmen*), Claude Debussy (*La Soiree dans Grenade* and *La Puerto del Vino*), and Emmanuel Chabrier (*España*).

Exercise 3 Class Exercise

Count and clap the following rhythms.

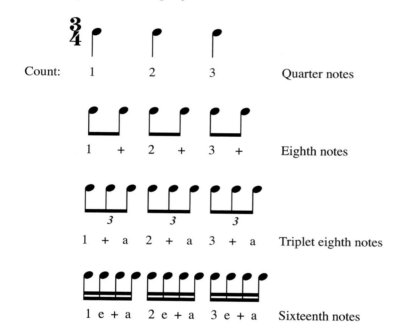

Count: 1   2   3   Quarter notes

1 + 2 + 3 +   Eighth notes

1 + a   2 + a   3 + a   Triplet eighth notes

1 e + a   2 e + a   3 e + a   Sixteenth notes

Exercise 4

Write the counts below each exercise. Clap the rhythms.

Exercise 5 Class Exercise

Write in the counts below each exercise. Clap the rhythms.

1. March (*The Nutcracker Suite*, Op. 71a) (P. Tchaikovsky)

2. "Esta Noche Voy a Verla" ("This Night I Am Going to See Her") (lyrics and music by J. Gabriel), Spanish love song

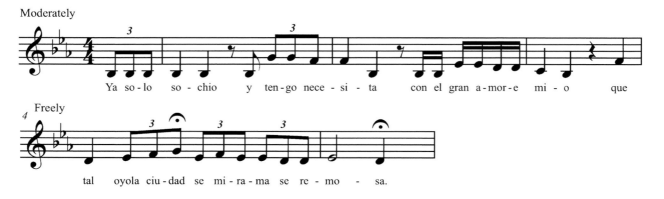

Moderately

Ya so - lo so - chio y ten-go nece - si - ta con el gran a-mor-e mi - o   que

Freely

tal   oyola ciu-dad se mi - ra - ma se re - mo - sa.

3. Sonatina, Op. 60, No. 2 (F. Kuhlau)

Allegro molto

4. "Honeysuckle Rose" (A. Razaf, T. "Fats" Waller)

Moderately slow

"Honeysuckle Rose" is rewritten below with a moderate "swing" beat in unequal triplet rhythms, which is how it might be performed by a jazz musician. Write counts below the notes and clap, feeling the easy swing of the beat. Notice that this also may be rewritten in 12/8.

Moderately slow (with a swing beat)

1(+)a 2(+)a 3 (4)

Vocabulary note

"SWING"

In many jazz, blues or rock genres, music written as two equal time values is generally played or sung in unequal values, with the first note held longer than the second. For example, two eighth notes may be played with a triplet feel: ♪♪ = ♩ ♪

In jazz or related music, the altered rhythm swings, resulting in a foot-tapping groove. As in some earlier Baroque and Classical music (called "*notes inégales*"), the rhythmic alteration is improvised.

---

5. The Pink Panther (H. Mancini)

•   Above the music, bracket the three sets of tied notes.
•   How many counts should you hold each set of ties? _____ _____ _____

6. Symphony in F Sharp Minor, No. 45 ("Farewell"), Fourth Movement (Coda) (F.J. Haydn)

Adagio

7. "Bésame Mucho" ("Kiss Me Much") (music and Spanish words by C. Velazquez)

In this time signature, determine what note value will equal these three quarter note triplets.

Bé— sa—me,— — bé—sa—me mu — cho, —

co- mo si fue —raes —ta no —che la úl— ti— ma vez. —

Theory Trainer

Exercise 12b Rhythm tapping with eighth note triplets

Workbook Exercises 12.5 and 12.6

The Duplet

Less frequently in compound meter, the **duplet**, or the division of two equal parts, is used where you normally have groups of three.

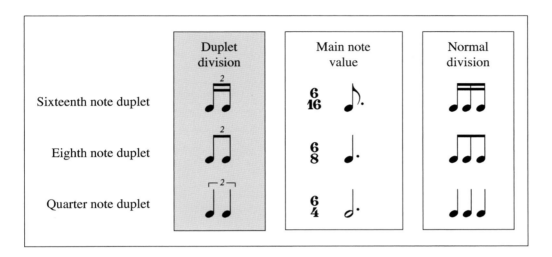

Exercise 6 Class Exercise

Identify the meter and write in the counts for the following exercise. Clap the rhythm.

1. "Angngidudue" (R.C. Vinluan) (Gaddang dialect), Filipino lullaby

    ". . . Go to sleep . . . Your mother went to the stream to catch mud fish so she can have fish to cook for the children."

Workbook Exercises 12.7–12.11

Name _____

Exercise 12.1 Class Exercise

Identify the meter, the main pulse note and the subdivided beat for the following time signatures.

	Meter	Main pulse	Subdivided beat
Example **6/4**	Compound duple	𝅗𝅥.	𝅘𝅥
1. **12/8**			
2. **9/4**			
3. **6/8**			
4. **6/16**			
5. **9/8**			
6. **12/16**			

Exercise 12.2 Class Exercise

Write the counts below each exercise and clap the rhythms. Identify the meter.

Example:
Meter: Compound triple

1. Meter _____

         1   2   3   4

OR   1(2 3)   4(5 6) 7(8 9) 10(11 12)

         >   >   >   >

2. Meter _____

3. Meter _____

4. Meter _____

Exercise 12.3

On the line given below each exercise, rewrite the rhythms adding barlines and beams as needed. All measures are complete. Count and clap.

1.

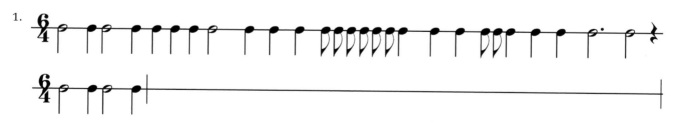

2.

NAME: _____

Exercise 12.4

Each of the following seven time signatures will be used once. In the boxes above each melody, write the missing time signature. Write the counts below each melody. Clap and sing. Which examples begin with anacrusis measures? _____ Which ones end with incomplete measures? _____

1. "Skye Boat Song," Scottish melody

2. "hãta yo" ("Clear the Way"), Teton Sioux Indian war song

ha - ta yo - wa-ka-ya hi - bu we - lo e

Cultural note

This is the song that an American Indian medicine man had sung in the late 1800s while painting war paint on the forehead of the Sioux warrior Bear Eagle. Singing for the warrior, the medicine man voiced: *"Clear the way! In a sacred manner I come!"* To the Sioux, war was a sacred act.

3.   Prelude in G Sharp Minor, Op. 32, No. 12 (S. Rachmaninoff)

4.   "Ride of the Valkyries" (R. Wagner)

5.   Pas Espagnol (from *Dolly Suite*, Op. 56) (G. Fauré)

6.   Symphony No. 3 in F, Op. 90 (First Movement) (J. Brahms)

7.   English Suite in D minor, BWV 811 (Gigue) (J.S. Bach)

NAME: _____

Exercise 12.5

Compose rhythms to fill measures that are left blank using a combination of notes or rests that are similar to those in surrounding measures. Write the counts below each exercise. Clap the rhythms.

Exercise 12.6

Write the counts below each exercise. Clap the rhythms.

1. "Comin' Through the Rye," Scottish melody

Cultural note: The Scotch Snap ♪♩.

The second beat of "Comin' Through the Rye" (a sixteenth note followed by a dotted eighth) is called a **Scotch snap**, a characteristic of many Scottish songs and dances beginning with the eighteenth century.

2. "Carmen, Carmela," Spanish folk song

3. Moment Musical, Op. 94, No. 1 (F. Schubert)

4.   "Peter Gunn," Theme Song (H. Mancini)

In this time signature, determine what note value will equal the three quarter note triplets. Divide the class in two, each one clapping a different bass clef line. (Hint: To count and play the triplets, change the time signature in those measures to 2/2.) Listen to the audio and tap along. If possible, tap both lines yourself.

TRACK 95

🔊 *95. "Peter Gunn," Theme Song (H. Mancini)*

Exercise 12.7

Rewrite the following melody in the corresponding meter using triplets as needed. Count and clap. Compare the two versions, discussing the differences and similarities.

"When Johnny Comes Marching Home" (Originally in compound meter)

"When Johnny Comes Marching Home" (Rewrite in simple meter.)

Exercise 12.8

Rewrite the following melody in the corresponding meter using duplets as needed. Count and clap. Compare the two versions, discussing the differences and similarities.

Les Préludes (F. Liszt) (Originally in simple meter)

Les Préludes (F. Liszt) (Rewrite in compound meter.)

Exercise 12.9

Write the counts for Claude Debussy's "Clair de lune." Does the excerpt begin with an anacrusis measure? _____ How many slurs are used in this excerpt? _____

Clair de lune (from *Suite Bergamasque*) (C. Debussy)

Exercise 12.10

Compose a melody incorporating duplet rhythms in a compound meter, or triplets in a simple meter. Notate the melody on your own manuscript paper.

- Select a clef, time signature, and key.
- Begin with a motive; use repetition for unity, variation for interest.
- Note: to help you incorporate triplets or duplets into your melody, say a three syllable word to represent a triplet in simple meter rhythm, or a two syllable word for a duplet in compound meter. Perform the melody for the class, or ask a classmate or your instructor to play it for you.

Exercise 12.11

Match the word with the definition.

1. Compound meter   _____   Note that represents the beat; note that receives one count

2. Duplet   _____   Music written as two equal time values played or sung in unequal values. Often used in jazz, blues or rock genres

3. Pulse note   _____   Scotch snap; characteristic of many Scottish songs and dances beginning in the eighteenth century

4. Simple meter   _____   When the top number of a time signature is 6, 9, or 12; the main pulse note is a dotted note that divides into groups of 3 or 6

5. "Swing" music   _____   Triplets; division of the note into three equal parts where you normally have two equal parts

6.   _____   When the top number of a time signature is 2, 3, or 4; the main pulse note divides into groups of 2 or 4

7.   _____   Subdivision of a note into two equal parts where you normally have three equal parts

MODULE 13

TRIADS: ROMAN NUMERALS

Triads of the Major Scale: Use of Roman Numerals

Each note of a major scale may be used as the root of a triad. There are three ways of labeling these triads. In Module 11, we used **chord symbols** to discuss the four qualities of triads: the letter name of the root and the triad quality. For example, EM tells us that the root is E and the triad is major. There are two other ways of labeling triads: **roman numerals** and **scale degree names**. Because many musicians use any of these three ways to label and discuss triads, it is important to know these methods of labeling.

Vocabulary note

ROMAN NUMERALS

are used to indicate triads in relation to the tonic note. For example, the tonic is roman numeral I.

SCALE DEGREE NAMES

are the names given to each note of the scale (see Module 6).

CHORD SYMBOLS

are the letter names and qualities of a triad. For example, the letter name and quality of a triad may be "D major" (DM).

Exercise 1 Class Exercise

Listen to your instructor play the triads formed from each note in the C major scale. Since the scale does not have any sharps or flats, the triads also do not have any accidentals.

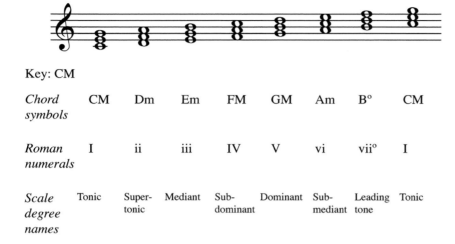

Key: CM

Chord symbols	CM	Dm	Em	FM	GM	Am	B°	CM
Roman numerals	I	ii	iii	IV	V	vi	vii°	I
Scale degree names	Tonic	Super-tonic	Mediant	Sub-dominant	Dominant	Sub-mediant	Leading tone	Tonic

Notice:

• The key of the scale is identified at the beginning just below the clef sign.
• The quality of the triad (major, minor, or diminished) is indicated by the use of upper case or lower case roman numerals (or °).

Major triads are indicated **by upper case roman numerals**. In a major scale there are **three major triads**.

> CM = I
> FM = IV
> GM = V

Minor triads are indicated by **lower case roman numerals**. In a major scale there are **three minor triads**.

> Dm = ii
> Em = iii
> Am = vi

Diminished triads are indicated by **lower case roman numerals accompanied by the "degree" sign**. In a major scale there is **one diminished triad**.

> B diminished = vii°

• The roman numerals, triad qualities, and scale degree names are the same for every major scale. Only the triad letter names (A, B, C) change with each key.

Exercise 2 Class Exercise

1. Using **accidentals**, draw the triads of the D major scale. Below each triad, label the roman numerals and the chord symbols. The first triad is given.

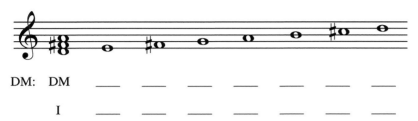

DM: DM　＿＿　＿＿　＿＿　＿＿　＿＿　＿＿　＿＿

　　　I　　＿＿　＿＿　＿＿　＿＿　＿＿　＿＿

2. After the clef, draw the **key signature** and triads for the E major scale. Below each triad, label the roman numerals and chord symbols.

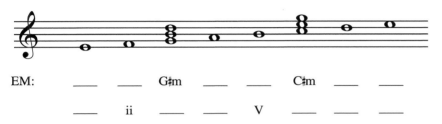

EM:　＿＿　＿＿　G#m　＿＿　＿＿　C#m　＿＿　＿＿

　　＿＿　ii　＿＿　＿＿　V　＿＿　＿＿

Exercise 3 Class Exercise Singing

"Vamudara," a Shona Shangra dance song from Zimbabwe, is not in a traditional compound quadruple meter.

- Tap the rhythm with two hands, accenting the left hand. Feel the irregularity of the rhythm, which is typical of many African songs. Be sure to keep the eighth notes steady.

- Write the solfège, chord symbols, and roman numerals below.
- Sing the song using letter names or solfège syllables.
- Divide the class in two: one half will tap while the other half sings. Reverse parts. Then sing and tap at the same time.

Solfège Syllable　　Do Mi Sol ＿＿　Fa ＿＿ ＿＿ ＿＿　Do ＿＿ ＿＿ ＿＿　Sol ＿＿ ＿＿

Chord Symbol　CM　＿＿＿＿　＿＿＿＿　＿＿＿＿

Roman Numeral　_I_　＿＿＿＿　＿＿＿＿　＿＿＿＿

Primary and Secondary Triads of the Major Scale

Triads of a scale can be divided into two groups: primary and secondary triads. The **primary** triads are those that are most closely related to the tonic: tonic, subdominant, and dominant. The **secondary** triads are less closely related to the tonic: supertonic, mediant, submediant, and leading tone.

MAJOR SCALE TRIADS

Primary triads		Secondary triads	
I	Tonic	ii	Supertonic
IV	Subdominant	iii	Mediant
V	Dominant	vi	Submediant
		vii°	Leading tone

Exercise 4 | Class Exercise

Using the chord symbols written above each song, label the roman numerals beneath each chord. Remember: when a chord symbol is not written at the beginning of a measure, continue the harmony of the previous measure. Notice that only primary triads are used in these pieces. Sing each song with a piano or guitar accompaniment playing the chords that are given; listen for the chord changes.

1. "For He's a Jolly Good Fellow," traditional song

Using the chord symbols and roman numerals as shown in Exercise 2, label the roman numerals beneath each chord in this song.

🔊))) **TRACK 96**

"Matilda, Matilda" (N. Span), West Indies folk song

2.   "Matilda, Matilda," West Indies folk song, Calypso rhythm

Cultural note: Calypso rhythm

Calypso is a type of music that arose in the early 1900s in Trinidad and Tobago (islands in the West Indies about seven miles northeast of Venezuela.) Its roots (called "Creole") were African mixed with Spanish, French, and English musical traditions. Its lyrics, sometimes satirical, were originally useful as a means to discuss politics and news of the day. (In "Matilda, Matilda" the lyrics bemoan a jilted man's loss of his girlfriend. Not only does she take his money, she takes his horse and cart and runs away to Venezuela!)

   Calypso rhythms are noted for their syncopations.

Play these rhythms by tapping the accents (>) on a hard surface using the heel of the hand; tap notes without accents using the fingers.

Listen to "Matilda, Matilda" a folk song from the West Indies. Then sing it again with a piano or guitar accompaniment playing the chords that are given; listen for the chord changes.

"Matilda, Matilda," West Indies folk song, Calypso rhythm

![Companion Website] **Theory Trainer**

Exercise 13a Identify roman numerals when given a triad: major keys

Harmonizing Music in a Major Key Using Roman Numerals

We can use roman numerals to add triads as an accompaniment to a melody; this is called "harmonization" of a melody. Earlier in this module, we harmonized melodies using chord symbols.

Exercise 5

Draw triads in the bass clef to accompany the melody of "Kum Ba Yah," a gospel song.

- Begin by determining the major key.
- Using the roman numerals given below each line, draw the corresponding triad; you may refer back to Exercise 2 (triads of the D major scale) to assist you.
- Place the triads in the bass clef directly beneath the melody note in the treble clef that corresponds to the triad. Be sure each measure has the correct number of beats (or rests).
- Play your composition, if possible.

Cultural note

Originally a Nigerian folk melody, this African-American gospel song was titled "Come By Here, Oh Lord." Over time, it was rephrased and became known as "Kum Ba Yah."

"Kum Ba Yah," African-American spiritual

Questions to consider:

*   How is the key established in this piece?
*   Which triads are not used?

 Theory Trainer

> **Exercise 13b** Draw triads when given a roman numeral: major keys

Workbook Exercises 13.1–13.4

Triads of the Harmonic Minor Scale: Use of Roman Numerals

As with the major scale, each note of the harmonic minor scale may be used as the root of a triad. Triads may be formed from each note of the natural and melodic minor scales as well, but the harmonic form is most useful when discussing the harmonies used in pieces written in minor keys (hence the designation "harmonic" minor).

The quality of the triads formed on each note of the harmonic minor scale are the same for every minor key. In addition to the sharps or flats (if any) in the key signature, the seventh note is always raised a half step. The seventh note is found in three triads: the mediant, dominant, and leading tone.

Exercise 6

Play and listen to the triads formed from each note in the A minor scale, **harmonic form**. Although A minor does not have any sharps or flats in its key signature, the seventh note (G♯) will be raised in the mediant, dominant, and leading tone triads.

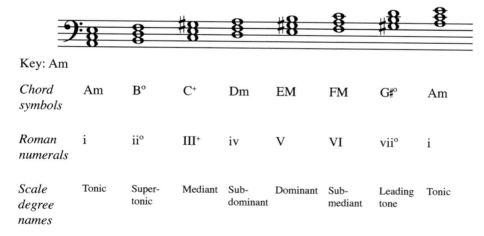

Key: Am								
Chord symbols	Am	B°	C⁺	Dm	EM	FM	G♯°	Am
Roman numerals	i	ii°	III⁺	iv	V	VI	vii°	i
Scale degree names	Tonic	Super-tonic	Mediant	Sub-dominant	Dominant	Sub-mediant	Leading tone	Tonic

Notice:

*   The key of the scale is identified at the beginning.
*   The quality of the triad (major, minor, augmented, or diminished) is indicated by the use of upper case or lower case roman numerals; there are two major, two minor, two diminished, and one augmented triad in the harmonic minor scale.

QUALITY OF TRIADS IN MINOR SCALES

Major triads are V and VI.

Minor triads are i and iv.

Diminished triads are ii° and vii°.

The **augmented** triad (III⁺) is indicated by an upper case roman numeral followed by a + sign. Composers of the Common Practice period (approximately the seventeenth to nineteenth centuries) did not use the augmented form of the median triad except in passing. Even today, the mediant is usually a major triad which is formed from the natural minor form of the scale.

- The roman numerals, triad qualities, and scale degree names are the same for every harmonic minor scale. Only the triad letter names (A, B, C) change with the key.

Exercise 7 Class Exercise

1. Using **accidentals**, draw the triads of the E harmonic minor scale. Below each triad, label the roman numeral and the chord symbol. Note that the F♯ comes from the E minor key signature; the D is raised because it is the seventh note of the scale.

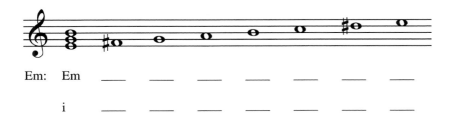

Em: Em   ____   ____   ____   ____   ____   ____   ____

      i   ____   ____   ____   ____   ____   ____   ____

2. After the clef, draw the **key signature** and triads for the D harmonic minor scale. Below each triad, label the roman numerals and chord symbols. When using a key signature, the only accidental that is needed is the raised seventh; three triads will be affected (III⁺, V, and vii°).

Key signature

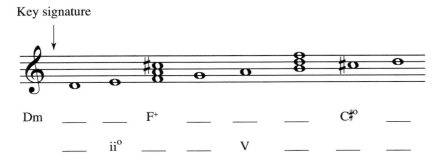

Dm   ____   ____   F⁺   ____   ____   ____   C♯°   ____

    ____   ii°   ____   ____   V   ____   ____   ____

Primary and Secondary Triads of the Harmonic Minor Scale

Triads of a minor scale can be divided into primary and secondary triads. Just as in the major scale, the **primary** triads are the tonic, subdominant, and dominant. The **secondary** triads are the supertonic, mediant, submediant, and leading tone.

MINOR SCALE TRIADS (Harmonic Form)	
Primary triads	**Secondary triads**
i Tonic	ii° Supertonic
iv Subdominant	III⁺ Mediant
V Dominant	VI Submediant
	vii° Leading tone

 Theory Trainer

      Exercise 13a Identify roman numerals when given a triad: major and minor keys

Harmonizing Music in a Minor Key Using Roman Numerals

Exercise 8 Class Exercise

Draw triads in the bass clef to accompany the given melody.

1. Volksliedschen (Little Folk Song), Op. 68, #9 (R. Schumann)

- Using the roman numerals given below the bass clef, notate the corresponding triad; you may refer back to Exercise 7, #2 (triads of the D minor scale) to assist you.
- Place the triads in the bass clef directly beneath the melody note in the treble clef that corresponds to the triad. Be sure each measure has the correct number of beats.
- Play your composition. Did it sound like what you expected?

Volksliedchen (R. Schumann)

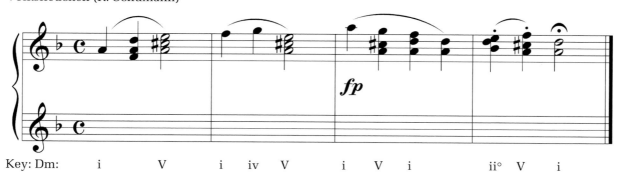

Key: Dm: i   V   i   iv V   i V   i   ii° V   i

2. "Charade" (H. Mancini)

- Using the roman numerals given below each bass clef line, notate the corresponding triad; you may refer back to Exercise 6 (triads of the A minor scale) to assist you.
- Notice the unusual extended use of the tonic triad in the first line and the "fleeting" use of the III+ in m. 14. (Both are used to create "color" in the composition.)

"Charade" (H. Mancini)

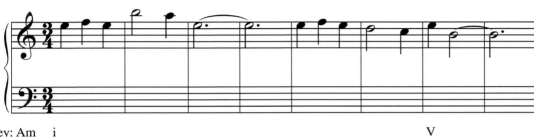

Key: Am   i   V

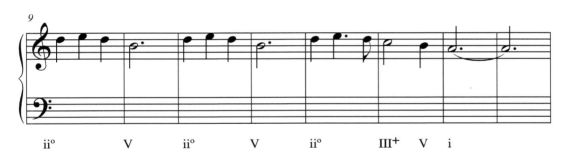

ii°   V   ii°   V   ii°   III⁺   V   i

@ **Theory Trainer**

    Exercise 13b Draw triads when given a roman numeral: major and minor keys

Workbook Exercises 13.5–13.9

Name _____

Exercise 13.1

Draw primary triads for the given major key signatures. Below the staff, label the key and roman numerals. Play the triads on the keyboard.

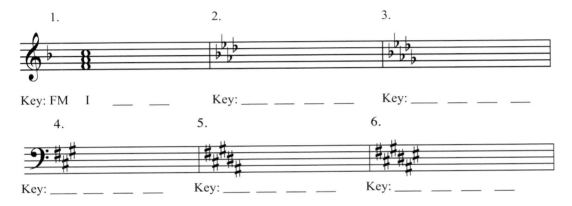

Key: FM   I   ___ ___   Key: ___ ___ ___ ___   Key: ___ ___ ___ ___

Key: ___ ___ ___ ___   Key: ___ ___ ___ ___   Key: ___ ___ ___ ___

Exercise 13.2

Label the major key and write the roman numerals and chord symbols for the given triads. Note the different key signatures.

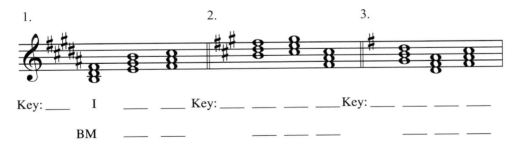

Key: ___   I   ___ ___   Key: ___ ___ ___ ___   Key: ___ ___ ___ ___

BM   ___ ___   ___ ___ ___   ___ ___ ___

Exercise 13.3

Identify the scale degree name and triad quality for the following roman numerals in a major key.

	Roman Numeral	Scale Degree Name	Triad Quality
1.	V	_____	_____
2.	iii	_____	_____
3.	vii°	_____	_____
4.	I	_____	_____
5.	ii	_____	_____
6.	IV	_____	_____
7.	vi	_____	_____

Exercise 13.4

Harmonize the following song by writing triads on the bass staff. Use the roman numerals written below the melody. Label the key at the beginning of the piece.

"Gaudeamus Igitur" ("Let Us All Be Joyful Now"), German student drinking song

Key: _____

Historical note

Properly titled "De Brevitte Vitae" ("On the Shortness of Life"), this song is also called "Gaudeamus." It is a popular song used at commencement exercises in many European countries, but was originally a boisterous drinking song. Several composers have used this piece in longer works, including Johannes Brahms in his *Academic Festival Overture*.

NAME: _____

Exercise 13.5

Identify the minor key. Draw the primary triads for the harmonic minor form and label with roman numerals. Play these triads on the keyboard.

1.

2.

3.

Key: Em   i   ___   ___   Key: ___   ___   ___   ___   Key: ___   ___   ___   ___

4.

5.

6.

Key: ___   ___   ___   ___   Key: ___   ___   ___   ___   Key: ___   ___   ___   ___

Exercise 13.6

For each exercise, label the minor key. Using the harmonic form of the minor, write the roman numerals and chord symbols of the following triads. Note the three different key signatures. Locate the mediant triad; is its quality major or augmented? _____

Key: ___   i   ___   ___   Key: ___   ___   ___   ___   Key: ___   ___   ___   ___

Bm   ___   ___   ___   ___   ___   ___   ___   ___

Exercise 13.7

Identify the scale degree name and triad quality for the following roman numerals in a minor key.

	Roman Numeral	Scale Degree Name	Triad Quality
1.	III	_____	_____
2.	iv	_____	_____
3.	vii°	_____	_____
4	i	_____	_____
5.	ii°	_____	_____
6.	VI	_____	_____
7.	V	_____	_____

Exercise 13.8

Harmonize "Erster Verlust" ("First Sorrow") by Robert Schumann using the roman numerals written below and adding accidentals as needed. Identify the key at the beginning.

"Erster Verlust" ("First Sorrow"), Op. 68, No. 16

Key: _____   i   iv   i   ii°   V   i   V   i

Exercise 13.9

Match the word with the definition.

1. Chord symbol

_____ Names given to each note of the scale; for example, supertonic is the second note of the scale

2. Dominant

_____ Fourth note of the scale, five notes below the tonic

3. Harmonization

_____ First note of the scale, names the key

4. Leading tone

_____ Numbers representing the number note of a scale on which a chord is based; for example, I = tonic, V = dominant

5. Primary triads

_____ Triads less closely related to the tonic: supertonic, mediant, submediant, and leading tone (or subtonic in natural minor)

6. Roman numeral

_____ Fifth note of the scale, second note of importance after the tonic

7. Scale degree

_____ Addition of triads to accompany a melody

8. Secondary triads

_____ Triads most closely related to the tonic: tonic, subdominant, dominant

9. Subdominant

_____ Letter name and quality of a chord, for example, "F minor"

10. Tonic

_____ Seventh note of the scale (subtonic in natural minor)

Defining Inversions: Root Position, First Inversion, and Second Inversion

We have been discussing triads in their simplest form: three notes that form consecutive thirds.

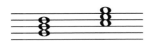

Triads may also be written as **inversions** ("invert" means "turn upside down"). There are three positions: root, first inversion, and second inversion. In all positions, the notes and therefore the quality (major, minor, augmented, diminished) remain the same; only the sequence of the notes from bottom to top changes. Composers use inversions to vary the harmonic sound and to create a smoother linear motion of the notes from chord to chord (called "voice leading.")

- In **root position**, the root is the lowest, or bass note.

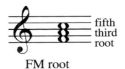

FM root

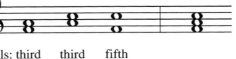

Intervals: third   third   fifth

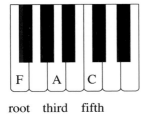

root   third   fifth

Chord Symbol: FM
(FM with F in the bass)

- In **first inversion**, the third of the triad is the bass note (bass = bottom).

FM first inversion   Intervals: third   fourth   sixth

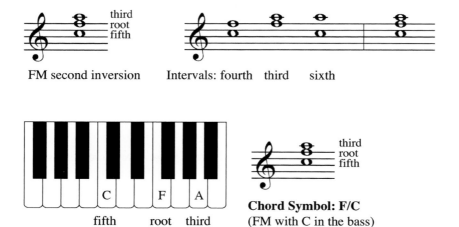

third   fifth   root

Chord Symbol: F/A
(FM with A in the bass)

- In **second inversion**, the fifth is the bass note.

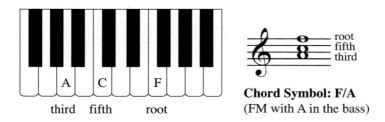

FM second inversion   Intervals: fourth third   sixth

fifth   root   third

Chord Symbol: F/C
(FM with C in the bass)

Exercise 1

Draw the root position and inversions for the following triads. Label the inversion below each triad. Your instructor may also ask you to provide chord symbols, which are used predominantly in popular songs.

Example   1.

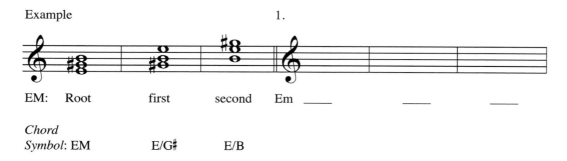

EM: Root   first   second   Em _____   _____   _____

Chord
Symbol: EM   E/G♯   E/B

2.

3.

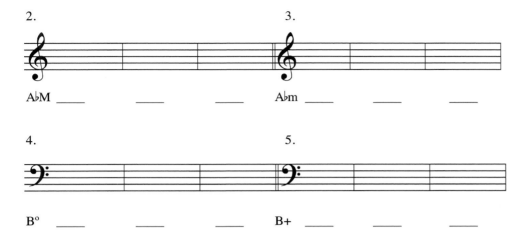

A♭M ____   ____   ____   A♭m ____   ____   ____

4.

5.

B° ____   ____   ____   B+ ____   ____   ____

Exercise 2 Class Exercise

Identify the root (letter name) of the triad, quality, and the inversion (root, first, second). Chord symbols may help to identify the inversion.

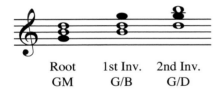

Root   1st Inv.   2nd Inv.
GM   G/B   G/D

- In root position, the root (the highlighted G in the triads above) is the bass note.
- In first inversion, the third of the triad is in the bass (and the root has moved to the top).
- In second inversion, the fifth of the triad is in the bass (and the root is in the middle of the triad).

Shortcut: In an inversion, locate the interval of the fourth. The root will be the upper note of the fourth.

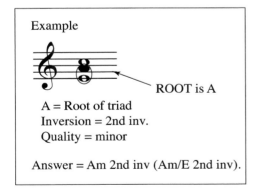

Example

ROOT is A

A = Root of triad
Inversion = 2nd inv.
Quality = minor

Answer = Am 2nd inv (Am/E 2nd inv).

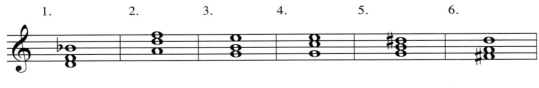

1.   2.   3.   4.   5.   6.

____   ____   ____   ____   ____   ____

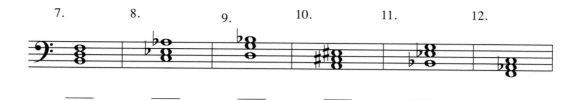

 **Theory Trainer**

Exercise 14a Identify root, quality, and triad inversions.

Exercise 3

Draw inverted triads using the letter name, triad quality, and inversion given below each staff.

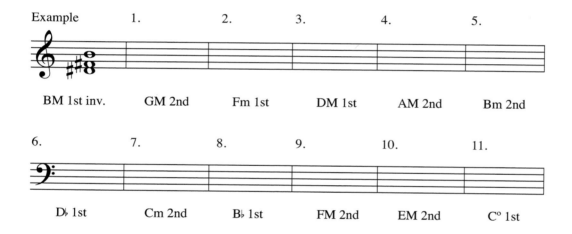

Example	1.	2.	3.	4.	5.
BM 1st inv.	GM 2nd	Fm 1st	DM 1st	AM 2nd	Bm 2nd
6.	7.	8.	9.	10.	11.
D♭ 1st	Cm 2nd	B♭ 1st	FM 2nd	EM 2nd	C° 1st

 **Theory Trainer**

Exercise 14b Draw triads with inversions.

Harmonizing Music Using Inversions

The following piece, "Tico, Tico," has been harmonized using a variety of triads, some inverted. Circle the inverted triads. Above the melodic line, triad letter names are provided. Compare the triads in the first two lines with those in the last two lines: in what ways are they similar to or different from each other? Discuss this as a class. (Note: some melody notes do not belong to the triads. They are called "non-harmonic" tones. The two notes circled in the first complete measure are non-harmonic tones.)

Cultural note: Choro

"Tico, Tico" is an example of a type of popular Brazilian song called a **choro** (literally "cry"). Despite their words of lament, *choro* melodies were usually played at a fast tempo with snappy, syncopated rhythms: "*If I'm on time—Cuckoo—but if I'm late—Woo-woo; the one my heart has gone to may not want to wait!*"

"Tico, Tico No Fuba" ("Bird in the Cornmeal") (Words and music Z. Abreu, A. Oliveira, E. Drake)

TRACK 97

Listen to "Tico, Tico No Fuba." Pay particular attention to the inverted triads that you have circled.

Exercise 4

Circle the non-harmonic tones in the previous exercise "Tico, Tico." The first measure is done for you. (As noted earlier, melody notes that do not belong to the harmony are called "non-harmonic" tones.)

Exercise 5 Class Exercise

Harmonize the following melodies using the letter name, triad quality and inversion (first and second) given above the treble clef. The first measure of each exercise is done for you.

- If an inversion is not indicated, the triad is root position.
- A measure that is left blank continues with the harmony of the previous measure.

1. "Steal Away," Spiritual
   Note: The harmony in m. 5 continues from the previous measure.

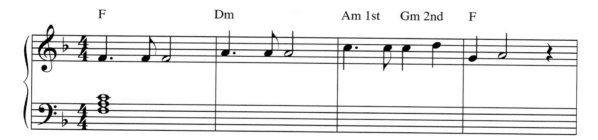

2. French Folk Song

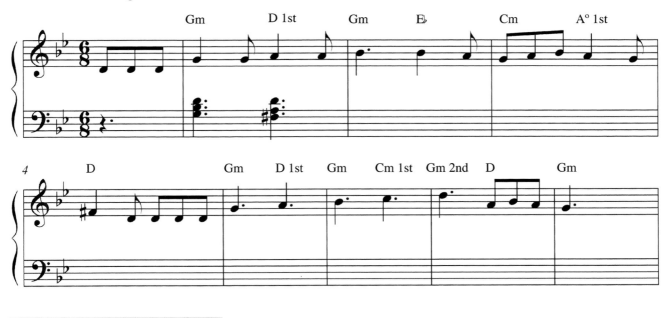

Workbook Exercises 14.1–14.4

Triads in Open and Close Position

Triads may be written in two different positions: **close** or **open**.

- **Close position** occurs when the distance between the lowest and highest notes in a triad is less than an octave.

Triads in close position

- **Open position** occurs when the notes exceed an octave in range. The triads in close position shown above are rewritten below in open position.

Triads in open position

As we have seen with inversions, composers use triads in open and close position to vary the sound and to assist with smooth voice leading. Notes of a triad may also be duplicated, and non-triad notes ("non-chord" or "non-harmonic" tones) may be added to expand the "color" of a harmony.

Exercise 6 Class Exercise

Listen to Track 98 or ask your instructor to play "Folk Song (with Open Triads)" by Ryan Dorin. Then listen to Track 99 where the song is harmonized with triads played in close position. The triad in parentheses in m. 1 shows the triad redrawn in close position. Discuss the differences and similarities of the two versions.

Folk Song (with Open Triads) (R. Dorin)

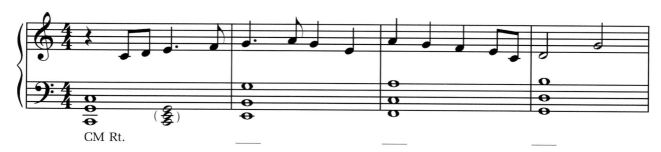

CM Rt.

🔊 **TRACK 98**

Listen to "Folk Song (with Open Triads)" by Ryan Dorin.

🔊 **TRACK 99**

Listen to "Folk Song" played with close position triads.

Exercise 7

Identify the root, quality, and inversion of each triad. Redraw the triad in close position by moving the upper note down an octave. Redraw melodic ("broken") triads harmonically ("blocked").

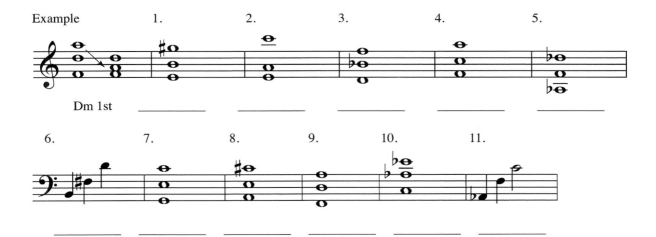

Dm 1st _____ _____ _____ _____ _____

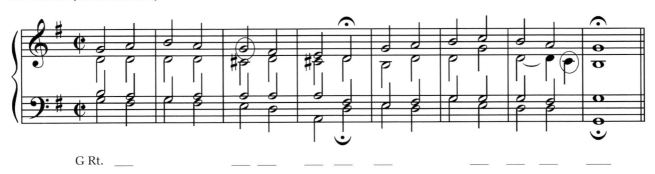

_____ _____ _____ _____ _____ _____

Exercise 8

Return to Exercise 6 on page 400 ("Folk Song") and draw the bass staff triads in close position. Below, identify the root, quality, and inversion of each triad. The first measure is done for you.

Exercise 9 Class Exercise

Robert Schumann's "Ein Choral" is a hymn composed of triads written in open position. Label the root, quality, and inversion of the underscored triads. Most of the triads have duplicated notes; two triads are incomplete. All notes that do not belong to the triad have been circled.

Ein Choral (R. Schumann)

G Rt. ____   ____ ____   ____   ____ ____

Theory Trainer

Exercise 14a Identify triad inversions (in open and close position).

Figured Bass Symbols

Figured bass symbols are interval numbers written below the bass staff to indicate triad quality and inversion, and were first used in published music starting around 1600. Musicians continue to use them today.

The following is an example of the use of figured bass symbols from Corelli's "Trio Sonata." Notice the numbers and naturals written below the bass clef of the "organo" (keyboard) part. Using these symbols, the performer would improvise the right hand above.

Trio Sonata in F major (A. Corelli)

Historical Note: Figured bass

A harpsichordist (most popular keyboard instrument during seventeenth and eighteenth centuries) used these figured bass symbols to improvise above a given bass line (called "realizing" a figured bass). This is similar to a jazz performer today using chord symbols/progressions to improvise.

Constructing and Identifying Triads Using Figured Bass Symbols

Figured bass symbols are numbers ("figures") that represent the intervals created above a bass (or "bottom") note. Here, the root of the triad is G.

A triad in **root position** consists of a fifth and a third above the lowest note.

Figured bass: 5 / 3

A triad in **first inversion** consists of a sixth and a third above the lowest note.

Figured bass: 6 / 3

A triad in **second inversion** consists of a sixth and a fourth above the lowest note.

Figured bass: 6 / 4

These symbols may be reduced even further as follows. Here, the root of the triad is F.

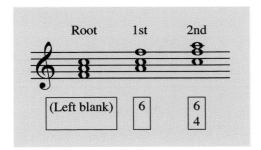

- In root position, the figured bass is left blank; *the fifth and the third above the bass are assumed.*
- In first inversion, only the number "6" is given to represent "6/3"; *the third above the bass is assumed.*
- In second inversion, both numbers are written ("6/4") *in order to differentiate this inversion from the first inversion.*

Exercise 10 Class Exercise

Complete the triad above the given note using the figured bass symbols written below the staff. Identify the letter name and quality of the triad. For this exercise do not add accidentals.

Note: a "6" written below the staff should not be confused with the jazz label "6" where the interval of the sixth is added to a root position triad.

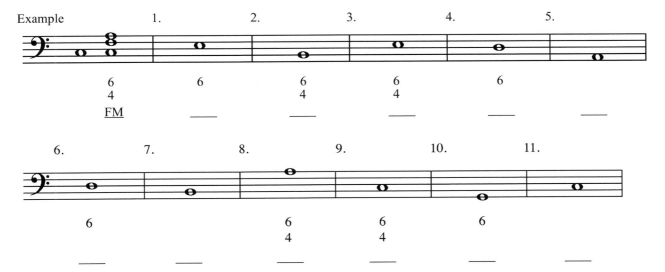

Exercise 11

Draw triads using the letter name and figured bass symbol given below the staff. Use accidentals as needed.

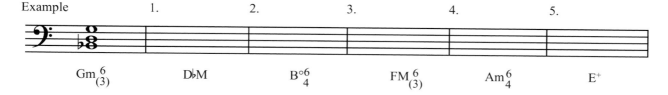

Example   1.   2.   3.   4.   5.

$Gm\frac{6}{(3)}$ D♭M $B°\frac{6}{4}$ $FM\frac{6}{(3)}$ $Am\frac{6}{4}$ E^+

Workbook Exercises 14.5–14.8

Harmonizing Music Using Roman Numerals and Figured Bass Symbols

In the previous section, we harmonized pieces using chord symbols (letter name and quality) written above the melody. We may also use roman numerals and figured bass symbols to harmonize a melody and to analyze the harmonies used by a composer.

Let's look at the first measures of J.S. Bach's "Prelude in F Major." We may analyze the harmonies that Bach uses in this Prelude and assign roman numerals and figured bass symbols to them.

- Broken triads use the same figured bass rules as blocked triads.
- Blocked triads have been written in the bass clef below the Bach piece to represent the broken triads.

Prelude in F Major, BWV 927 (J.S. Bach)

FM: F   B♭ 2nd   E° 1st   F

        I $IV\frac{6}{4}$ vii°6   I

- We begin by assigning roman numerals to each triad of the F major scale, as shown below. Circle the letter name of the triads that are used in Bach's Prelude in F.

Chord symbol:	FM	Gm	Am	B♭M	CM	Dm	E°	FM
Roman numeral:	I	ii	iii	IV	V	vi	vii°	I

- The position of a triad is determined by the lowest note: in root position, the root is the lowest note; in first inversion the third is the lowest note; in second inversion the fifth is the lowest note. Assign the figured bass accordingly. For example, locate the triad marked "B♭ 2nd" in the Bach piece above and find its corresponding roman numeral and figured bass symbols below.

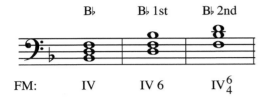

FM: IV   IV 6   IV$^6_4$

- Draw the inversions for the E° triad. Label each triad with roman numeral and figured bass symbols. Locate the triad marked "E° 1st" in the Bach piece above and find its corresponding roman numeral and figured bass in the inversions that you have drawn below.

FM: _____   _____   _____

Exercise 12 Class Exercise

"O Ewigkeit, du Donnerwort" (J.S. Bach)

- Identify the root, quality, and inversion for the underscored triads.
- Label the roman numeral and figured bass for each triad. The first triad is given.

FM: FM   ___ ___ ___ ___ ___ ___ ___
         I   ___ ___ ___ ___ ___ ___ ___

Workbook Exercises 14.9–14.11

Drawing Chord Progressions in Close Position

A **chord progression** is a series of chords (or triads). Music of the seventeenth and eighteenth centuries, jazz, and many popular songs use chord progressions as their harmonic basis. To see how the 12-bar blues progression uses a series of triads in a set order, refer to p. 453 in Module 16. Another chord progression that also uses primary triads is I IV V I. For example:

For example:

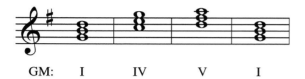

GM: I   IV   V   I

Below, the same chord progression is written using inversions. Notice how inversions allow the triads to progress more smoothly, without leaping from triad to triad.

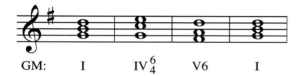

GM: I   IV$^6_4$ V6   I

Exercise 13 Class Exercise

Using the given roman numerals and figured bass symbols in the following keys, draw chord progressions first with root position triads and then with inversions.

1.

CM: I   IV   V   I   I   IV$^6_4$ V6   I

2.

AM: I   IV   V   I   I   IV$^6_4$ V6   I

3.

FM: I   IV   V   I   I   IV$^6_4$ V6   I

Exercise 14 Class Exercise

Sing the following triads using solfège, letter names, or numbers.

1.

2.

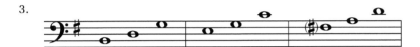

3.

4.

Workbook Exercises 14.12 and 14.14

Name _____

Exercise 14.1

Draw root position and inversions for the following triads. Label the inversion (root, first, second) below each triad. Your instructor may also ask you to provide chord symbols as shown below the first exercise.

1.

GM: _____   _____   _____
     G   G/B   G/D

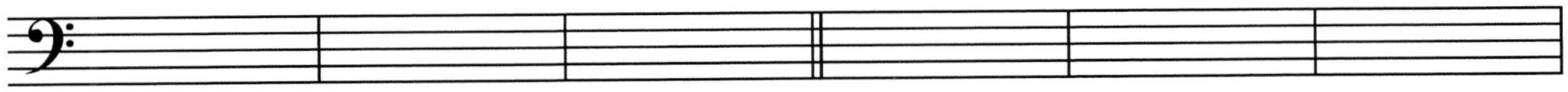

2.

Gm: _____   _____   _____

3.

AM: _____   _____   _____

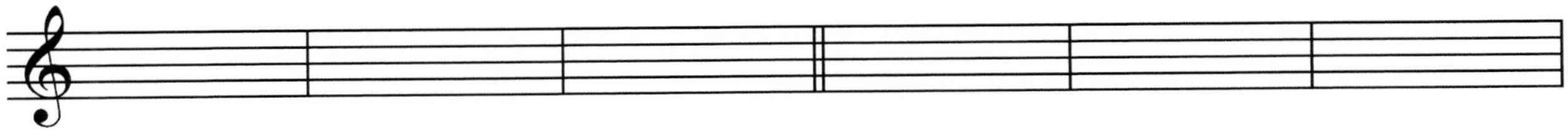

4.

Am: _____   _____   _____

5.

DbM: _____   _____   _____

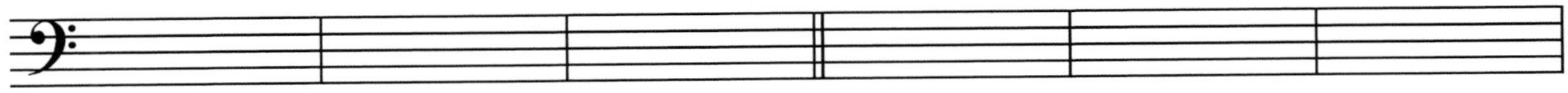

6.

Dbm: _____   _____   _____

7.

F°: _____   _____   _____

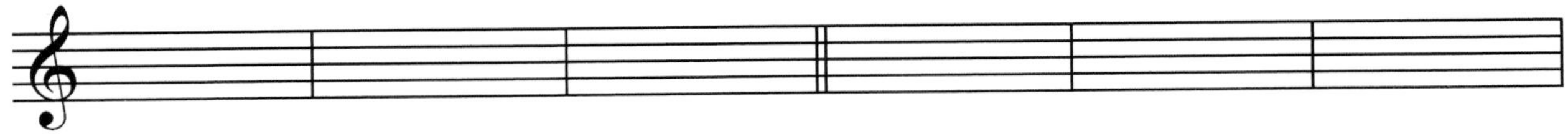

8.

F⁺: _____   _____   _____

Exercise 14.2

Identify the root (letter name) of the triad, quality (M, m, Aug, dim), and the inversion (root, first, second). Chord symbols may help to identify the inversion.

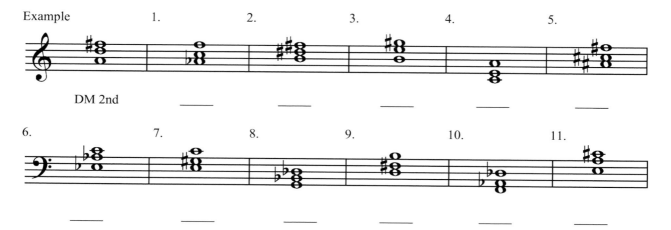

Example   1.   2.   3.   4.   5.

DM 2nd   _____   _____

6.   7.   8.   9.   10.   11.

Exercise 14.3

Draw triads using the letter names and inversion given below the staff.

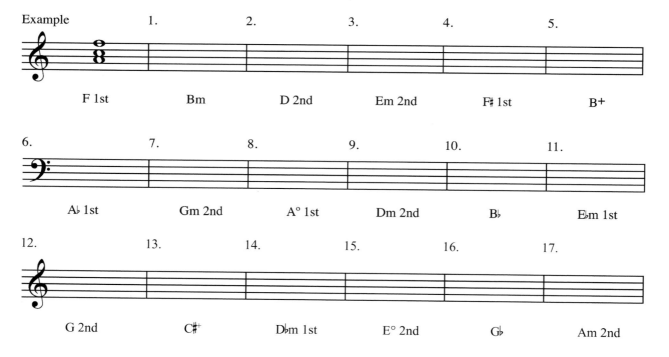

Example   1.   2.   3.   4.   5.

F 1st   Bm   D 2nd   Em 2nd   F♯ 1st   B+

6.   7.   8.   9.   10.   11.

A♭ 1st   Gm 2nd   A° 1st   Dm 2nd   B♭   E♭m 1st

12.   13.   14.   15.   16.   17.

G 2nd   C♯+   D♭m 1st   E° 2nd   G♭   Am 2nd

NAME: _____

Exercise 14.4

Harmonize the following melodies using the letter names given above the treble clef. The first measure has been done for you.

- Root position triads are indicated solely by letter name.
- A measure that is left blank continues with the harmony of the previous measure.
- Draw the bass staff triads directly under the corresponding treble staff notes.

1. "The Crime of Tom Dula" (A. Lomax, F. M. Warner), American folk song

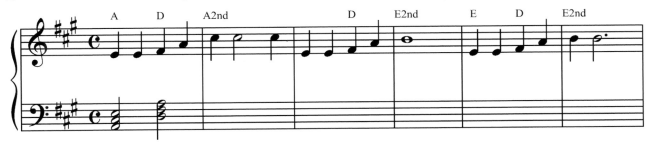

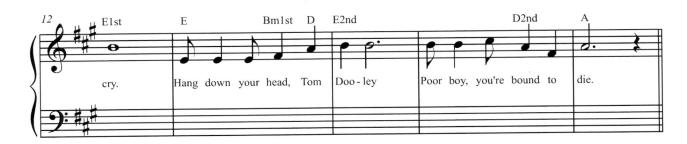

"THE CRIME OF TOM DULA"

This is a popular folk song thought to have been composed by Tom Dula (now called Tom Dooley) as he waited in prison to be hanged for stabbing a woman who rejected his love.

2. "Maria Elena" (L. Barcelata)

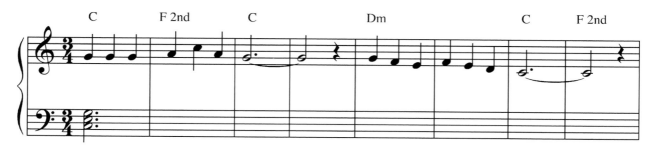

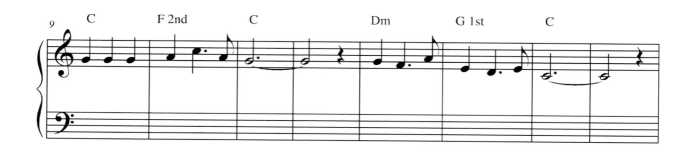

3. "Speak Softly, Love" (L. Kusik, N. Rota)

Exercise 14.5

Identify the root, quality, and inversion of each triad. Redraw the triad by moving the upper note down an octave. Redraw "broken" triads harmonically.

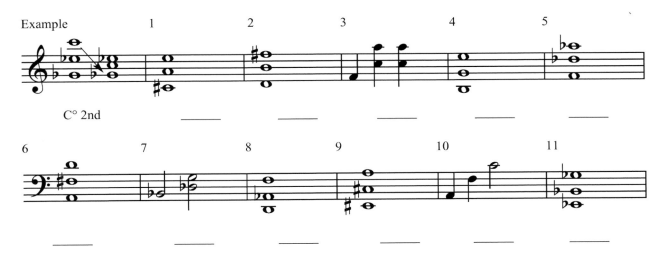

C° 2nd

Exercise 14.6

Identify the root, quality, and inversion for the underscored triads. The first one is done for you. Note:

- Although all triads have at least three notes, the first and last triads are missing the fifth note of the triad; these are called "incomplete" triads.
- Notes that are circled are non-harmonic tones and do not belong to the triad.

Soldiers' March, Op. 68, No. 2 (R. Schumann)

GM
Rt.

Exercise 14.7

Draw triads using the letter names and figured bass symbols given below the staff.

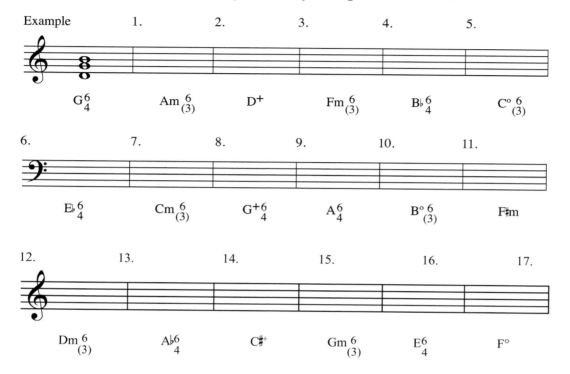

Example   1.   2.   3.   4.   5.

G$^6_4$ Am$^6_{(3)}$ D$^+$ Fm$^6_{(3)}$ B♭$^6_4$ C°$^6_{(3)}$

6.   7.   8.   9.   10.   11.

E♭$^6_4$ Cm$^6_{(3)}$ G$^{+6}_4$ A$^6_4$ B°$^6_{(3)}$ F♯m

12.   13.   14.   15.   16.   17.

Dm$^6_{(3)}$ A♭$^6_4$ C♯$^+$ Gm$^6_{(3)}$ E$^6_4$ F°

Exercise 14.8

Return to Exercise 14.2 on page 410 and label the inversions with figured bass symbols.

NAME: _____

Exercise 14.9

Harmonize the melody below using the letter names and figured bass symbols written above the melodic line.

- Root position triads are indicated solely by letter name. For this exercise, first inversion triads are indicated by a "6." Second inversion triads are labeled "6/4."
- Be sure to place the bass staff triads directly under the corresponding treble staff notes.
- Count and tap the rhythm of this piece, using the right hand for the treble staff and left hand for the bass staff.

"Mambo No. 5" (D. Pérez Prado)

Cultural note: Mambo

The **mambo** (or "*conversation with the gods*" in Yoruba, the language of the Cuban slaves from Africa) is a Cuban style of music and dance form. The Cuban band director and composer Dámasco Pérez Prado created the mambo dance steps in 1943, resulting in the mambo craze that swept New York City in the 1950s. The music was rhythmic with syncopations and full of energy.

Exercise 14.10

Identify the key. For the triads with underscores, write the letter name, quality, and inversion on the first line, followed by the corresponding roman numeral and appropriate figured bass symbol on the second line. (Notice: a duplicated triad note, either in unison or at the octave, will not affect the triad letter name, and circled pitches are non-harmonic tones that do not belong to the triad.) To assist with this analysis, draw the triads for the scale on your own staff paper as shown on pages 378 and 384.

1. "Freu dich sehr, o meine Seele" (J.S. Bach)

Letter name   GRt   __   __   __   __   __   __
Key: ____   I   __   __   __   __   __   __

2. "Wild Rider," Op. 68, No. 8 (R. Schumann)

Letter name: am   __ _____   __ __ __
Key: ____   i   __ __   __ __ __

416

NAME: _____

Exercise 14.11

Using tonic and dominant triads, complete the harmonization for "La Raspa," and label with roman numerals. Underscores indicate where the harmonies change. Play the harmonization yourself or ask another student or your instructor to play it for you. (The first measure is done for you. Notice that the harmonization is written in a common "dance style" or "oom-pah" accompaniment pattern: a low bass note followed by a triad, frequently in a higher octave.)

"La Raspa," Mexican hat dance

Key: B♭   I _____   _____   _____

Exercise 14.12

Harmonize Frederic Chopin's Mazurka, Op. 7, No. 1 in "dance style" (here, "oom-pah-pah") using the roman numerals and figured bass symbols given below the bass clef.

- Identify the key. Draw the primary triads for the key and label with roman numerals.
- Using the roman numerals and figured bass symbols given below the melody, harmonize the Mazurka, drawing the triads directly below the corresponding melody notes.
- To help maintain the dance character of this piece, experiment by placing triads in different octaves and inversions, and repeating triads on the third beat as shown in the first measure.
- Play the hamonization yourself or ask another student or your instructor to play it for you.

Mazurka, Op. 7, No. 1 (F. Chopin)

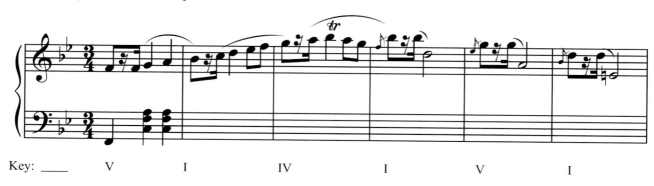

Key: ____   V   I   IV   I   V   I

V I^6_4 I   V   I   V   I

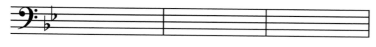

Key: _____   _I_   _____   _____

418

N A M E :

Exercise 14.13

Using roman numerals and figured bass symbols for the parallel keys (G major and G minor), draw the following chord progressions.

- Begin by drawing inversions for primary triads using the roman numerals and figured bass symbols written below the staves.
- For the final chord progression, draw the appropriate triads for the given roman numerals and figured bass symbols.
- Note the key signature at the beginning of each line. Accidentals should be added only in the minor key for the dominant triad; use the harmonic form of minor.

1.

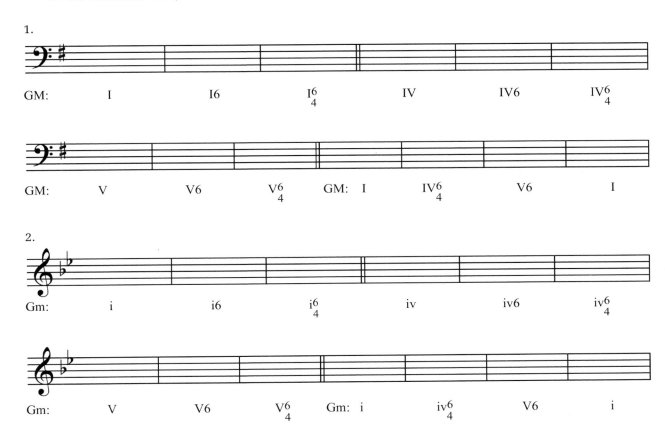

GM: I   I6   I$_4^6$ IV   IV6   IV$_4^6$

GM: V   V6   V$_4^6$ GM: I   IV$_4^6$ V6   I

2.

Gm: i   i6   i$_4^6$ iv   iv6   iv$_4^6$

Gm: V   V6   V$_4^6$ Gm: i   iv$_4^6$ V6   i

Exercise 14.14

Match the word with the definition.

1. Chord progression   _____   Interval numbers written below the bass staff indicating chord inversion

2. Close position   _____   Turning of a chord upside down

3. Figured bass symbols   _____   Distance from the lowest to the highest notes of a triad is an octave or less

4. First inversion   _____   Fifth of a chord is at the bottom

5. Harmonization   _____   Distance from the lowest to the highest notes of a triad is greater than an octave

6. Open position   _____   Series of chords

7. Root position   _____   Third of a chord is at the bottom

8. Second inversion   _____   Root of a chord is at the bottom

9. Triad inversion   _____   Chords accompanying a melody

MODULE 15

SEVENTH CHORDS

In Modules 11 and 13 we studied three-note chords called **triads** and used them to harmonize melodies, a defining feature of Western music called "tertian harmony," or harmonies built on the interval of the third. In addition to triads, composers have harmonized melodies using "tertian" chords made of four notes, and even five or more notes.

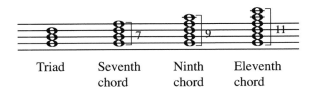

| Triad | Seventh chord | Ninth chord | Eleventh chord |

The four-note chord is called the **seventh chord**, named for the interval of the seventh created between the lowest and highest notes of the chord. Subsequent chords with more notes are named from the interval number between their root and highest notes.

Historical note: Seventh chords

Originally, composers used sevenths as added notes to a melody and its harmony—they were non-chord tones that created dissonances (intervals that required a resolution). By the eighteenth century, sevenths became an accepted part of a composer's harmonic vocabulary; eventually, they were used extensively by some composers (such as Claude Debussy) and in jazz and some popular music.

Exercise 1 Class Exercise

🔊 **TRACK 100**

Listening: "That's All" harmonized with seventh chords.

"That's All" (A. Brandt and B. Haymes)

Notice how "That's All" is harmonized with just one triad (C major) and many seventh chords. Listen to Track 100 or to your instructor perform the excerpt and pay attention to the sound of the chords created by the addition of a fourth note above the triads.

🔊 **TRACK 101**

Listening: "That's All" harmonized with triads.

Listen to Track 101 where only triads are used to harmonize the piece. Discuss the differences between the two performances: does one sound more "colorful?" More dissonant? More "interesting?"

Qualities of Seventh Chords

There are five qualities of seventh chords that can be created by drawing three notes above the pitches of a major scale or the three forms of a minor scale.

Note:

* In root position, the seventh chord consists of four notes, all consecutive thirds apart.
* The interval of the seventh is created between the root and the highest note.
* The **quality** of the seventh chord is determined by the quality of the triad (the lowest three notes) and the quality of the seventh (from the root to the highest note).

Following are the seventh chords for C as the root:

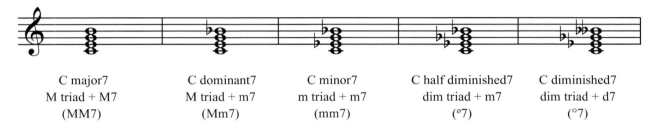

C major7	C dominant7	C minor7	C half diminished7	C diminished7
M triad + M7	M triad + m7	m triad + m7	dim triad + m7	dim triad + d7
(MM7)	(Mm7)	(mm7)	(ø7)	(°7)

We will discuss the seventh chord that is most commonly used in tonal music: the **dominant seventh**. (See Appendix 5 to learn more about the four other qualities of seventh chords.)

Dominant Seventh Chords

In Western tonal music the dominant seventh chord is the most frequently used seventh chord.
    Note:

* The dominant seventh, written V7, is constructed on the fifth scale degree of a scale—hence the name **dominant** seventh.

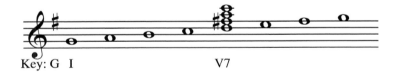

Key: G I   V7

* When the dominant seventh is identified by letter name, the letter name and a "7" are commonly used, for example, D7.

D7

* The dominant seventh chord consists of a major triad with the addition of a fourth note a minor seventh (m7) above the root. Jazz musicians might call this quality "Major-minor." For example:

D major triad with m7 above (Mm7)

423

Two Methods of Writing Dominant Seventh Chords

Method 1: Using the major key signature to draw a dominant seventh chord

Locate the dominant note of a major scale by counting up five notes from the tonic; construct the dominant seventh chord by drawing four notes above the dominant note. For example:

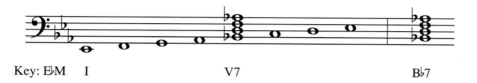

Key: E♭M   I   V7   B♭7

The key signature of E♭ major (B♭ E♭ A♭) provides the accidentals B♭ and A♭ in the dominant seventh chord.

Exercise 2

Draw dominant seventh chords using the major key signatures given below. Identify the key and letter name of the V7 chord.

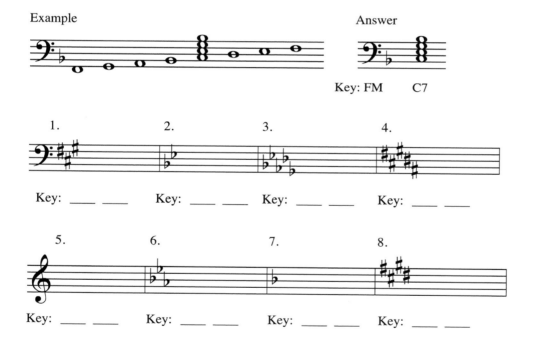

Example   Answer

Key: FM   C7

1.   2.   3.   4.

Key: ____ ____   Key: ____ ____   Key: ____ ____   Key: ____ ____

5.   6.   7.   8.

Key: ____ ____   Key: ____ ____   Key: ____ ____   Key: ____ ____

Theory Trainer

Exercise 15a Draw dominant sevenths with a major key signature.

Method 2: Using the size of intervals to construct a dominant seventh chord

• The dominant seventh chord consists of the following intervals:

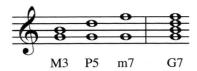

     M3   P5   m7   G7

• One may also draw a dominant seventh chord by adding a minor third (m3) above a major triad.

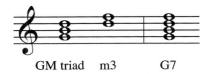

   GM triad   m3   G7

Exercise 3

Draw dominant seventh chords from the given root.

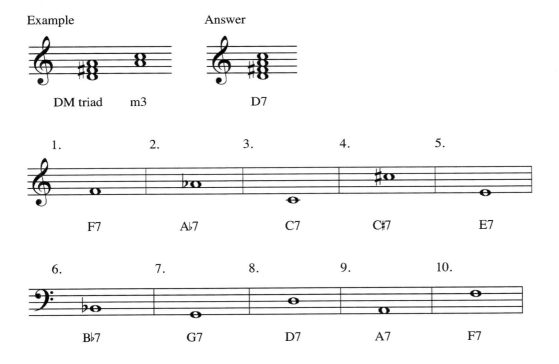

Note: One may also use the major key signature to assist in constructing a dominant seventh chord from a given root. To do this, **descend** a perfect fifth (P5) from the given chord root (the V) to the tonic (I) to determine the key signature. Apply the sharps or flats of the key signature to the chord.

Example   Answer

V   I   B7

Key: EM (sharps are F♯ C♯ G♯ D♯)

 **Theory Trainer**

Exercise 15c Draw dominant sevenths given a root.

Harmonizing Music in Major Keys Using Triads or Dominant Seventh Chords in Root Position

Exercise 4

Harmonize the following melodies with triads or dominant seventh chords using the given chord symbols or figured bass symbols.

1. "Surfin' U.S.A." (Chuck Berry)

D   A7   D   G/D   D7   G/D   D

2. Sonatina in C major, Op. 36, No. 1 (Second Movement) (M. Clementi)

F: I   IV $^6_4$ I   V7   I6   I   I$^6_4$ V

Workbook Exercises 15.1–15.3

Inversions of Dominant Seventh Chords

Dominant seventh chords, like triads, may be inverted.

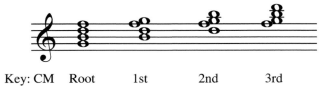

Key: CM   Root   1st   2nd   3rd

Notice:

- The seventh chord has four positions: root position and three inversions. (The triad, with only three notes, has three positions: root position and two inversions.)
- Unlike triad inversions, seventh chord inversions in close position will have an interval of a **second** at the top, the middle, or the bottom of the chord. It is this interval relationship of a major second in the inverted chords (the whole step between F and G), and the interval of the seventh in the root position chord, that provide the important dissonance which is essential and characteristic of a seventh chord.

In this example, the root is G, which is colored in. The interval of the second is circled. The root of the seventh chord (G) is the upper note of the second; you may use the interval of the second to identify the inversion and the root of the chord.

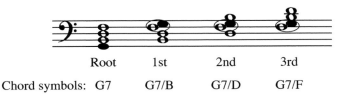

        Root   1st   2nd   3rd

Chord symbols: G7   G7/B   G7/D   G7/F

- In root position, notes are thirds apart.
- In first inversion, the interval of the second is at the top of the chord.
- In second inversion, the second is in the middle.
- In third inversion, the second is at the bottom.

Figured Bass Symbols for Seventh Chords

Following are the figured bass symbols of the dominant seventh chord and its inversions. Numbers are for all of the intervals ascending from the bass note.

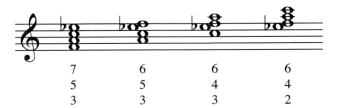

    7   6   6   6
    5   5   4   4
    3   3   3   2

As with figured bass symbols for triads, these symbols may be shortened; they will measure the interval of the bass note to the root and the bass note to the seventh of the chord. Memorize and use these numbers.

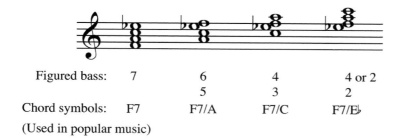

Figured bass:	7	6	4	4 or 2
		5	3	2
Chord symbols:	F7	F7/A	F7/C	F7/E♭

(Used in popular music)

(Note: Figured bass symbols are modified for minor keys; this subject is beyond the scope of this book.)

Exercise 5

Draw inversions for dominant seventh chords. Label the key and the figured bass symbols. Your instructor may also ask for the chord symbols (for example, F7).

Example   1.

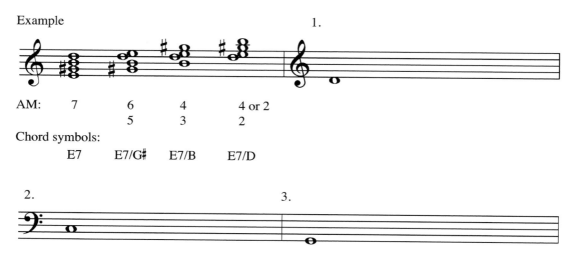

AM:	7	6	4	4 or 2
		5	3	2
Chord symbols:				
	E7	E7/G♯	E7/B	E7/D

2.   3.

Exercise 6

Identify the root and figured bass symbols for the following dominant seventh chords. Reminder: in an inversion, the root of the chord is the upper note of the interval of the second.

Example   1.   2.   3.   4.   5.

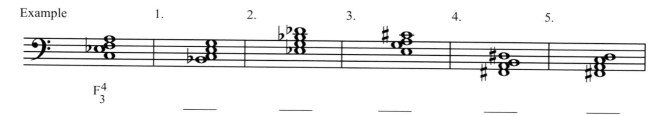

F$^4_3$

___   ___   ___   ___   ___

Theory Trainer

Exercise 15d Identify dominant seventh inversions.

Harmonizing Music in Major Keys Using Inverted Dominant Seventh Chords

Exercise 7

Harmonize the following melody with triads or dominant seventh chords using the given chord symbols or figured bass symbols.

"The Heavens Are Telling" (*The Creation*, originally in C) (F.J. Haydn)
(Note: The figured bass is derived from the composer's score.)

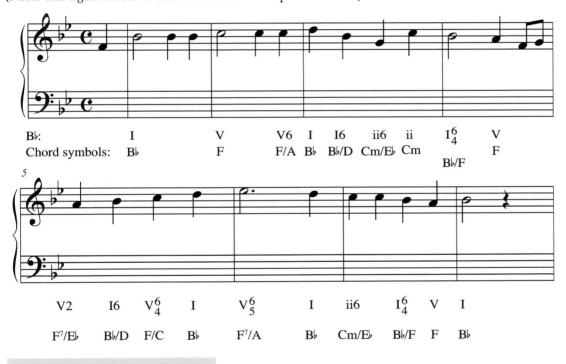

Chord Progressions Using Dominant Seventh Chords in Major Keys

Earlier, we discussed chord progressions using primary triads. A common chord progression using a dominant seventh chord is shown below.

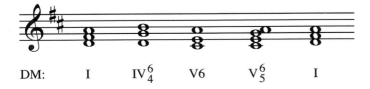

Workbook Exercises 15.4–15.8

429

Notice:

- The subdominant (IV) and dominant (V) are inverted to create a smooth voice leading between the chords.
- The V6/5 adds the seventh tone above the dominant to the triad. In the preceding chord progression, the added note is the G.
- Frequently the fifth of the dominant seventh chord may be omitted. Your instructor will play the following examples for you: listen for whether or not the chord is complete.

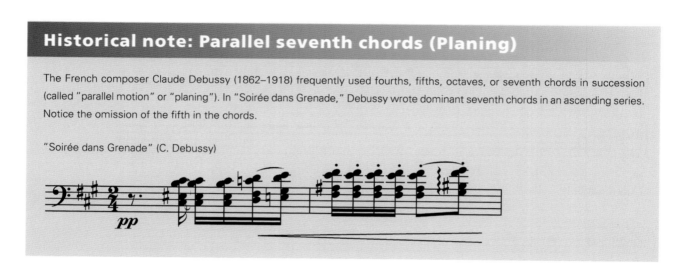

Historical note: Parallel seventh chords (Planing)

The French composer Claude Debussy (1862–1918) frequently used fourths, fifths, octaves, or seventh chords in succession (called "parallel motion" or "planing"). In "Soirée dans Grenade," Debussy wrote dominant seventh chords in an ascending series. Notice the omission of the fifth in the chords.

"Soirée dans Grenade" (C. Debussy)

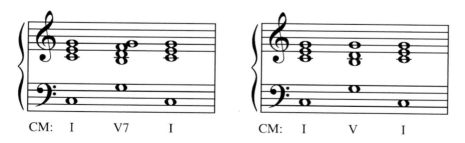

Exercise 8 Class Listening Exercise

Compare two similar chord progressions; the first one uses the dominant seventh chord while the second one uses a dominant triad. Your instructor will play the two progressions for the class. Notice the added tension in the V7 chord that does not exist in the dominant triad. Can you identify the notes that create this tension?

For example:

Your instructor will play a chord progression: tonic–dominant–tonic. Below, check whether the second chord is a triad or a seventh chord. The chords may be inverted.

I—V—I   I—V7—I

1. _____   _____
2. _____   _____
3. _____   _____
4. _____   _____
5. _____   _____

Exercise 9

Write the following chord progression in the given keys. Notice that the use of repeated notes between consecutive chords leads to a smoother chord progression; this is called "smooth voice leading."

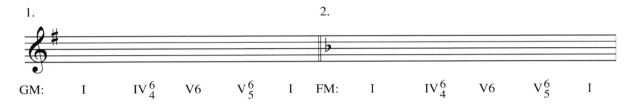

1.   2.

GM: I   IV$^6_4$ V6   V$^6_5$ I   FM: I   IV$^6_4$ V6   V$^6_5$ I

Workbook Exercises 15.9 and 15.10

Dominant Seventh Chords in Minor Keys

The **harmonic form** of the minor scale is used to construct the dominant seventh chord in minor keys.

- By raising the seventh note in the minor scale, the dominant triad becomes major.

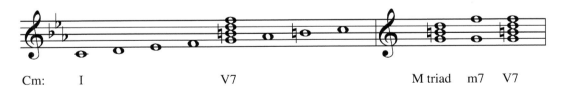

Cm: I   V7   M triad   m7   V7

- The dominant seventh chord is the same for parallel keys (keys that have the same tonic).

DM: V   V7 Dm: V   V7

431

The dominant seventh in D major has a C♯ because of the key signature. The dominant seventh in D minor has a C♯ because of the raised seventh used in the harmonic minor.

Exercise 10 Class Exercise

Write root position dominant seventh chords for the following minor keys. Name the key. The first has been done for you.

Key: Em B7   Key: __ __   Key: __ __   Key: __ __   Key: __ __   Key: __ __

 **Theory Trainer**

Exercise 15b Draw dominant sevenths with a minor key signature.

Exercise 11 Class Exercise

Using the harmonic form of F minor, harmonize the following melody. Listen to Track 102 of Chopin's original *Nocturne* where the melody is harmonized with a bass "dance style" pattern. (Refer to Exercise 14.11 on page 417 for the definition of "dance style.")

Nocturne in F Minor, Op. 55, No. 1 (F. Chopin)

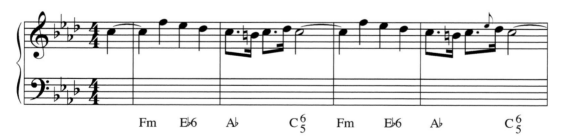

Fm   E♭6   A♭   C$^6_5$ Fm   E♭6   A♭   C$^6_5$

🔊 **TRACK 102**

Listening: Nocturne in F Minor, Op. 55, No. 1 (F. Chopin)

Workbook Exercises 15.11–15.14

Name _____

Exercise 15.1

Write root position dominant seventh chords in the following **major** keys. Identify the key. Label the letter name of the chord.

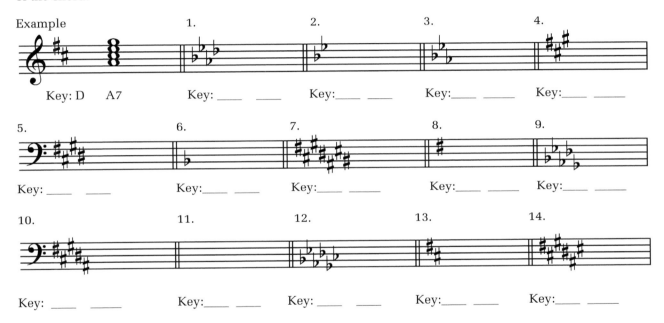

Example   1.   2.   3.   4.

Key: D   A7   Key: ____ ____   Key:____ ____   Key:____ ____   Key:____ ____

5.   6.   7.   8.   9.

Key: ____ ____   Key:____ ____   Key:____ ____   Key:____ ____   Key:____ ____

10.   11.   12.   13.   14.

Key: ____ ____   Key:____ ____   Key: ____ ____   Key:____ ____   Key:____ ____

Exercise 15.2

Write dominant seventh chords from the given root. Label the letter name of the chord.

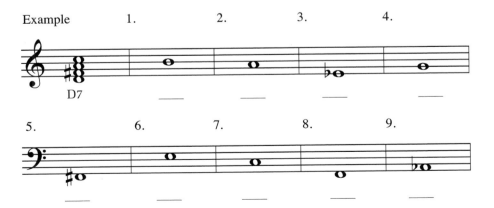

Example   1.   2.   3.   4.

D7   ____   ____   ____   ____

5.   6.   7.   8.   9.

____   ____   ____   ____   ____

Exercise 15.3

Harmonize the following melody with triads or dominant seventh chords using the figured bass symbols. Label the key.

"To Jerez We Will Go," Mexican folk song

Key: _____   I   V7   I   V7   I   IV$^6_4$

I   V6   V   V7   I

Exercise 15.4

Draw inversions for dominant seventh chords. Label the key and the figured bass symbols. Your instructor may also ask for the chord symbols (for example, F7).

1.

2.

Key: ___   ___   ___   ___   ___   Key: ____   ___   ___   ___   ___

Chord Symbol _____   ___   ___   ___   Chord Symbol ___   ___   ___   ___

3.

4.

Key: ___   ___   ___   ___   ___   Key: ____   ___   ___   ___   ___

Chord Symbol _____   ___   ___   ___   Chord Symbol ___   ___   ___   ___

Exercise 15.5

Write dominant seventh chords in the following **major** keys using the roman numerals and figured bass symbols given below each staff. Identify the key.

Exercise 15.6

Identify the root and figured bass for the following dominant seventh chords.

Exercise 15.7

Write dominant seventh chords using the chord symbols given below each staff.

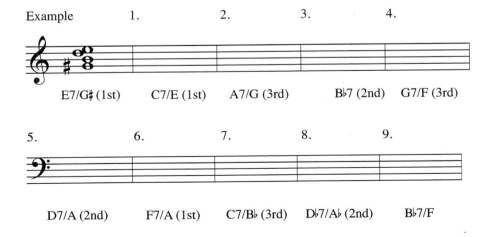

Exercise 15.8 | Class Exercise

The melody "That's All" has been harmonized below with C major triads and seven different seventh chords, some of which are dominant seventh chords. Circle the dominant seventh chords. Your instructor may play the triads and seventh chords to assist you or you can listen to Track 100.

"That's All" (A. Brandt, B. Haymes)

Exercise 15.9

Write the following chord progression in the given keys. Notice that the use of repeated notes between consecutive chords leads to a smoother chord progression.

1.   2.

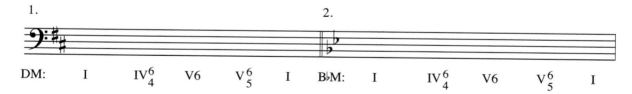

DM: I   IV$^6_4$ V6   V$^6_5$ I   B♭M: I   IV$^6_4$ V6   V$^6_5$ I

Exercise 15.10

Label the key and analyze the following piece by giving roman numerals and figured bass symbols for the underscored chords. The circled notes are non-harmonic tones.

1.   "German Dance" (L.v. Beethoven)

Key: ____   _____ (V_3^4) _____   _____

Exercise 15.11

Write root position dominant seventh chords in the following **minor** keys. Identify the key and letter name of the dominant seventh chord. The first one is done for you.

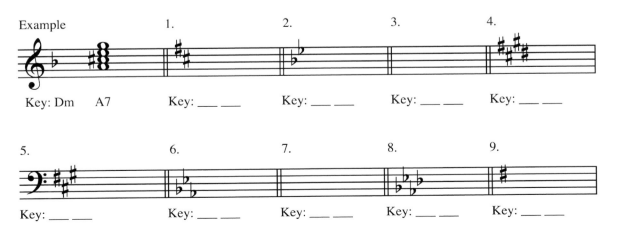

Key: Dm   A7   Key: ___ ___   Key: ___ ___   Key: ___ ___   Key: ___ ___

Key: ___ ___   Key: ___ ___   Key: ___ ___   Key: ___ ___   Key: ___ ___

Exercise 15.12

Using the given chord symbols, harmonize the following melody. (Note: use the harmonic minor scale.)

"Bethena" (S. Joplin)

Key: _____ 　　Bm 　　　Bm6 　　　F#$^4_3$ 　　　Bm6 　　　Bm 　　　Bm6 　　　G$^6_4$ 　　　F#$^6_4$

Exercise 15.13

Harmonize "Bésame Mucho," writing primary triads or dominant seventh chords on the bass staff below the melody. (Select triads or chords that incorporate the melody notes that are found on the main beats; harmonies change where indicated by underscores. Use root or inverted chords to facilitate smooth "voice leading." Refer to Exercise 9 on page 401.) On the underscores, write roman numeral and figured bass symbols. The first measure is done for you. Play the harmonization or ask another student or your instructor to play it for you.

"Bésame Mucho" (C. Velazquez)

Key: Dm 　　i 　　iv$^6_4$ _____ 　　　iv$^6_4$ 　　　_____ _____ _____ _____

Exercise 15.14

Match the word with the definition.

1. Dominant seventh chord _____ Chord consisting of four notes, named for the interval created by the lowest and highest notes

2. Figured bass _____ Chord consisting of three notes

3. Harmonization _____ Harmonies using triads; harmonies based on the interval of a third

4. Planing _____ Seventh chord based on the fifth note of a scale

5. Seventh chord _____ Interval numbers written below the bass staff used to indicate the inversion of chords

6. Triad _____ Seventh chords used in parallel motion

7. Tertian harmony _____ Chords accompanying a melody

438

MODULE 16

FORM IN MUSIC

In previous modules, we studied the basic components of music: melody (pitch), rhythm (meter), and harmony. These aspects of music give one the tools to study and create music, just as understanding grammatical rules gives one the tools to write sentences. In this module we will discuss how to use this knowledge to understand a musical composition or to create one of your own.

Phrase Structure: Antecedent, Consequent

Musical lines or melodies are often compared to sentences. Just as a sentence may divide into clauses, a musical line may divide into **antecedent** and **consequent phrases**. A **phrase** may be defined as a "musical sentence." Just as a comma or a semicolon is used in a sentence to separate clauses, or a period is used at the end of a sentence, **cadences** are used in music to mark or delineate phrases. (Cadences will be discussed later in the module.)

For example, in the Trio of Mozart's "Menuette," we hear the melody divide into two four-measure phrases.

Trio from Menuette (W.A. Mozart)

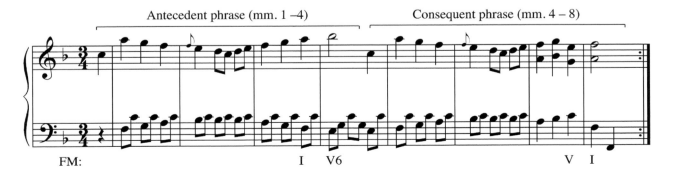

Listen to the Mozart excerpt, noticing that:

- Beginning with an anacrusis ("pick-up") note and ending in measure 4, the first phrase is an **antecedent phrase**. Although the phrase ends on a longer note value (a half note), it has an unfinished or incomplete quality to it because it does not end on a note of the tonic triad.
- Beginning on the third beat of measure 4 until measure 8, the second phrase is a **consequent phrase**. It is almost identical to the first phrase; however, it ends on an F tonic note in both the bass and the melody. This gives the phrase a feeling of completion.
- The two phrases together form a **period**. When two phrases begin identically as in this song, they form a **parallel period**.

Musical note: Phrase structure

PHRASE

A "musical sentence" usually 4–8 measures long that is concluded by a cadence (to be discussed beginning on page 441).

ANTECEDENT PHRASE

The "question," with an ending that sounds momentary. The antecedent phrase usually does not end on the tonic note.

CONSEQUENT PHRASE

The "answer," with an ending that sounds final. The consequent phrase usually ends on the tonic note.

PERIOD

Two phrases, the antecedent followed immediately by the consequent. The phrases may be **parallel** (phrases begin alike) or **contrasting** (phrases begin differently).

Exercise 1 Class Exercise

Sing the following melodies.

- The combination of lyrics and music contributes to the phrase structure of a melody; begin by looking for repetition and contrast in the lyrics and the melody. Say the words aloud and then sing the words with the melody.
- Each of the melodies divides into two phrases. Identify the phrases and then label them "antecedent" or "consequent."
- The two phrases form a period. Name the type of period: parallel or contrasting.

1. "Georgia on My Mind" (words by S. Gorrell, music by H. Carmichael)

2. "Cielito Lindo" (Q. Mendoza y Cortés)

Cadences: Authentic, Half, Plagal, Deceptive

Phrase endings, called **cadences**, are identified by the last two different kinds of chords that are used to harmonize the final notes of a phrase. If we compare cadences in music to the punctuation marks that are used in sentences, cadences may correspond to commas, periods, question marks, or exclamation marks. We will study four cadences: the authentic, half, plagal, and deceptive cadence.

Authentic Cadence

When the last two chords of a phrase are V–I, the result is an **authentic cadence**. This gives a conclusive ending to a phrase, much like a period marks the end of a sentence. The consequent phrase of a musical period frequently ends with an authentic cadence. Listen to your instructor play the following authentic cadences.

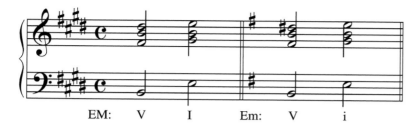

EM: V   I   Em: V   i

Notice:

- In a major key, the authentic cadence is V–I.
- In a minor key, the authentic cadence is V–i. In E minor the raised seventh from the harmonic minor creates the leading tone, D♯, and the dominant triad becomes a major triad.

🔊 **TRACK 103**

Listening: Piano Sonata in F Major, K.332 (Third Movement, excerpt) (W.A. Mozart)

Exercise 2 Class Exercise

Listen to Track 103 or your instructor play the following Mozart example; listen to the alternating dominant seventh and tonic chords.

Sonata in F Major, K.332 (Third Movement) (W.A. Mozart)

Notice that:

- This melody forms a period; the first phrase is an antecedent phrase and the second is the consequent phrase.
- Not every V–I (or V7–I) chord progression forms an authentic cadence; only the last two chords at the end of a phrase establish a cadence.
- Both phrases end with an authentic cadence, but the final melodic notes are different. The first phrase ends on the dominant (C), while the second phrase ends on the tonic (F), giving the final cadence a feeling of completion or finality. Listen to the example again to hear the difference.
    fp dynamic marking meaning *loud, then immediately soft*.
- The circled notes are non-harmonic tones; they do not belong to the tonic triad or the dominant seventh chord.

🔊 **TRACK 104**

Listening: Moment Musical, Op. 94, No. 3 (F. Schubert)

Exercise 3

Listen to Track 104 or to your instructor play the Schubert example. Notice that the two phrases (mm. 1–8 and mm. 9–16) are in different keys, one major and one minor. Both end with authentic cadences. On the underscores below, label the key, roman numerals, and cadence.

Moment Musical, Op. 94, No. 3 (F. Schubert)

Key: _____   _____   _____

Cadence: _____

Key: _____   _____   _____

Cadence: _____

443

 Theory Trainer

Exercise 16a Cadence drawing: authentic cadence.

Half Cadence

In a **half cadence**, a phrase ends with a dominant chord, which is usually preceded by the tonic, the supertonic, or the subdominant chord.

Listen to your instructor play the following half cadences.

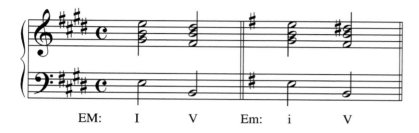

EM: I   V   Em: i   V

As the name implies, the half cadence sounds incomplete.

🔊)) **TRACK 105**

Listening: Variations on Paisiello's "Nel Cor Più Non Mi Sento" (L.v. Beethoven)

Exercise 4 Class Exercise

Listen to Track 105 or your instructor play the beginning of Beethoven's Variations on "Nel cor più non mi sento."

Six Variations on Paisiello's "Nel Cor Più Non Mi Sento" (L.v. Beethoven)

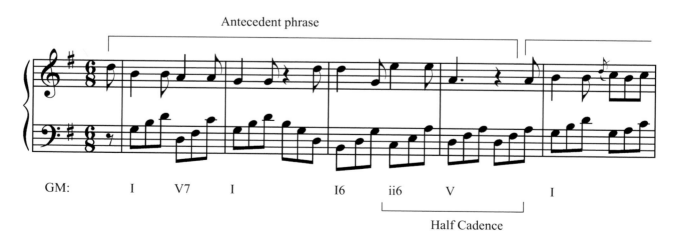

GM: I   V7   I   I6   ii6   V   I

Half Cadence

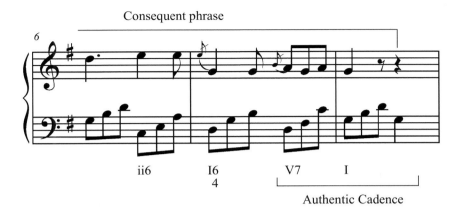

Consequent phrase

ii6   I6   V7   I
       4
Authentic Cadence

Notice that:

- This melody consists of two dissimilar phrases that form a **contrasting period**.
- The first phrase ends with a **half cadence** (ii V), creating the antecedent phrase. This phrase sounds inconclusive; if you play only the antecedent phrase, it will sound incomplete.
- The second phrase ends with an **authentic cadence** (V I), creating the consequent phrase. Because the last chord is the tonic triad with the tonic G in the melody and the bass, the phrase sounds complete, or final.

🔊 **TRACK 106**

Listening: Rondo (W.A. Mozart)

Exercise 5 | Class Exercise

Listen to Track 106 or to your instructor play Mozart's "Rondo." This melody is another example of a period; is it parallel or contrasting? Identify the cadences below the underscored notes: are they authentic or half cadences?

- Label the key at the beginning of the piece.
- Write the letter name and roman numeral of the underscored notes. The last triad is not complete.

Notice:

- The grand staff consists of two treble clefs until the last measure.
- The circled notes are non-harmonic tones.

Rondo (W.A. Mozart)

Key: _____

Cadence: _____

Cadence: _____

@ **Theory Trainer**

Exercise 16a Cadence drawing: authentic and half cadences.

Plagal Cadence

Plagal cadences are used less frequently as final cadences in a piece or a large section of music. The final chord is the tonic preceded by the subdominant (IV–I). This is sometimes called the "Amen" cadence because of its use at the end of hymns. Listen to your instructor play the following plagal cadences.

Notice:

*   In a major key, the plagal cadence is IV–I; both chords are major.
*   In a minor key, the plagal cadence is iv–i; both chords are minor.

🔊 **TRACK 107**

Listening: "Good King Wenceslas," traditional hymn

Exercise 6 | Class Exercise

The ending of the hymn "Good King Wenceslas" is given below. Listen to Track 107 or your instructor play the excerpt, paying attention to the plagal cadence at the end of the phrase.

"Good King Wenceslas," traditional hymn

@ **Theory Trainer**

Exercise 16a Cadence drawing: authentic, half and plagal cadences.

Deceptive Cadence

In a **deceptive cadence**, the dominant chord resolves to an unexpected chord, rather than the tonic. In the second example (a deceptive cadence), the dominant (V) resolves to the submediant (vi or VI), the most common resolution.

Listen to your instructor play the following authentic and deceptive cadences.

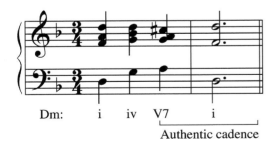

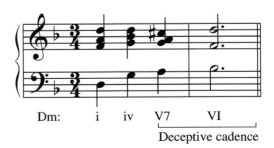

Notice that:

- In the above examples, the last triads in both cadences share two notes; only the bass clef note (the root of the triad) is different. This is because the tonic and submediant triads have two notes in common.
- In a major key, the deceptive cadence is V–vi (the submediant is minor).
- In a minor key, the deceptive cadence is V–VI (the submediant is major).

🔊 **TRACK 108**

Listening: Two Part Invention in D minor, BWV 775 (J.S. Bach)

Exercise 7 Class Exercise

Listen to Track 108 or your instructor play Bach's "Two Part Invention" in D minor. Notice:

• The first cadence is a deceptive cadence (V–VI); the second cadence is an authentic cadence (V–i). Listen to the "deceptive" quality in the first cadence, and the conclusive sound of the final cadence.

Two Part Invention in D minor, BWV 775 (J.S. Bach)

Workbook Exercises 16.1 and 16.2

 Theory Trainer

Exercise 16a Cadence drawing: all cadences.

Forms

Form is the organizing structure of a piece, which is determined by musical elements such as melody, harmony, rhythm (meter), and character (mood). We will discuss four forms: binary, ternary, the 32-bar form, and 12-bar blues. These forms divide into sections, each of which will each be given identifying letter names like "A" and "B."

Binary Form: Two-part Form

Binary form consists of two sections of similar lengths which repeat.

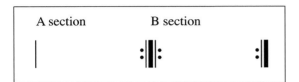

The melodic material in the B section may be similar to that of the A section, but the key in the B section may change to a related key, such as the dominant. For a piece in a minor key, the B section may change to the relative major. This key change, called a modulation, occurs without a change in key signature. The composition will return to the tonic key before the end of the piece.

🔊)) **TRACK 109**

Listening: Minuet in C, K.6 (W.A. Mozart)

Exercise 8 **Class Exercise**

Listen to Track 109 or your instructor play "Minuet in C" (W.A. Mozart)

Minuet in C, K.6 (W.A. Mozart)

A section

B section

Notice that:

- The Minuet has double bars and repeat signs that separate the two sections.
- The A section begins in C major and modulates to the dominant (G). The C♯ and D♯ in mm. 2, 4, and 6 embellish the melody, while the F♯ in mm. 5, 7, and 8 indicates a modulation to G major.
- The B section uses identical melodic and rhythmic material as the A section, but begins in G major and returns to C major before the end of the piece.

Ternary Form: Three-part Form

Ternary form is a three-part form (ABA) where the A and B sections are contrasting in key and frequently in mood or character. A change in the key signature may accompany the change in key.

 **TRACK 110**

Listening: "Wild Rider" (R. Schumann)

Exercise 9 Class Exercise

Listen to Track 110 or your instructor play "Wild Rider" by Schumann. Notice:

- This piece is in ternary form. How does the B section differ from the A section; in what ways are the sections the same?

"Wild Rider" (R. Schumann)

32-Bar Form (AABA)

The **32-bar form**, so-called because of the number of measures (bars) in the song, is an AABA pattern. It is one of the most common forms used for songs, including popular, folk, and rock. In its simplest form, it consists of four eight-measure segments. The first A section ends on the tonic and repeats. The B section, which is sometimes called the bridge in pop songs, may be contrasting in key and mood; it ends with a half cadence, which leads back to the final A section.

Exercise 10 Class Exercise

Sing "Over the Rainbow" by Harold Arlen.

"Over the Rainbow" (H. Arlen)

Notice that:

• Each section is eight measures long.

A Section	Mm. 1–8
A Section	Mm. 9–16
B Section	Mm. 17–24
A Section	Mm. 25–32

- The repetition of the lyrics and the melodic line contributes to the division of the song into the sections A A B A. Consider how the octave leap at the beginning of each A section also helps one to identify the section.
- In m. 16 just prior to the B section, the time signature changes to 5/4. Discuss how this change may affect the form of this song.

Workbook Exercise 16.3

12-Bar Blues

The **12-bar blues** is a chord progression used not only in many blues songs (for which it is named) but is also the harmonic basis of many popular songs. In its simplest form, it uses the primary triads in a key (I IV V). Following is a common blues progression.

12 bar blues progression in 4/4:			
I	I	I	I
IV	IV	I	I
V	IV	I	I

🔊 **TRACK 111—CLASS EXERCISE**

Listen to the 12-bar blues progression on Track 111 or to blues performers such as Muddy Waters and Bessie Smith. With your instructor's assistance, follow the chord changes by singing along with the bass.

Cultural note: The blues

The blues emerged out of the African–American musical tradition, which included spirituals, "call and response" and field songs, and ballads. Many were slow, melancholy songs expressing feelings about loss, oppression, or troubled lives.

Exercise 11

Read the lyrics out loud, then sing "St. Louis Blues" by William Handy. Listen for the chord changes; the roman numerals are given for the first line. Complete the roman numeral analysis for the remainder of the piece; sing the piece once more, adding triads on the piano or another instrument.

Notice:

- The lyrics for lines 1 and 2 are identical; the last syllable of lines 1 and 3 rhyme.
- This song uses a modified 12-bar blues progression; the second triad in the first and last lines is the modified triad.

12 bar blues progression in 4/4:

I	IV	I	I
IV	IV	I	I
V	V	I	I

"St. Louis Blues" (W. Handy)

I hate to see ___ the eve-ning sun go down, _____

I hate to see the eve-ning sun go down _____

'Cause my wo-man ___ she has left this town. _____

Repeat Signs

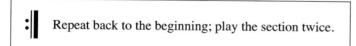

Repeat back to the beginning; play the section twice.

Exercise 12 Class Exercise

Sing the following songs, observing the repeat signs.

1. "O Tannenbaum," German traditional melody

2. "Ma Gazelle," Algerian folk song

Cultural note: Moorish scale

Sing the **Moorish scale** that is used in the above song. Notice that there are three half steps and an augmented second (A2). Indicate these intervals in the scale below.

𝄆 : 𝄇　Repeat the section between the two signs (play this section twice.)

Exercise 13 Class Exercise

Listen to "Pastorale" by J. Burgmüller; repeat the measures between the two repeat signs.

🔊 **TRACK 112**

Listening: "Pastorale," Op. 100, No. 3 (J. Burgmüller)

• Play mm. 1–10, then 3–10.

"Pastorale," Op. 100, No. 3 (J. Burgmüller)

First Ending, Second Ending

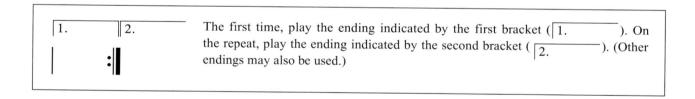

The first time, play the ending indicated by the first bracket (⌐1.————⌐). On the repeat, play the ending indicated by the second bracket (⌐2.————⌐). (Other endings may also be used.)

Exercise 14 Class Exercise

🔊 **TRACK 113**

Listening: "To a Wild Rose" (E. MacDowell)

Listen to Track 113 or your instructor play MacDowell's "To a Wild Rose."

• Play measures 1–3, followed by the first ending. The repeat sign at the end of m. 8 instructs one to return to the beginning. Repeat mm. 1–3, skip the first ending and finish with the second ending. (Play measures 1–8, 1–3, 9–13.)

"To a Wild Rose" (E. MacDowell)

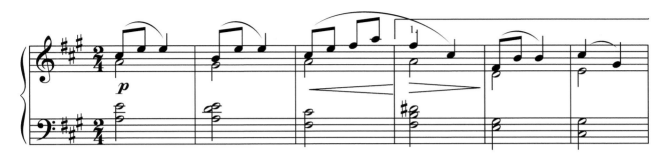

Da Capo al Fine

D.C. al Fine	*D.C. (Da Capo)*: Italian meaning "to the head"; return to the beginning.
	Fine: Italian meaning "the end." Pronounced "Fee-nay."
	Play from the beginning to the measure marked "D.C. al Fine." Return to the beginning and end at the measure marked "Fine."

Exercise 15 Class Exercise

◀))) **TRACK 114**

> *Listening: "Amor, Amor, Amor" (G. Ruiz)*

Listen to Track 114 or your instructor play "Amor, Amor, Amor" by Gabriel Ruiz, following the "D.C." and "Fine" signs.

- Play from the beginning to m. 24 (marked "D.C. al Fine"). Return to the beginning and end at m. 16 where the "Fine" is written. (Play A, mm. 1–24, A, 1–16.)

"Amor, Amor, Amor" (G. Ruiz)

Dal Segno al Fine

D.S. al Fine   D.S. (*Dal Segno*): Italian meaning "to the sign."

Play from the beginning to the measure marked "D.S. al Fine." Return to the sign (𝄋) and repeat, ending at "Fine."

Only a portion in the middle of the piece is repeated.

Exercise 16 Class Exercise

🔊 **TRACK 115**

Listening: "Qing Hai Ming Ge," Chinese folk song

Listen to Track 115 or your instructor play "Qing Hai Ming Ge," a Chinese folk song from Qing Hai province.

• Play from the beginning to m. 12 (marked "D.S. al Fine.") Return to the sign in m. 5 and end at Fine (m. 8). (Play mm. 1–12, 5–8.)

"Qing Hai Ming Ge," a Chinese folk song

Coda

Coda	An Italian word meaning "tail"; an "extended ending," a section at the end of a piece.
D.C. al Coda	Play from the beginning until the measure marked "D.C." Return to the beginning and play until the words "To Coda." Continue at the coda (⊕) to complete the song.
D.S. al Coda	Play from the beginning until the measure marked "D.S." Return to the sign (𝄋) and play until the words "To Coda." Continue at the coda ⊕ to complete the song.

Workbook Exercises 16.4 and 16.5

Exercise 17

Match the word with the definition.

1. Antecedent phrase   _____ Return to the sign (𝄋) and end at "Fine"

2. Authentic cadence   _____ AABA; commonly used for songs

3. Binary form   _____ Italian. "tail": an extended ending

4. Cadence   _____ Return to the beginning and end at "Fine"

5. Coda   _____ Two phrases; may be parallel or contrasting

6. Consequent phrase   _____ Short musical idea consisting of a particular rhythm and/or intervals

7. Contrasting period   _____ Three-part form: ABA

8. Deceptive cadence   _____ Phrase ending with IV–I (or iv–i)

9. D.C. al Fine   _____ Musical sentence ending with a cadence

10. D.S. al Fine   _____ Form used for blues songs and many popular songs

11. Form in music   _____ First section of a period ending with the dominant; the "question"

12. Half cadence   _____ Two-part form: AB

13. Motive   _____ Phrase ending with I–V (or i–V)

14. Period   _____ Organizing structure of music, determined by musical elements such as melody, harmony, rhythm, character (mood)

15. Plagal cadence   _____ Period where the phrases begin differently

16. Phrase   _____ Multiple endings

17. Ternary form   _____ Phrase ending with V–I (or V–i)

18. 12-bar blues   _____ Second section of a period usually ending on the tonic; the "answer"

19. 32-bar form   _____ Ending point at the end of a phrase identified by the last two chords used to harmonize the final notes

20. [1.] [2.]   _____ Phrase ending with V–VI (or V–vi)

Workbook Exercises 16.6 and 16.7

Name _____

Exercise 16.1

Write the roman numerals below each triad. Then identify the cadence: Authentic, Half, Plagal, or Deceptive. The first one is given.

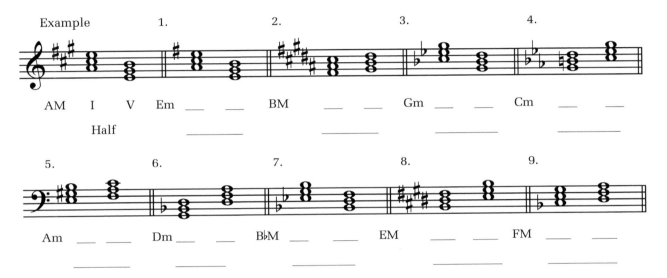

Example   1.   2.   3.   4.

AM   I   V   Em ___ ___   BM ___ ___   Gm ___ ___   Cm ___ ___

Half   _____   _____   _____   _____

5.   6.   7.   8.   9.

Am ___ ___   Dm ___ ___   BbM ___ ___   EM ___ ___   FM ___ ___

_____   _____   _____   _____   _____

Exercise 16.2

Draw the following cadences using root position triads. Label the roman numerals below each triad.

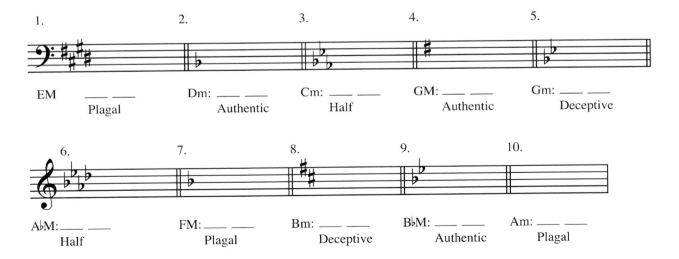

1.   2.   3.   4.   5.

EM ___ ___   Dm: ___ ___   Cm: ___ ___   GM: ___ ___   Gm: ___ ___

Plagal   Authentic   Half   Authentic   Deceptive

6.   7.   8.   9.   10.

AbM: ___ ___   FM: ___ ___   Bm: ___ ___   BbM: ___ ___   Am: ___ ___

Half   Plagal   Deceptive   Authentic   Plagal

Exercise 16.3

Identify the form of the following pieces: binary, ternary, 32-bar form. In the music, write letter names (A or B) for the major sections.

1.   "Till There Was You" (M. Wilson)

Form: _____

There were bells   on the hill,   but I   nev-er heard them ring-ing,   no I   nev-er heard them at

all till there was   you. _____   There were birds   in the   sky,   but I   nev-er saw them wing-ing, no I

nev-er saw them at   all 'till there was   you.   And there was   mus-ic   and   there were won-der-ful

ros-es,   they   tell me,   in   sweet   fra-grant mea-dows   of   dawn   and   dew.   There were

birds   in the   sky,   but I   nev-er saw them wing-ing,   no I   nev-er saw them at   all 'till there was   you.

🔊 **TRACK 116**

Listening: "Till There Was You" (M. Wilson)

462

NAME: _____

2. Waltz in A♭ (F. Schubert)

    Form: _____

Identify the cadence at the end of each section.

Cadence: _____

Cadence: _____

🔊 **TRACK 117**

Listening: Waltz in A♭ (F. Schubert)

3. Ecossaise ("Scottish") (L.v. Beethoven)

    Form: _____

Identify the cadence at the end of each section.

Cadence: _____

Cadence: _____

Cadence: _____

🔊 **TRACK 118**

Listening: Ecossaise (L.v. Beethoven)

Exercise 16.4 | Repeat Signs

1. Playera, Op. 5, No. 5 (E. Granados)

Describe or give measure numbers to explain how the music repeats.

_____

_____

2. "All Through the Night," Welsh folk song

What does "D.C." mean in Italian? _____

What does "Fine" mean? _____ Describe or give measure numbers to explain how the music repeats.

_____

_____

3. "Gui Zhou Shan Ge" (Zhen Ya), Chinese folk song

What does "D.S." mean in Italian? _____

Describe or give measure numbers to explain how the music repeats. _____

_____

NAME: _____

Exercise 16.5 | Class Exercise

Improvise a melody to a 12-bar blues progression in C major; perform this for the class.

There are only three rules:

- Play notes of the scales that have been notated.
- Always maintain a steady beat. (If a "wrong" note is played, do not stop.)
- For the bass, play the 12-bar blues progression. (You may also use Track #111.)

> The **12-bar blues** pattern may use just the primary triads of the scale: I, IV, V. The melody may use a variety of blues scales including the five-note (pentatonic) scale, the six-note (hexatonic) scale, or ten-note chromatic scale.

1. Notate the triads using a C major blues progression. The first measure is done for you.

Key: CM   I   I   I   I

IV   IV   I   I

V   IV   I   I

2. Using the blues scale patterns shown in the box below, notate the blues scale of your choice (or the instructor's) on the staff below for the tonic, subdominant, and dominant keys.

Blues scale on tonic: C

Blues scale on subdominant: F

Blues scale on dominant: G

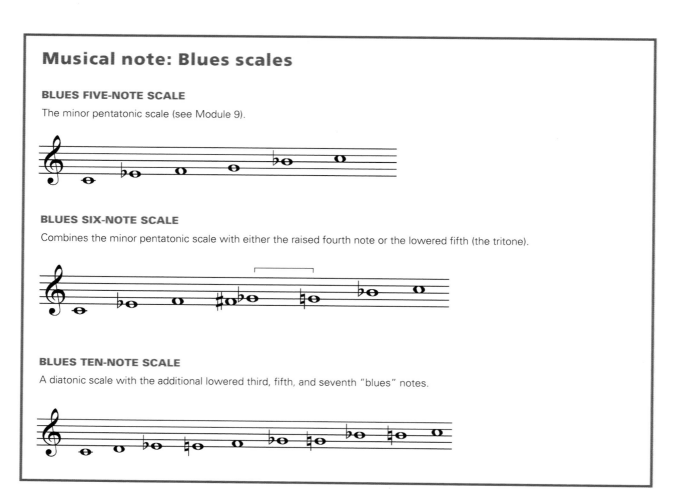

Musical note: Blues scales

BLUES FIVE-NOTE SCALE

The minor pentatonic scale (see Module 9).

BLUES SIX-NOTE SCALE

Combines the minor pentatonic scale with either the raised fourth note or the lowered fifth (the tritone).

BLUES TEN-NOTE SCALE

A diatonic scale with the additional lowered third, fifth, and seventh "blues" notes.

Exercise 16.6

Analyze the pieces in Appendices 8–11 on the website. Discuss how cadences, phrase structure, the melodic line, and underlying harmony contribute to the form of the piece.

Exercise 16.7

Using your knowledge of keys, scales, rhythm, and phrase structure, compose your own melodies in binary, ternary, 32-bar, and 12-bar blues forms. Lyrics may be added to the 32-bar song or 12-bar blues. (Some composers prefer to write the lyrics first, and compose a melody to accompany the words.) Harmonize your melodies using your knowledge of triads and seventh chords. Share your compositions with the class.

APPENDIX 1 **MUSICAL TERMS**

12-bar blues   A musical genre of African-American origin based on blues scales, with chord progressions 12 measures long.

32-bar form   A song form (AABA) consisting of 32 measures divided into four 8-measure sections, with a repeating A section and a contrasting B section.

Accent   A sign (>) placed above or below a note head indicating to play that note louder than surrounding notes.

Accidental   A sign used to alter a pitch. There are five accidentals: sharp, flat, natural, double sharp, and double flat.

Adagio   Italian. "At ease"; a slow tempo marking.

Alla breve   Italian. The time signature ¢ or 2/2 time; simple duple meter with the half note as the pulse note.

Allegro   Italian. Fast tempo indication.

Alto clef (see C clef)   The sign (𝄡) indicating that the middle line (line 3) is middle C.

Anacrusis   Note or notes of an incomplete measure at the beginning of a piece of music (also called "pick-up"). (See **Upbeat**.)

Andante   Italian. "Moving along"; a walking tempo.

Antecedent phrase   The first section of a period which ends on the dominant (a half cadence), an inconclusive ending.

Articulation   An indication of how smoothly or detached notes are to be played. Symbols or words may be used; for example, *staccato* (detached) and *legato* (connected).

Augmented interval   The perfect interval or major interval increased by a half step. For example, a perfect fourth (P4) is C–F; an augmented fourth (A4) is C–F♯.

Authentic cadence   A resting or ending of a section of music with the last two chords consisting of a dominant (V) to a tonic (I). Occasionally, the leading tone chord (vii°) may be used as a substitute chord instead of the dominant.

Bar line   A vertical line through the horizontal lines of a staff or staves separating music into measures.

Bass clef (F clef)   The sign (𝄢) indicating that the fourth line from the bottom is the F below middle C.

Beam   A horizontal line connecting the end of note stems of rhythmic values smaller than a quarter note; replaces the flag on individual notes.

Beat   The steady pulse of music.

Binary form   A two-part form (AB) with each section repeated, and the B section in a contrasting but related key.

C clef   Movable clefs that designate the line to represent middle C. (See **Alto clef** and **Tenor clef**.)

Cadence   The ending point of a phrase or section of music.

Changing meter (also Polymeter or Complex meter)   Meters that change within a piece of music. For example, when the beginning time signature is 3/4 and changes to 3/8 and then to 4/8.

Chord   Three or more pitches that sound simultaneously. (See **Seventh chord** and **Triad**.)

Chord progression   A series of adjacent chords.

Chromatic half step   A half step using the same letter names, but with different accidentals; for example, A (natural)–A♯ or B♭–B (natural).

Chromatic scale   A scale consisting only of half steps.

Circle of Fifths   Shows the 15 major and 15 minor keys with their increasing number of sharps or flats. The keys move by perfect fifths (the major keys moving from CM and the minor keys moving from Am) with the sharp keys clockwise to the right, and the flat keys counter clockwise to the left.

Clef   A sign placed at the beginning of a staff that names particular pitches: F, G, or C.

Coda   Italian. "Tail": an extended ending.

Common time   The time signature C or 4/4 time; simple quadruple meter with the quarter note as the pulse note.

Compound interval   An interval larger than an octave.

Consequent phrase   The second half of a period following an antecedent phrase which ends on the tonic chord, usually with an authentic cadence.

Consonance   In Western tonal music, consonant intervals are P1, M3, m3, P4, P5, M6, m6, P8. (See **Dissonance**.)

Crescendo   (< or *cresc.*) A dynamic marking meaning to become gradually louder.

Cut time (see Alla breve)

D.C. al Fine   Italian. "*Da Capo*" ("to the head") directs the musician to return to the beginning and repeat, ending at the word *Fine* (the end).

D.S. al Fine   Italian. "*Dal Segno*" ("to the sign") directs the musician to return to the sign (𝄋) and repeat, ending at the word *Fine* (the end).

Deceptive cadence   A momentary and unexpected ending to a section of music where the dominant goes to the submediant (for example, V to VI in a minor key) instead of to the tonic (for example, V to I in a major key).

Decrescendo   (*Decres.* or >) A dynamic marking meaning to grow softer. Same as *diminuendo*.

Diatonic   Different consecutive letter names for pitches, for example A–B.

Diatonic half step   A half step using different consecutive letter names; for example, B–C or A♯–B. (See **Chromatic half step**.)

Diminished interval   The perfect interval or minor interval decreased in size by a half step. For example, a perfect fourth (P4) is C–F; a diminished fourth (dim4) is C–F♭.

Diminuendo   (*Dim.*) A dynamic marking meaning to become gradually softer. Same as *decrescendo*.

Dissonance   In Western tonal music, dissonant intervals are the augmented and diminished intervals, M2, m2, M7, and m7. (See **Consonance**.)

Dominant   The fifth note (or chord) of a major or minor scale.

Dominant seventh chord   The quality of seventh chord built on the fifth note (dominant) of a major scale or the harmonic minor scale; consists of a major triad and a minor seventh from the lowest note to the highest note.

Double bar line   Two vertical lines on a staff or staves used to indicate the end of a section of music.

Double flat sign   An accidental (𝄫) that lowers a note a whole step.

Double sharp sign   An accidental (𝄪) that raises a note a whole step.

Downbeat   The first beat of a measure, named for the conductor's downward motion used to indicate the first beat.

Duple meter   The recurring pattern of beats: a strong beat followed by a weak beat. For example, music written in 2/4, 2/2, and 6/8.

Duplet   Subdivision of a note, which would normally subdivide into three equal parts, into two equal parts.

Dynamics   The volume (loudness or softness) of a sound. Signs or words such as *p* (*piano* in Italian), for soft, are used to indicate dynamics.

Enharmonic   Different names for the same pitch; for example, F♯ and G♭.

Fermata   A sign (𝄐) placed above or below a note or a rest indicating to hold the note or rest longer than its normal rhythmic value.

Figured bass A method of labeling chords and their inversions by counting the interval number (figure) up from the lowest note (bass note).

Final bar line Two vertical lines (a thin line followed by a thicker line) used at the end of a piece.

First and second endings The first time, play the ending indicated by the first bracket ([1.   ]). On the repeat, play the ending indicated by the second bracket ([2.   ]). (Other endings may also be used).

First inversion A chord position where the third of the chord is the lowest pitch; for example, BDG, where B is the third in the triad GBD.

Fixed Do A method of singing solfège where "Do" is "C," "Re" is "D," and so forth. If "Do" corresponds to a scale's tonic, this is "Movable Do."

Flag The part of a note attached to the stem that changes the note's value by half. For example, adding a flag to a quarter note (♩) changes it to an eighth note (♪).

Flat An accidental (♭) used to lower a note a half step.

Form The organizing structure of a piece, which is determined by musical elements such as melody, harmony, rhythm (meter), and character (mood). Examples of form are binary (AB), ternary (ABA), and sonata form.

Forte (𝒇) Italian. A dynamic marking meaning *loud*.

Fortissimo (𝒇𝒇) Italian. A dynamic marking meaning *very loud*.

Grand staff The treble staff above and bass staff below joined together by a bar line and with a brace; used in notating keyboard music.

Half cadence A momentary ending of a section of music that ends with a dominant chord; for example, tonic-dominant (I–V) or subdominant–dominant (IV–V).

Half step On the keyboard, two adjacent keys. In Western tonal music, the half step is the smallest interval; also called the *semitone*.

Harmonic interval The interval created by the simultaneous sounding of two pitches. (See **Melodic interval**.)

Harmonic minor scale The form of the minor scale with the seventh note raised a half step from the natural minor, creating the leading tone and 1½ steps (A2) between the sixth and seventh notes. Half steps are between 2 and 3, 5 and 6, and 7 and 8.

Harmonic series (also Overtone series) The lowest frequency (the fundamental) and a series of higher frequencies (harmonics or overtones) sounding as one pitch.

Harmonization Chords or triads accompanying a melody.

Harmony The vertical arrangement of notes forming chords; the succession of chords.

Improvisation The art of spontaneously creating a melody, harmony, and/or rhythm; found in many styles of music including jazz, Baroque music with figured bass symbols and South Asian music.

Interval The numeric distance between two notes. Intervals may be further defined by quality (perfect, major, minor, augmented, diminished) and whether they sound simultaneously (harmonic) or consecutively (melodic).

Inversion The turning of an interval or chord upside down.

Irregular meter A meter other than duple, triple, or quadruple; for example, 5/4 or 8/8.

Key signature The sharps or flats placed in a specific order after the clef at the beginning of a line of music indicating the key of a piece.

Leading tone The seventh note or chord in a major scale, harmonic minor, or ascending melodic minor scale; a half step below the tonic, the leading tone "leads" to the tonic.

Ledger line Short lines above or below a staff that extend the pitch range of the staff.

Legato Italian. "Binding"; to play notes smoothly and connected.

Lento Italian. A slow tempo.

Major scale A pattern of eight notes made of whole steps and half steps with the half steps occurring between 3 and 4 and between 7 and 8.

Measure   The grouping of metered beats (strong and weak beats) separated by lines called bar lines.

Mediant   The third note (or chord) in a major or minor scale.

Melodic interval   The interval created when two pitches are written or sounded consecutively. (See **Harmonic interval**.)

Melodic minor scale   In the ascending melodic minor, the sixth and seventh tones of the natural minor scale are raised a half step, resulting in half steps between 2 and 3 and between 7 and 8. In the descending form, the sixth and seventh notes are lowered a half step, resulting in a return to the natural form of the minor scale.

Melody   The horizontal succession of pitches. Additional elements include rhythm and the shape or contour formed by ascending or descending pitches.

Meter   The recurring division of the pulse into a pattern of strong and weak beats; for example, duple, triple or quadruple.

Mezzo forte (*mf*)   Italian. A dynamic marking meaning *medium loud.*

Mezzo piano (*mp*)   Italian. A dynamic marking meaning *medium soft.*

Minor scale   A pattern of eight notes in three different forms: natural (pure), harmonic and melodic. All three forms share the same key signature and the first five notes.

Modal music   A musical system based on the church modes.

Moderato   Italian. A moderate tempo.

Modes   The eight-note medieval "church" scales used until the end of the Renaissance around 1600. Two of these modes became the major and natural minor scales (Ionian and Aeolian, respectively). Frequently folk songs, jazz, and modern pieces are modal.

Modulation   The changing of a key within a piece of music. Accidentals may be used to indicate the change, or a double bar and new key signature may be used.

Motive   A short rhythmic and melodic idea used in a phrase.

Movable Do   A method of singing solfège where "Do" corresponds to the scale's tonic, "Re" is the supertonic, and so forth. If "Do" is "C," "Re" is "D," this is "Fixed Do."

Natural   An accidental (♮) used to cancel a previous sharp, flat, double sharp or double flat for that note.

Natural (pure) minor scale   The form of the minor scale which follows the key signature, resulting in half steps between 2 and 3 and between 5 and 6.

Note head   The part of a note that is oval; the placement of the note head on the staff indicates the pitch of the note. Stems and flags may be added, and the note head may be filled in. If the note head is used alone, it is a whole note.

Parallel key   A major and minor key that share the same tonic, or beginning note, but not the same key signature; for example, A major and A minor.

Pentatonic scale   A pattern of five notes within the octave; for example, the five black keys comprise a pentatonic scale.

Period   The grouping of two or more phrases. When two phrases are combined, the first usually ends with a momentary conclusion (the antecedent phrase) and the second ends with a definitive conclusion (the consequent phrase).

Phrase   A musical sentence, frequently four to eight measures long, ending with a feeling of closure called a cadence.

Pianissimo (*pp*)   Italian. A dynamic marking meaning *very soft.*

Piano (*p*)   Italian. A dynamic marking meaning *soft.*

Pitch   The frequency, or rate of speed, of sound vibrations. For example, the pitch A has a frequency of 440 vibrations per second.

Plagal cadence   A resting or ending of a section of music with the last two chords consisting of subdominant (IV or iv) to tonic (I or i). This is sometimes called the "Amen" cadence because it is used at the end of some hymns.

Planing   Use of stepwise, successive triads or seventh chords in parallel motion.

Primary triads   Triads of the scale that are the most frequently occurring and closely related to the tonic; these are the tonic, subdominant, and dominant.

Pulse   The steady beat in music.

Quadruple meter   The recurring pattern of beats: a strong beat followed by three weak beats. Music written in 4/4 or 12/8 are examples of quadruple meter.

Relative key   A major and minor scale that share the same key signature but not the same tonic note; for example, C major and A minor.

Repeat sign   (‖: :‖) Two vertical lines with two dots placed in front or after the lines, instructing the musician to repeat a section.

Rest   A symbol to represent a specific duration of silence.

Rhythm   The movement of music in time; the relative duration of sounds or silence.

Rhythmic value   The duration of pitches; for example, a quarter note is half the value of the half note, and a half note is half the value of a whole note.

Roman numerals   Roman numerals are drawn below the staff to represent the number note in the scale (scale degree) on which a chord is based. For example, the roman numeral IV or iv represents the subdominant triad in a major and minor key, respectively.

Root   The note on which a chord is built; the root gives the chord its letter name.

Root position   A chord position with the root of the chord in the lowest note; for example, GBD, with G as the lowest note of the G triad.

Scale   A pattern of notes consisting of a variety of intervals, usually whole steps and half steps. Some examples include the major, three forms of minor, whole tone, pentatonic, and chromatic scales.

Scale degree   Names given to specific notes of major and minor scales; for example, in G major the first note of the scale (G) is the tonic.

Second inversion   A chord position with the fifth of the chord as the lowest note; for example, DGB, with D being the fifth of the triad GBD.

Secondary triads   Triads of the scale that are less frequently occurring and less closely related to the tonic; these are the supertonic, mediant, submediant, and leading tone.

Seventh chord   In its simplest form, four notes, consecutive thirds apart. There are five qualities of seventh chords: major, dominant seventh, minor, half diminished, and diminished.

Sharp   An accidental (♯) used to raise a note a half step.

Simple interval   An interval of an octave or less.

Slur   A curved line above or below two or more different pitches indicating to play those notes smoothly or connected.

Solfège   Singing with syllables as described by the eleventh-century monk Guido d'Arezzo. Today, there are seven syllables: Do Re Mi Fa Sol La Ti.

Staccato   Italian. An articulation (∙) above or below a note head indicating to play that note detached or unconnected.

Staff   (pl. staves) A system of five parallel lines and four spaces on which notes are written to represent pitches; the higher the pitch, the higher it will be placed on the staff.

Stem   A vertical line attached on the right above a note head, or on the left below a note head. All rhythmic values shorter than the whole note use stems.

Subdominant   The fourth note (or chord) in a scale.

Submediant   The sixth note (or chord) in a scale.

Subtonic   The seventh note (or chord) in a natural minor scale and the descending form of the melodic minor.

Supertonic   The second note (or chord) in a scale.

Syncopation   The shift in accent from what is normally a strong beat in a measure, to a weak beat; the rhythmic emphasis on a weak beat.

Tablature   A type of notation that uses symbols, letters, or figures to describe how fingers are to be placed to produce a pitch, rather than the pitch as shown on a staff.

Tempo   The rate of speed of the pulse. Frequently, Italian words are used; for example, *Allegro* for fast, and *Lento* for slow.

Tendency tone   Notes of a scale or chord that "tend" to lead up or down to another note; for example, the leading tone "leads" up to the tonic.

Tenor clef (see C clef)   The sign (𝄡) indicating that the fourth line from the bottom of the staff is middle C.

Ternary form   A three-part form (ABA) with the B section in a contrasting but related key.

Tetrachord   A pattern of four adjacent notes spanning a perfect fourth; from the Greek words *tetra* ("four") and *chordē* ("string").

Third inversion   A chord position with the seventh of the chord as the lowest note; for example, FGBD, with the F as the seventh note in the seventh chord GBDF.

Tie   A curved line above or below, connecting notes of the same pitch so that the first note is played only once and is held for the combined rhythmic value of all the tied pitches.

Timbre   The tone quality ("color") of an instrument or voice; every instrument has its own unique sound or timbre.

Time signature   (sometimes called Meter signature) The two numbers placed at the beginning of a piece that indicate the number of beats in a measure (top number) and the note value of the basic pulse (lower number).

Tonal music   A musical system based on the major or minor scales.

Tonic   The note (or chord) based on the first note of a scale. The tonic note names the key of the piece.

Transposition   Changing a piece or section of music from one key to another; for example, in transposing a piece from D major to E major, all pitches would be written or played a whole step higher.

Treble clef (G clef)   The sign (𝄞) indicating that the second line from the bottom of the staff is the G above middle C.

Triad   In its simplest form, three notes consecutive thirds apart. There are four qualities of triads: major, minor, augmented, and diminished.

Triple meter   The recurring pattern of beats: a strong beat followed by two weak beats. Pieces written in 3/4 or 9/8 are examples of triple meter.

Triplet   Division of a note into three equal parts where you normally have two equal parts.

Tritone   "Three tones," an interval spanning three whole steps; for example, C–F♯ or C–G♭.

Unison   ("One sound") Two notes that are the same pitch.

Upbeat   The last beat preceding the bar line, and before the downbeat.

Whole step   The interval consisting of two adjacent half steps. On the keyboard, skip one key between two notes to create a whole step.

Whole tone scale   A six-note scale consisting only of whole steps. Also called a hextonal scale.

APPENDIX 2 **ACOUSTICS**

Acoustics (from the Greek verb *akouo* or "to hear" or "to listen") is a branch of science that studies sound. In music, sound is defined in four ways: pitch, duration, volume and timbre. We studied these musical components in the earlier modules; in this appendix we will briefly discuss the science of these components.

Pitch (Frequency)

Sound is determined by the number of vibrations per second (**frequency**) created by a vibrating object. If the vibrations are regular, a pitch is produced. Random vibrations produce non-pitched sounds, for example, the sound of a jet or a tambourine.

Note:

- Frequency may be defined as the number of times a pattern repeats (or cycles); frequency is measured in Hertz (Hz), which is the number of cycles per second. Humans hear sounds between 20 Hz and 20,000 Hz.
- Frequency determines pitch; the higher the frequency, the higher the pitch. Today we use 440 Hz (the A above middle C) as the pitch for tuning.
- Octave pitches are created by doubling or halving a frequency. For example, a piano string vibrating at 220 Hz will produce the A below middle C. A string half as long will vibrate at 440 Hz, or twice the frequency, and produce the A above middle C, or an octave higher. In fact, all octave pitches vibrate at a ratio of 2:1; therefore all A's will be a multiple of 440.
- All intervals may be expressed as the ratio of the frequency of vibration from one pitch to another; notice that the harmonic series shown below is derived from these ratios. For example, octaves vibrate at the ratio of 2:1. The perfect fifth vibrates at the ratio of 3:2.

Harmonic Series

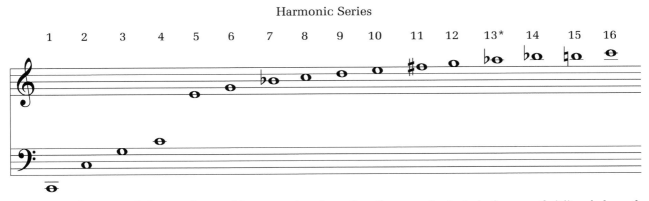

* *Note*: The A♭ is particularly out of tune with tempered tuning; other discrepancies include the seventh (B♭) and eleventh (F♯) partials, or "parts" of the fundamental pitch.

- Intervals may be described as consonant (sounds that are stable, "pleasing" to the ear) or dissonant (sounds that are needing to be resolved, "displeasing" to the ear). As described in frequency ratios, consonant intervals are expressed in simpler ratios (for example, 2:1 is an octave, and 3:2 is a P5), and dissonant intervals are expressed in more complex ratios, (for example, 15:8 is a M7, and 16:15 is a m2).
- Each pitch consists of the lowest frequency (the fundamental) and a series of higher frequencies (harmonics or overtones). The entire series is called a harmonic series (or overtone series). It is the relative strength, or "amplitude," of each of the frequencies that determines the "color" or "timbre" of an instrument.

Duration

Musicians refer to rhythmic values when speaking of duration: how long does a note (or silence) last? Duration also may be affected by the attack, decay, sustain and release of the note.

- The **attack** is the initial creation of the sound. For example, is the flute "tongued" giving the note a sharp attack? How does the pianist strike the key: with a sharp accent or a gentle drop?
- The **decay** is the decrease in volume after the attack. Some instruments like wood blocks have an immediate decay and the sound disappears immediately after the attack. Other instruments like the organ can maintain their volume indefinitely.
- The **sustain** is the length of time before the sound becomes inaudible. This aspect of duration is different from the rhythmic value of a note. For example, the quarter note receives one beat.
- The **release** is the end of the note. On a piano, the key is released; the flutist stops the flow of air.

Volume (Intensity)

When a sound is created, air molecules are set in motion, resulting in vibrations; the higher the frequency of vibrations, the higher the pitch. The **volume** of the sound, however, is determined by how much the air molecules expand and compress (the **amplitude**), which affects the air pressure. The greater the increase and decrease in air pressure, the greater the sound's **intensity**. A sound wave's intensity is related to its amplitude. Musicians use the term **dynamics** when talking about intensity.

Note:

- Intensity is measured in **decibels** (dB) beginning with 0 dB, which is the softest sound that humans can hear.
- Examples of sounds measured in dB include a whisper (20 dB) to the sound of a large orchestra (98 dB). Sounds at 160 dB will cause instant and irreparable hearing loss.

Color (Timbre)

Each sound created by an instrument consists of more than one frequency. These frequencies are not heard as discrete ones, but as a combination of the frequencies. The instruments from around the world are classified by type:

- Aerophones (flutes, brasses, reeds) where air vibrates through a column;
- Chordophones (stringed instruments) where a string vibrates;
- Idiophones (percussive instruments such as bells and shakers) where the instrument produces the sound (*idio* means "itself");
- Membranophones (drums) where a membrane vibrates.

Similar instruments within each classification have a similar series of frequencies. This aspect of sound is called **timbre**, or **color**; for example, a trumpet has a distinctly different sound from a violin, and a singer sounds noticeably different from a sitar.

APPENDIX 3 C CLEFS (ALTO AND TENOR)

Beginning in the Middle Ages, C clefs, in addition to F and G clefs, were used. Today, music continues to be written using C clefs in order to avoid the excessive use of ledger lines and octave signs. The most common C clefs are the alto and tenor clefs, which are used by instruments such as the viola (alto clef) and, for higher passages on the cello (tenor clef). Notice that middle C is the third line in the alto clef, and the fourth line in the tenor clef.

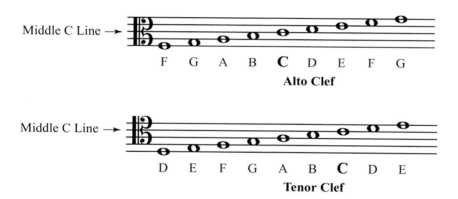

Following is an excerpt from Franz Schubert's String Quartet in D, D. 74. Here, the viola part is written in the alto clef, where the third line is middle C. Unlike the two violins that play the melody an octave apart, the viola and cello play in unison for the first two measures. In mm. 3–4, the viola plays an octave higher than the cello. In writing the viola part in the alto clef, the range of the music may be more easily notated within the staff.

String Quartet in D, D. 74 (F. Schubert)

In the cello and piano transcription below of Camille Saint-Saëns' "Le Cygne" ("The Swan") from *Le Carnaval des Animaux*, the cello solo is notated in the tenor clef (where the fourth line is middle C). In using the tenor clef, Saint-Saëns reduces the need for ledger lines.

"Le Cygne" ("The Swan"), *Le Carnaval des Animaux* (C. Saint-Saëns)

Exercise 1

Write the letter name of the following notes in the alto clef. (Keep track of middle C.)

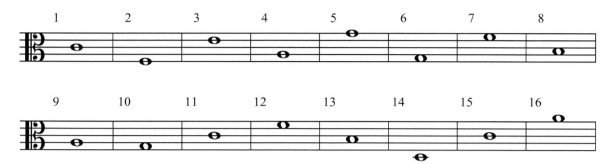

Exercise 2

Draw the following **treble clef** notes as the same pitch in the **alto clef**.

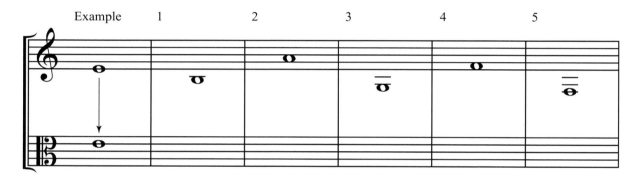

Exercise 3

Draw the following **bass clef** notes as the same pitch in the **alto clef**.

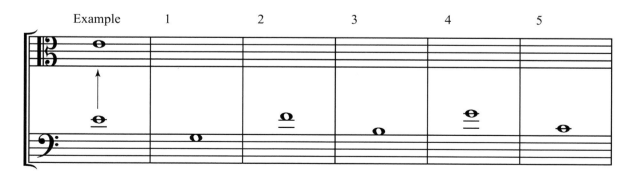

Exercise 4

Redraw the Orlando Lassus melody written in the alto clef as the same pitches in the treble clef.

"Qui Sequitur Me," motet (O. Lassus)

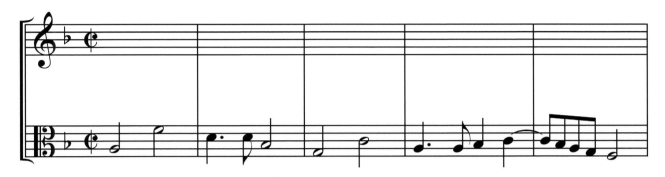

Theory Trainer

Exercise Appendix 3a Find white keys on the staff.
Exercise Appendix 3b Find white keys on the keyboard.

APPENDIX 4 MODES

The music of Europe from the Middle Ages to the end of the Renaissance (from the Fall of Rome in 476 to around 1600) was based on a system of scales called modes; we identify this music as **"modal music."** Two of these modes, the Ionian and Aeolian modes, continued to be used in Western music from around 1600 through much of the nineteenth century, creating the major-minor system; we identify this music as **"tonal music."** Beginning in the late nineteenth century, composers began to use modes again as the basis of their pieces. Popular music from the Middle Ages to the present, including folk and some jazz melodies, has roots in the modes.

There are seven modes. Notice that:

- Modes span an octave, beginning and ending on the same pitch.
- Each mode consists of a different arrangement of whole steps and half steps.
- Medieval theorists gave Greek names to the modes although they do not resemble Greek modes.
- The modes are written without accidentals. In practice, Medieval musicians added the Bb and later, other accidentals, to avoid the tritone (A4 or d5). Adding accidentals contributed to the eventual breakdown of the modal system.

Ionian mode (presently the major scale); has half steps between 3–4 and 7–8.

Dorian mode has half steps between 2–3 and 6–7.

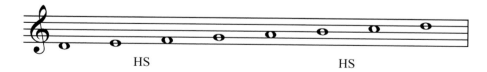

Phrygian mode has half steps between 1–2 and 5–6.

Lydian mode has half steps between 4–5 and 7–8.

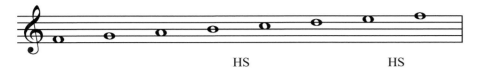

HS HS

Mixolydian mode has half steps between 3–4 and 6–7.

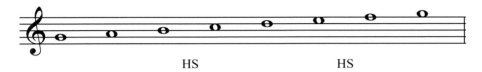

HS HS

Aeolian mode (presently the natural minor scale) has half steps between 2–3 and 5–6.

HS HS

Locrian mode has half steps between 1–2 and 4–5.

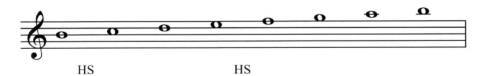

HS HS

Historical note

Gregory the Great, the first great pope of the Middle Ages, solidified papal power (c. 590–604). He is credited with composing much of the music used in the Roman liturgy, resulting in the label "Gregorian chant." It is more likely that Pope Gregory codified these chants, rather than composing them. To the original four modes described by St. Ambrose, the fourth century theorist, Pope Gregory added four others.

Exercise 1

Following are two examples of Gregorian chant from the 11th–13th centuries. In these examples, the first and last pitch of each example is the first note of the mode of the piece. Medieval theorists called this note the *finalis* (comparable to our tonic). Notice that the chants are written without time signatures or barlines.

1. Kyrie, Easter Mass (Mixolydian mode)

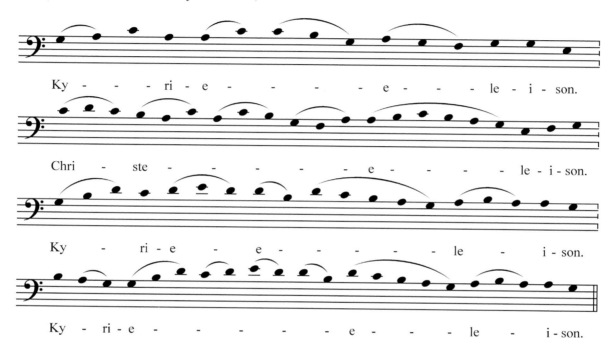

2. Alleluia (Dorian mode)

Exercise 2

Many folk songs are modal; frequently, composers wrote melodies based on folk song or dance elements. Identify the mode of the following examples.

1. "Wayfaring Stranger," American spiritual

2. "D'ror Yikra," Middle Eastern folk song

Notice the changing time signatures. Keep the quarter note beat constant throughout the song.

3.   Mazurka, Op. 24, No. 2 (F. Chopin) (Originally written an octave higher.)

> ## Vocabulary
>
> **MAZURKA**
>
> A mazurka ("mazurek" in Polish), is a Polish dance in triple meter, usually with an accent on the second or third beat. It frequently uses trills, triplets, two eighth notes followed by two quarter notes, or a dotted eighth followed by a sixteenth note. Like many Polish folk songs, mazurkas are modal, usually Lydian. Chopin, whose mother was Polish, composed over 50 stylized mazurkas.
>
> **RITEN**
>
> (Italian: *ritenuto*) means 'held back', to suddenly slow the tempo.

Transposing Modes

Modes originally were sung without any accidentals; on the keyboard, we would only use the white keys from C to C (Ionian), D to D (Dorian), and so forth. Just as major and minor scales may be played beginning on any note (called transposition), modes may also be transposed to different pitches. There are two methods to transpose modes: 1) using the arrangement of whole and half steps; 2) using the key signature.

First Method of Modal Transposition: Using Whole and Half Steps

Begin by reviewing the arrangement of whole and half steps for each mode given at the beginning of this appendix. For example, the Phrygian mode has half steps between 1–2 and 5–6. Notice the accidentals that would be needed to create these half steps when the Phrygian mode begins on G, rather than E.

G Phyrgian mode

HS   HS

The Mixolydian mode has half steps between 3–4 and 6–7. To transpose the Mixolydian mode from G to F, two flats would be needed as shown below.

F Mixolydian

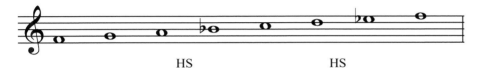

HS   HS

Second Method of Modal Transposition: Using the Key Signature

When only the white keys of the keyboard are used to write the modes, the Ionian mode begins on C. When we transpose the Ionian mode to a different note, we can use the key signature of the corresponding major scale of the Ionian mode. For example, if the Ionian mode begins on E♭, the major key signature for E♭ is three flats: B♭, E♭ and A♭. All other modes now begin on subsequent notes of the E♭ major scale as shown below.

E♭ Ionian mode: half steps between 3–4 and 7–8.

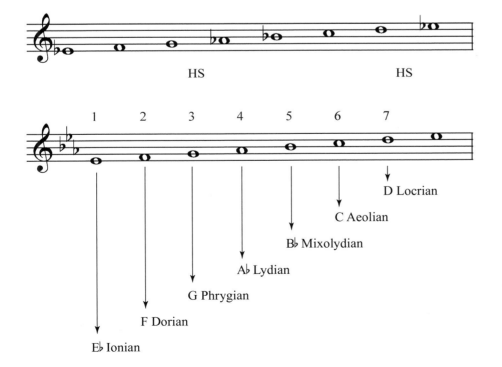

To write the G Phrygian mode, we begin on G and use three flats in the key signature. (Note that the Phrygian mode is a M3 above the Ionian mode; G is a M3 above E♭.) Compare this with G Phrygian written using the first method of constructing modes using whole and half steps.

G Phrygian mode with a key signature

HS   HS

To write the B♭ Mixolydian mode, we begin on B♭ and use three flats in the key signature. (Note that the Mixolydian mode is the fifth note (P5) above the Ionian mode; B♭ is a P5 above E♭.) Compare this with the B♭ Mixolydian written using whole and half steps.

B♭ Mixolydian mode with a key signature

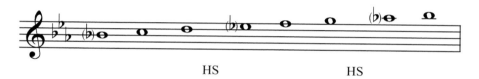

HS   HS

Notice:

- In order to use a key signature to determine the accidentals in a mode, establish the interval of the first note of the mode (which we will call the "tonic") in relation to the "tonic" of the Ionian mode.
- Study the following list.

Ionian	Tonic note of a major scale.
Dorian	Second note of a major scale, M2 above the tonic
Phrygian	Third note of a major scale, M3 above the tonic
Lydian	Fourth note of a major scale, P4 above the tonic
Mixolydian	Fifth note of a major scale, P5 above the tonic
Aeolian	Sixth note of a major scale, M6 above the tonic
Locrian	Seventh note of a major scale, M7 above the tonic

Exercise 3

Using the list given above, you can determine the mode of a song by determining the interval of tonic of the major scale to the tonic of the mode.

Example: "Black Is the Color of My True Love's Hair," American folk song

This folk song was popular in the Appalachian Mountains from 1915, but probably came from Scotland and is part of the Celtic (Scottish) music tradition.

Black, black, black   is the co-lor - of my true love's   hair.   Her lips -

- are some-thing - won-drous fair.   -   The - pur - est eyes and the neat - est -

hands.   -   I   love   the   ground   where - on she - stands.

To find the mode of "Black Is the Color," follow the steps given below.

1. Name the major key with one sharp. <u>G major</u>
2. Identify the interval of the last note of song (A) to the major tonic note (G). <u>M2</u>
3. Using this interval, determine the mode. <u>'A' Dorian is the second note (M2) above the major tonic note.</u>
4. Draw the 'A' Dorian mode. (Note: HS between 2–3 and 6–7.)

HS   HS

1. "Old Joe Clark," American folk song

Using the following steps, determine the mode of "Old Joe Clark."

1. Name the major key with two sharps.
2. Identify the interval of last note of song to the tonic note of the major scale.
3. Using this interval, determine the mode.
4. Draw the mode and indicate the half steps (HS).

2. "Hitragut," Middle Eastern folk song

Using the following steps, identify the mode of "Hitragut."

1. Name the major key with two flats.
2. Identify the interval of last note of song to the tonic note of the major scale.
3. Using this interval, determine the mode.
4. Draw the mode and indicate the half steps (HS).

 Theory Trainer

Exercise Appendix 4a Input modes.
Exercise Appendix 4b Identify modes given a key signature.
Exercise Appendix 4c Identify modes by ear.

Modes and Blues Harmony

Beginning in the 1950s and 1960s, jazz, rock and blues musicians began to use modal harmonies in their songs. Listen to Miles Davis (including "So What" and the album "Kind of Blue"), The Rolling Stones ("I'm Crying"), The Who, or Crosby, Stills and Nash for examples of modal influences in jazz, rock, or blues music.

APPENDIX 5   OTHER SEVENTH CHORDS (MAJOR, MINOR, HALF DIMINISHED, DIMINISHED)

There are five qualities of seventh chords. In Module 15 we studied the **dominant seventh** chord. In this appendix, we will study the other four seventh chords: major seventh, minor seventh, half diminished seventh, and diminished seventh.

In their simplest form, seventh chords have four notes, consecutive thirds apart. It is the quality of each of the thirds that determines the quality of the seventh chord. Additionally, determining the quality of the triad of the lowest three notes of the seventh chord and the quality of the seventh (from the lowest to the highest note) helps to determine the quality of the seventh chord.

The seventh chords for C as the root are shown below.

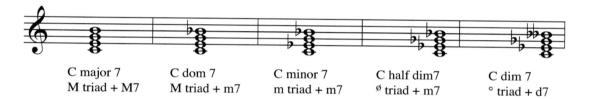

| C major 7 | C dom 7 | C minor 7 | C half dim7 | C dim 7 |
| M triad + M7 | M triad + m7 | m triad + m7 | ⌀ triad + m7 | ° triad + d7 |

Major Seventh Chords

Major seventh chords consist of a **major triad** and a **major seventh** (M7) from the root of the chord up to the seventh.

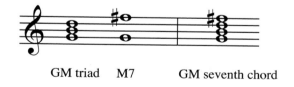

GM triad   M7   GM seventh chord

In a major scale, major seventh chords are formed on the tonic and subdominant notes.

Exercise 1

Draw major seventh chords from the given root.

Minor Seventh Chords

Minor seventh chords consist of a minor triad and a minor seventh (m7) from the root of the chord up to the seventh.

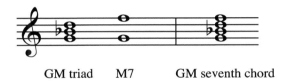

GM triad   M7   GM seventh chord

In a major scale, minor seventh chords are formed on the supertonic, mediant, and submediant notes.

Exercise 2

Draw minor seventh chords from the given root.

Half Diminished Seventh Chords

Half diminished seventh chords consist of a **diminished triad** and a **minor seventh** (m7) from the root of the chord up to the seventh. The half diminished seventh chord may also be identified by the "degree" sign slashed with a forward stroke (for example Gø7).

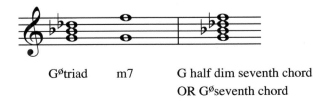

Gø triad   m7   G half dim seventh chord
                         OR Gø seventh chord

In a major scale, half diminished seventh chords are formed on the leading tone note.

Exercise 3

Draw half diminished seventh chords from the given root.

Diminished Seventh Chords

Diminished seventh chords (also called "fully diminished" seventh chords), consist of a **diminished triad** and a **diminished seventh** (d7) from the root of the chord up to the seventh. The diminished seventh chord may also be identified with the "degree" sign (for example Gᵒ7).

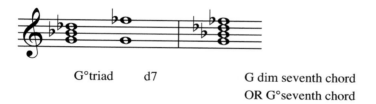

G°triad   d7   G dim seventh chord

OR G°seventh chord

Diminished seventh chords are formed on the leading tone of the harmonic minor scale. In a major scale, half diminished seventh chords are formed on the leading tone note; in a harmonic scale, half diminished seventh chords are formed on the supertonic note.

Exercise 4

Draw diminished seventh chords from the given root.

Exercise 5

Below each chord, write the letter name (A, B, C) and quality (M7, Dom7, m7, or ᵒ̸7) for the seventh chords of the F major scale. The first one is done for you.

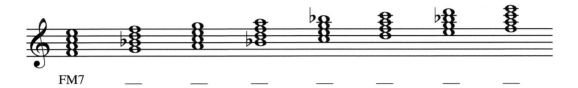

FM7 ___ ___ ___ ___ ___ ___ ___

Exercise 6

Below each chord, write the letter name (A, B, C) and quality (M7, Dom7, m7, or ᵒ̸7) for the seventh chords of the A natural minor scale. The first one is done for you.

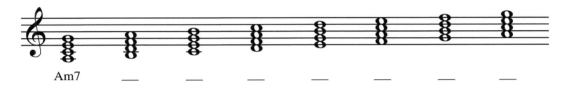

Am7 ___ ___ ___ ___ ___ ___ ___

APPENDIX 6 BASIC GUITAR CHORDS

Guitar music may be notated in four ways:

- Fretboard diagrams (also called chord diagrams) showing the vertical arrangement of the six guitar strings with numbers indicating the finger that will play on a specific guitar string and fret.
- Chord symbols (for example, G or D7) written above a song.
- Tablature showing the horizontal arrangement of the six guitar strings where fret numbers are printed on the specific string to be played. Music may be notated in the treble clef above the tablature.
- Treble clef notation where the written notes sound an octave lower than written.

This section will focus on fretboard diagrams to show the chords that are commonly used in musical styles such as folk, blues, and rock.

- In fretboard diagrams, the guitar's six strings are drawn vertically beginning with the lowest string on the left (E), and ending two octaves higher on the right (E).

Guitar Strings

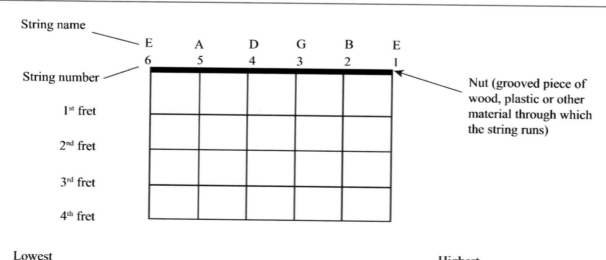

- Fingers are numbered as follows:

  1. Index finger
  2. Middle finger
  3. Ring finger
  4. Little finger ("pinky")

- To read a fretboard chart, study the various symbols shown below.

C chord (one finger)

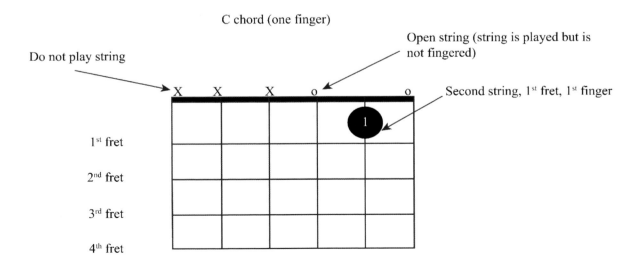

Do not play string

Open string (string is played but is not fingered)

Second string, 1st fret, 1st finger

1st fret

2nd fret

3rd fret

4th fret

Guitar Chords

The chords shown below are called "open position chords" because they have at least one string that remains "open" ("o"); open strings are not fingered but are free to resonate.

- Major Chords

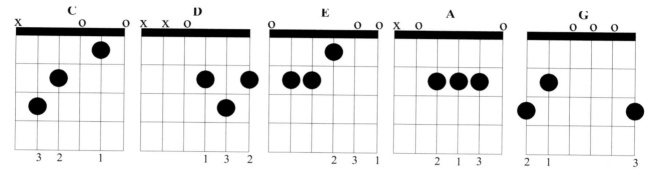

- Minor Chords (Compare these with D, E, A above; although only one pitch is lowered, the fingerings change to facilitate the new hand position.)

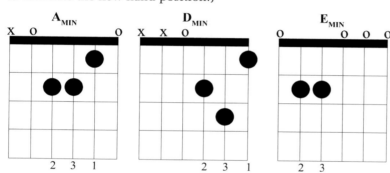

- Dominant Seventh Chords

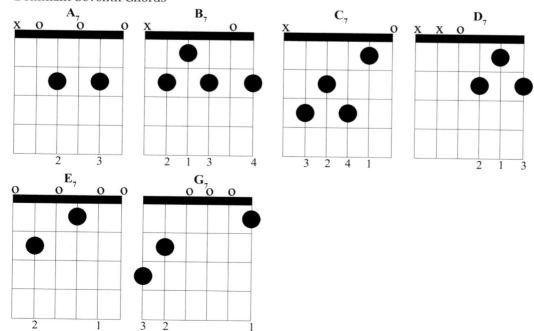

- Minor Seventh Chords and FM (Compare D7, E7, A7 with Dm7, Em7, Am7.)

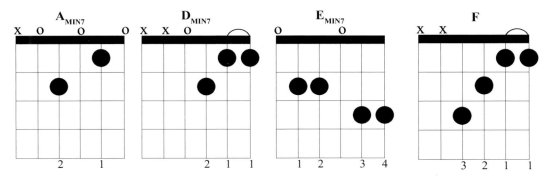

Exercise 1

Practice chord progressions in various keys.

1. Primary chords: I   IV   I   V

    Key: G   G   C   G   D   ("The Great Pretender" by Buck Ram of The Platters)

    Key: D   D   G   D   A   ("Roll Over Beethoven" by Chuck Berry)

                                             ("See You Later, Alligator" by Robert Charles Guidry and sung by Bill Haley and the Comets)

    Key: A   A   D   A   E   ("Rock Around the Clock" by Bill Haley)

                                             ("Mabellene" by Chuck Berry)

2. Add submediant: I   V   vi   IV

    Key: G   G   D   em   C   ("Can You Feel the Love Tonight?" by Elton John)

    Key: C   C   G   am   F   ("Let It Be" by Paul McCartney)

3. Add Dominant Seventh: I   V7   I

Key: G   G   D7   G

4. Add supertonic: I   V   ii   I   V   IV   ("Knockin' on Heaven's Door" by Bob Dylan)

Key: G   G   D   Am(7)   G   D   C

5. Blues chords: I7   IV7   V7

Key: A   A7   D7   E7

499

Exercise 2

1. Play the chords to "Brown Eyed Girl" by Van Morrison.

Intro:	G	C	G	D	
Verse:	G	C	G	D	
	G	Em	C	D	G	D7
Bridge:	G	C	G	D	

CREDITS

"What Kind of Fool Am I"; From the Musical Production *"Stop The World – I Want To Get Off"*; Words and Music by Leslie Bricusse and Anthony Newley; (c) Copyright 1961 (Renewed) TRO Essex Music Ltd., London, England; TRO – Ludlow Music, Inc., New York, controls all publication rights for the U.S.A. and Canada; International Copyright Secured. Made In U.S.A.; All Rights Reserved Including Public Performance For Profit. Used by permission

"James Bond Theme." By Monty Norman. © 1962 United Artists Music Ltd. Copyright Renewed by EMI Unart Catalog, Inc. Exclusive Print Rights Controlled and Administered by Alfred Music. All Rights Reserved. Used by Permission.

"Charade." Lyrics by Johnny Mercer. Music by Henry Mancini. © 1963 (Renewed) The Johnny Mercer Foundation and Northridge Music Company. All Rights for The Johnny Mercer Foundation Administered by WB Music Corp. All Rights Reserved. Used by Permission.

"My Heart Will Go On" from *Titanic*, by James Horner (music) and Will Jennings (lyrics). © 1997 Sony/ATV Music Publishing LLC, T C F Music Publishing, Inc., Fox Film Music Corporation and Blue Sky Rider Songs. All rights on behalf of Sony/ATV Music Publishing LLC administered by Sony/ATV Music Publishing LLC, 8 Music Square West, Nashville, TN 37203. All rights on behalf of Blue Sky Rider Songs administered by Irving Music, Inc. International copyright secured. All rights reserved. Reprinted with permission of Hal Leonard Corporation.

"Stand By Me," by Jerry Leiber, Mike Stoller, and Ben King. All rights reserved. Reprinted with permission of Hal Leonard Corporation.

"Layla Layla" by Mordechai Zeria. Words by Nathan Alterman. Published by Tarbut-Vechinuch Ed. © Mordechai Zeria and ACUM.

"María Elena" English by S.K. Russell (words) and Lorenzo Barcelata (music and Spanish words). © 1932 by Peer International Corporation. Copyright renewed. International copyright secured. All rights reserved. Reprinted with permission of Hal Leonard Corporation.

"Take Me Out to the Ball Game" by Jack Norworth (words) and Albert von Tilzer (music). © 1909 Broadway Music Corp. and Bienstock Publishing Co. Copyright renewed. This arrangement © 2009 Broadway Music Corp. and Bienstock Publishing Co. All rights on behalf of Broadway Music Corp. administered by Sony/ATV Music Publishing LLC, 8 Music Square West, Nashville, TN 37203.

"Tiny Bubbles" by Leon Pober. © 1966-1994. Granite Music Corporation. Reprinted with permission by Criterion Music Corporation.

"Ma Omrot Enayich ("What Are Your Eyes Saying?")" by Mordechai Zeira. © Mordechai Zeira and ACUM.

"That's All" (from *Tootsie*). Words and Music by Bob Haymes and Alan Brandt. © 1953 (Renewed) Warner-Tamerlane Publishing Corp. and Mixed Bag Music, Inc. All Rights Administered by Warner-Tamerlane Publishing Corp. All Rights Reserved. Used by Permission.

"Esta Noche Voy A Verla" ("This Night I Am Going to See Her") by Juan Gabriel. © 1983 by Universal Music – MGB Songs. International copyright secured. All rights reserved. Reprinted with permission of Hal Leonard Corporation.

"Bésame Mucho" ("Kiss Me Much") by Consuelo Velazquez. © 1948 Promotora Hispano Americana de Musica , S.A. administered by Peer International Corporation. All rights reserved. Used by permission of Peer International Corporation.

"The Pink Panther," by Henry Mancini. All rights reserved. Reprinted with permission of Hal Leonard Corporation.

"Vamudara" arr. & additional words and music by Dumisani Maraire from Let Your Voice Be Heard! by Abraham Kobena Adzenyah, Dumisani Maraire, and Judith Cook Tucker © 1986 World Music Press/© 2009 Assigned to Plank Road Publishing, Inc. All Rights Reserved. www.musick8.com

"Tico Tico" ("Tico Tico No Fuba") by Zequinha Abreu, Aloysio Oliveira and Ervin Drake. © 1943 by Irmaos Vitale S.A. Copyright renewed. All rights administered by Peer International Corporation. International copyright secured. All rights reserved. Reprinted with permission of Hal Leonard Corporation.

"The Crime of Tom Dula"; Words and Music Collected, Adapted and Arranged by Frank Warner, John A. Lomax. From the singing of Frank Proffitt. TRO-© Copyright 1947 (Renewed) 1958 (Renewed) Ludlow Music, Inc., New York, NY. International Copyright Secured, Made in U.S.A. All Rights Reserved Including Public Performance for Profit. Used by Permissions.

"Speak Softly, Love" (Love Theme) by Larry Kusik (words) and Nino Rota (music). © 1972 Sony/ATV Music Publishing LLC, Copyright renewed. All rights administered by Sony/ATV Music Publishing LLC, 8 Music Square West, Nashville, TN 37203. International copyright secured. All rights reserved. Reprinted with permission of Hal Leonard Corporation.

"Mambo No. 5" by Damaso Perez Prado. Copyright © 1948 by Editorial Mexicana de Musica Internacional S.A. Administered by Peer International Corporation. Used by Permission of Peer International Corporation. All Rights Reserved.

"Surfin' USA" by Chuck Berry. © 1958, 1963 (renewed) by Arc Music Corp. (BMI) and Isalee Music Inc. (BMI), Arc Music Corp. Administered by BMG Rights Management (US) LLC for the world excluding Japan and Southeast

TRACK LISTING

TRACK 35	"Jingle Bells"
TRACK 36	"My Favorite Things" (R. Rodgers, O. Hammerstein II)
TRACK 37	"Love Me Tender" (E. Presley, V. Matson)
TRACK 38	Waltz in A Minor (F. Chopin)
TRACK 39	Anglaise (Anon.)
TRACK 40	Dance of Slovaks (B. Bartók)
TRACK 41	"Toryanse," Japanese folk song
TRACK 42	Menuet in G Major (J.S. Bach)
TRACK 43	"Lady Sant' Ana," Mexican-American folk song

Module 3 Basics of Rhythm: Extending Duration, Anacrusis, Rests

TRACK 44	Sing: Simple triple meter
TRACK 45	Sing: Simple quadruple meter
TRACK 46	Sing: Simple duple meter
TRACK 47	Sing: Simple triple meter
TRACK 48	Tap: Whole rest
TRACK 49	Tap: Whole rest
TRACK 50	Tap: Half rest
TRACK 51	Tap: Quarter rest
TRACK 52	Tap: Eighth rest
TRACK 53	Tap: Sixteenth rest

Module 4 Accidentals

TRACK 54	Hindustani jor improvisation
TRACK 55	Sing: Ascending chromatic scale, sing with note names
TRACK 56	Sing: Descending chromatic scale, sing with note names
TRACK 57	Sing: C to C, ascending and descending
TRACK 58	Sing: Ascending chromatic scale
TRACK 59	Sing: Descending chromatic scale
TRACK 60	Sing: The blues
TRACK 61	Sing: Two Japanese pentatonic scales

Module 6 Major Scale

TRACK 62	Sing scale: in F major
TRACK 63	Sing scale: in E major
TRACK 64	Sing scale: in D major
TRACK 65	Sing scale: Pentatonic
TRACK 66	Sing scale: Pentatonic
TRACK 67	Sing scale: Chromatic ascending
TRACK 68	Sing scale: Chromatic descending
TRACK 69	Sing scale: Whole tone

Module 8 Compound Meter

TRACK 70	"A Little Hunting Song" (R. Schumann)
TRACK 71	"Mirrors" (Count: 1 2) (R. Finney)
TRACK 72	"Mirrors" (Count: 1 2 3 4 5 6) (R. Finney)

Module 9 Minor Scale

TRACK 73 "James Bond Theme" in A minor (M. Norman)
TRACK 74 Symphony No. 40 in G minor, K. 550 (First Movement) (W.A. Mozart)
TRACK 75 "The Entertainer" in C major (S. Joplin)
TRACK 76 "Moonlight" Sonata in C♯ minor (L.v. Beethoven)
TRACK 77 "Die Forelle" ("The Trout") in D♭ major (F. Schubert)
TRACK 78 "El Choclo" in D minor (A. Villoldo)
TRACK 79 Sing: Natural minor (pure)
TRACK 80 Sing: Harmonic minor
TRACK 81 Sing: Melodic minor

Module 10 Intervals

TRACK 82 Sing: C to C
TRACK 83 Sing: Ascending intervals from C
TRACK 84 "Ting Song" ("Listening to the Pine Tree")
TRACK 85 Water Music, Suite No. 2 in D (G.F. Handel)
TRACK 86 "True Life Blues" (B. Monroe)
TRACK 87 "Pizza's Not for Breakfast" (Skeleton Closet)
TRACK 88 "Heartsong Aria" (F. Ho, R. Margraff)
TRACK 89 "Sabá Medley" (Ali Jihad Racy, Souhail Kaspar)
TRACK 90 "Benedicamus Domino" (Schola Cantorum of Amsterdam)

Module 11 Triads

TRACK 91 "Love Me Tender" (E. Presley, V. Matson)
TRACK 92 Karnatak "Budham aśrayami"
TRACK 93 "Black Girl (in the Pines)" (Lead Belly)
TRACK 94 Vai Call to Prayer (Liberia)

Module 12 Rhythm: Compound Meter Expanded

TRACK 95 Theme from "Peter Gunn" (H. Mancini)

Module 13 Triads: Roman Numerals

TRACK 96 Matilda, Matilda (N. Span)

Module 14 Inversions

TRACK 97 "Tico, Tico No Fuba" (Abreu, Oliveira, Drake)
TRACK 98 "Folk Song" (with open position triads) (R. Dorin)
TRACK 99 "Folk Song" (with close position triads ((R. Dorin)

Module 15 Seventh Chords

TRACK 100 "That's All" harmonized with seventh chords (A. Brandt, B. Haymes)
TRACK 101 "That's All" harmonized with triads (A. Brandt, B. Haymes)
TRACK 102 Nocturne in F Minor, Op. 55, No. 1 (F. Chopin)

Module 16 Form in Music

TRACK 103 Piano Sonata in F, K. 332 (3rd Mvt.) (W.A. Mozart)
TRACK 104 Moment Musical, Op. 94, No. 3 (F. Schubert)
TRACK 105 "Nel Cor Più Non Mi Sento" Variations (L.v. Beethoven)
TRACK 106 Rondo (W.A. Mozart)
TRACK 107 "Good King Wenceslas," traditional hymn
TRACK 108 Two Part Invention in D minor, BWV 775 (J.S. Bach)
TRACK 109 Minuet in C, K. 6 (W.A. Mozart)
TRACK 110 "Wild Rider" (R. Schumann)
TRACK 111 12-bar blues (guitar)
TRACK 112 "Pastorale," Op. 100, No. 3 (J. Burgmüller)
TRACK 113 "To a Wild Rose" (E. MacDowell)
TRACK 114 "Amor, Amor, Amor" (G. Ruiz)
TRACK 115 "Qing Hai Ming Ge," Chinese folk song
TRACK 116 "Till There Was You" (M. Wilson)
TRACK 117 Waltz in A♭ (F. Schubert)
TRACK 118 Ecossaise (L.v. Beethoven)

INDEX

INDEX

dominant seventh chord 423; chord progressions using 429–431; definition of 470; and figured bass symbols 427–428; harmonization in major keys 426, 429; inversions of 437; methods of writing 424–426; in minor keys 431–432; parallel 430

Dorian mode 482

dotted note 75–76; dotted eighth note 355, 439; dotted half note 355

dotted rest 83, 226

double bar lines 25–26, 54; definition of 470

double flat 106, 119–122, 348; definition of 470

double sharp 106, 119–122, 270, 348; definition of 470

downbeat 57; definition of 470

D.S. al Fine (Dal Segno al Fine) 215, 458; definition of 470

duple meter: compound 222, 224; definition of 470; simple 55, 223

duplet 365; definition of 470

dynamics 476; definition of 470

eighth notes 49–51, 131–132, 143–144, 149, 222, 225–227, 239

eighth rest 83

enharmonic 106, 110, 122, 178–179, 205; definition of 470

enharmonic scale 178–179, 205

enharmonic spellings 106–107, 110

F clef *see* bass clef (F clef)

fermata 80; definition of 470

figured bass symbols 401–402; and chord progression 407–408; definition of 401, 471; harmonization with 404–405; triad identification with 402–403

final bar line 471

Fine *see* D.S. al Fine

first ending 149, 153, 215, 243, 456; definition of 474

first inversion 393–395, 402–403, 405, 415, 427; definition of 471

"fixed Do" 176, 180; definition of 471; *see also* solfège

flags 49–52, 131, 227; definition of 471

flats 105–108, 119, 122, 178–181, 200–202, 259–260; definition of 471

forms 448–449; 12-bar blues 453–454; 32-bar form (AABA) 451–453; binary (two-part) (AB) 449–450; definition of 471; ternary (three-part) (ABA) 450–451

forte (*f*) 471

fortissimo (*ff*) 471

frequency *see* pitch

G clef *see* treble clef (G clef)

grace note *see* appoggiatura (grace note)

grand staff 25–26, 28, 445; definition of 471

guitar chords 496–500

half cadences 444–445; definition of 471

half diminished seventh chords 493–494

half note 48, 141, 149, 236; dotted 355

half rest 83

half step 105–106, 179–180, 269–270; chromatic 111–112; definition of 87, 471; diatonic 111–112; on keyboard 109; and major scale 169–170

harmonic interval 309–310; definition of 471

harmonic minor scale 384–385, 386; definition of 471

harmonization 335–336, 383–384, 386–387, 396–397, 404–405, 417, 426, 429; definition of 471

harmony 291, 329–330; definition of 471

hemiola 235

hextonal scale *see* whole tone scale

implied chords 329–330

improvisation 471

intensity *see* volume

interval 122, 291–292; augmented 307–310; compound 313–314; definition of 122, 471; descending 315; diminished 307–310; harmonic 309–310; inversion of 315; major 296, 299, 302–304, 307; melodic 309–310; minor 302–304, 307; octave as 295; perfect 296, 298, 309–310; quality 292, 296, 288; quantity 291–292; shortcuts 339; simple 313–314; unison as 292

inversion 393–394; definition of 471; of dominant seventh chords 427; and harmonization 396; of interval 315; of triads 393–420

Ionian mode 167, 482

irregular meter 471

keyboard 3; and bass clef 21; black keys 3–4; half steps on 105, 122; relating accidentals to 109, 293; and treble clef 13; white keys 4; whole steps on 115–116

key signature 193–196; definition of 471; determining 302–303; flat 200–201; major scale 197, 200–202, 256; minor scale 255–259, 263–264, 266; parallel 261; sharp 197–198; transposition 209–210

key tone 197, 257

Kundiman songs 134

leading tone 471

leading tone scale degree 172–173, 180

ledger lines 7–8, 28; definition of 471

legato 471

lento 471

Locrian mode 483

Lydian mode 483

major interval 296–298, 302–304, 307–308

major key signature 193–196, 209; and dominant seventh chord 424; in major triads 333; parallel 261; relative 256

major scales: changing the tonic 173; circle of fifths 205–206; definition of 165–166, 179, 472; enharmonic 177; finding the tonic 197, 202; with flats 200–201; intervals of 296–297; key signature 193–194; scale degrees 171–172, 179–180; with sharps 195–196; transposition 177, 209-210; triads of 332–333, 377–378, 380; using tetrachords 166; using whole and half steps 169

major seventh chords 492

major triad 332–333, 335–336, 339, 344, 346, 378, 385, 392

measures 26, 54, 81; definition of 472

mediant 172–173, 179, 380, 384–386; definition of 472

mediant scale degree 171–172

melodic form 263–266; musical examples of 266–267; natural (pure) form 263–264; scale degrees 171–172, 274; with sharps 265; triads 384–387

melodic interval 309–310; definition of 472

melodic minor scale 265–266; definition of 472